Essential
Theological
Terms

Essential
Theological
Terms

Justo L. González

WESTMINSTER
JOHN KNOX PRESS
LOUISVILLE • KENTUCKY

Unless otherwise noted, Scripture quotations are from the New Revised Standard Version of the Bible, copyright © 1989 by the Division of Christian Education of the National Council of the Churches of Christ in the U.S.A. and are used by permission.

Book design by Sharon Adams
Cover design by Mark Abrams

First edition
Published by Westminster John Knox Press
Louisville, Kentucky

This book is printed on acid-free paper that meets the American National Standards Institute Z39.48 standard. ∞

06 07 08 09 10 11 12 13 14 — 10 9 8 7 6 5 4 3 2

Library of Congress Cataloging-in-Publication Data

González, Justo L.
    Essential theological terms / Justo L. González.
       p. cm.
    ISBN-13: 978-0-664-22810-1 (alk. paper)
    ISBN-10: 0-664-22810-0 (alk. paper)
    1. Theology—Terminology.   I. Title.

   BR96.5.G66   2005

Contents

A Word of Introduction

I have written a number of books. Some took just a few months to write, and some several years. This one has taken half a century! It was exactly fifty years ago, in the fall of 1954, that I began my theological studies. It was with excitement that my first week of classes began, and with frustration that it ended. As I dove into my books and read them avidly, I found much of interest; yet I also found much that was puzzling. Words did not always mean exactly what I thought, or they were used in strange contexts where their common meaning made little sense. I had to stop and reread many a sentence, often leaving its exact meaning in abeyance until further reading clarified it. General dictionaries were not always helpful. I knew the meaning of many of these words I read—or at least I knew what the dictionary would say about them. But the meaning didn't always fit. Luther had begun the Protestant Reformation; yet Lutheranism is not Reformed! How can that be? Then, every once in a while, a Latin phrase appeared in the text: *simul justus et peccator; reformata semper reformanda; communicatio idiomatum*. I had studied Latin, and could read it fairly well. I could easily translate these phrases; but even the translation did not make much sense! These were phrases laden with meaning that had accrued through the centuries, and no knowledge of Latin, nor even the best Latin dictionary, was of much help in trying to discover what they meant in the context where I now found them.

Thus, one of the first tasks I had to face in my theological studies was to begin developing a mental dictionary—one in which many old words had new meanings, and many new words were employed for old meanings. That task I have not completed, and do not expect ever to complete. Language keeps evolving. New issues emerge, and these in turn require new words and new meanings. Old issues that had long been forgotten take new life as changing circumstances shed new light on them, and with them words and phrases long forgotten are revived, to be added to my mental dictionary.

In this task I was not left to fend for myself. Not only did my teachers help; there were also several dictionaries of theology—some in many volumes, and some in pocketbook size—that clarified many a point. Some of these I still use regularly. Yet, I also find that, since theological vocabulary evolves, every such dictionary or wordbook reflects the time when it was written and the burning issues of that time. A simple comparison of two or three of them, written twenty years apart from each other, will prove this point. As a result, a theological wordbook written twenty years ago, while still useful, will not include many of the words and phrases that are now relatively common in theological discourse. I certainly do not expect it to be otherwise with this book. It has been written early in the twenty-first century and, unless it is periodically revised and perhaps even rewritten, it will bear the marks of its birth date. At the same time, being a historian of doctrine by training and by avocation, I believe that this book also offers the essential vocabulary necessary for a budding theologian to be in dialogue with the theology of centuries past.

It is therefore as a tool for theological students early in the twenty-first century that I now offer this book. As I wrote it, I tried to remember and relive my puzzlement half a century ago and to make the task simpler for present-day students. With those students in mind, I have tried to clarify the meaning of words in theological discourse, both present and past. I can imagine a student who reads the newspapers regularly, and so is aware of the current use of a word such as "creationism," being confused when she reads that Augustine was a creationst, but Tertullian was not, and yet they both believed in the doctrine of creation! I can also imagine another student—even one with the best educational background—suddenly coming upon a reference to womanist theology, or to contextual theologies, and wondering what is meant by such phrases.

If this book somehow eases the burden of such students, and opens the way for them to be excited about the beauty of theology when one does not have to stop at every word to guess what it means, I shall consider my efforts more than worthwhile!

Now a word about what is included in the pages that follow. You will find that the list of words and phrases discussed includes four main sorts of entry. Some of these are words used almost exclusively in theology, and refer to specific theological issues. Examples of this sort of entry are "Arminianism" and "Nestorianism." In such cases, I have tried to include enough data so that the reader may be aware of the meaning of the term, as well as some of its implications. Some are relatively common words that, when used in theology, or in a particular theological or historical context, mean something different than they do in common usage. Examples of this sort of entry are "Creationism" and "Reformed." In such cases, I have tried to clarify the specific meaning of a term in a given context, and to distinguish it from wider, less technical meanings. A third sort of entry is a bit more technical, and is intended to make this book useful for the more advanced student of theology. Examples: "Theopaschism" and "Majoristic controversy." Finally, a fourth type of entry refers to theological subjects that are so basic that a general review of some of the issues connected with them may be helpful to a theological student. The obvious example is "God." In such cases, I have sought to offer a brief overview of the ways in which theologians deal with the subject, and what are some of the related issues and terms.

This leads to the matter of cross-references. These are clearly marked with an asterisk symbol (*), which indicates that an entry for this or a closely related term can be found in the text. To avoid interrupting the text with too many cross references between parentheses, I have often trusted the reader to realize that the entry cross-referenced will not always appear in exactly the same way. Thus, the cross-reference "*Hegelian" will refer to the entry "Hegelianism," and "*Lutheran" should lead the reader to "Lutheranism." When a cross-reference appears at the end of an entry, this usually means that it has to do with the subject of the entire entry. When it appears at the end of a paragraph or a sentence, it has to do with that paragraph or sentence.

Finally, a word to those for whom this is one of your first tools in theological education and research. If you find yourself as puzzled as I did fifty years ago, do not despair. Who knows? Perhaps in a few decades you will be writing a new wordbook of theological terms, including subjects and issues that at present I cannot even suspect. May God bless your studies and your service!

JUSTO L. GONZÁLEZ

Absolution   In its original meaning, the act of setting free. Theologically, the act of setting the sinner free. From very early times, it was customary for the church to pray for the absolution of sinners who confessed their sin, that God would pardon them, set them free. In the eighth and ninth centuries, it became customary, rather than simply to pray for the absolution of the sinner, for the priest to declare that the sinner was set free. It thus became one of the stages of the sacrament of *penance, where the priest declares: "I absolve you of your sins in the name of the Father, and the Son, and the Holy Spirit."

Accident   Besides its common meaning—something that happens by chance or without design—in philosophical and theological discourse an accident is usually a property of a *substance that is not essential to its nature. The roundness of a ball is not an accident, but a substantial property of the ball. On the other hand, the whiteness of a ball is an accident or an accidental property, for a ball may well exist without being white. In theology this term is found most often in two contexts: first, in the affirmation that there are no accidents in God, for accidents are by definition *contingent, and there is no contingency in the divine. Secondly, the term is much used in discussions regarding the presence of the body and blood of Christ in the *Eucharist, particularly in explanations of the doctrine of *transubstantiation.

Accommodation   A term with two very different meanings, according to its context. In discussions about *revelation it refers to the need for God's revelation to be adapted (accommodated) to human capabilities of understanding and reception. Thus, when dealing with the authority of Scripture, or with the teachings of Jesus, the principle of accommodation is often used to claim that Scripture, though infallible, adjusts its wording for its readers—and that Jesus does likewise with his listeners. An example of such accommodation is when Calvin explains that Joshua is said to stop the sun and the moon, when in fact it is the earth that moves, because an astronomically accurate statement would have been unintelligible at the time.

Today this term is used most often in the context of *missiology, where it means the efforts of missionaries to present their teachings in ways that take into account the culture they are addressing (*Acculturation). Early Jesuit missionaries Roberto de Nobili in India and Matteo Ricci in China proposed such accommodation. They were resisted by more traditional elements in the Roman Catholic Church, thus giving rise to the "Controversy of the Malabar Rites" and to the "Controversy over the Chinese Rites."

Acculturation   The process whereby missionaries and others trying to communicate the faith in other cultures seek to build bridges between their faith and the receiving cultures (*see* *Accommodation). When contrasted with *inculturation, usually the main difference lies in that, while in acculturation it is the missionary who seeks to adapt, in inculturation it is the receiving parties that, in accepting the *gospel, do so in terms of their own culture—sometimes intentionally and sometimes quite unconsciously.

Act (Pure Act; Actuality)   In *Aristotelian and medieval philosophy, a realized potentiality. An acorn is a potential oak, although in actuality it is an acorn. When the potentiality of the acorn is realized, then it is an oak in actuality. The distinction between potency and act is traditionally used to explain movement, as well as any other change in beings. Thus, when something moves from one place to another, that is because potentially it was already there. *Contingent beings may be potentially in many places, but actually only in one. *God, on the other hand, being pure act, is everywhere.

Adiaphora Literally, indifferent things. In theology, it refers to things that are neither commanded nor forbidden by Scripture, as well as to theological views that, while not strictly part of orthodox doctrine, do not contradict it. The adiaphora became a subject of controversy among Lutherans in the sixteenth century, after Luther's death, when Melanchthon and his followers declared that it was licit to accept certain practices for the sake of peace and unity, while the more strict among the Lutherans, led by Matthias Flacius, insisted that to do so was to fail to give faithful witness to the true faith. In the end, the Formula of Concord (1577), while affirming Melanchthon's understanding of the adiaphora, also declared that in times of persecution, when a firm witness is required, the adiaphora may become a matter of obligation for all true believers.

Adoptionism Strictly speaking, the view of a number of theologians in eighth-century Spain—notably Félix of Urgel and Elipandus of Toledo—who held that, while the Second *Person of the *Trinity is eternal, the man Jesus was adopted as God's son through grace. In a way, this is a medieval expression of earlier *Antiochene theology, which sought to preserve the humanity of Jesus by clearly distinguishing it from his divinity. Although the views of the Spanish adoptionists were repeatedly condemned by a number of Frankish synods under Charlemagne, this doctrine continued existing in Spain, particularly among those who lived under Moorish rule and therefore beyond the reach of Carolingian authorities.

More commonly, the term "adoptionism" is used to refer to any doctrine that holds that Jesus was a man whom God adopted into sonship. Thus, the Ebionites (*Ebionism) and many Antiochene theologians of the fourth and fifth centuries are sometimes called adoptionists. For similar reasons, some accuse nineteenth-century liberal theology of having adoptionistic tendencies (see *Liberalism).

Affusion *See *Infusion.*

Agape The word most often used in the New Testament for love, and sometimes for the love feast of early Christians (see also *Eucharist). In the context of the history of worship, it is most often used in this latter sense. When used in the context of contemporary theological and ethical discussions, its meaning stems from the very influential book by *Lundensian theologian Anders Nygren (1890–1978), *Agape and Eros.* In that work, Nygren sought to clarify the Christian understanding of love by contrasting the meaning of *agapē* with two other Greek words that can be translated as "love": *erōs* and *philia*. According to Nygren, *erōs* is love for the desirable, the beautiful, that which is worthy of love. Although it does not always refer to sexual desire—as in "eroticism"—it is love that in one way or another seeks to possess the beloved. Significantly, the New Testament never speaks of Christian love as *erōs*. It does speak on occasion of *philia*. This is typically the love that exists among friends. It includes an attraction that is often based on admiration, or at least on compatibility—as in the case of the *philo*sopher, who is a friend and follower of wisdom, *sophia*. Still, it is *agapē* that the New Testament uses almost uniformly to refer first of all to God's love for creation and for humankind, and then, as a reflection and response to God's love, to the love of Christians among themselves. *Agapē*, in sharp contrast to *erōs* and also to *philia*, does not love because the beloved is worthy, or because it desires to possess the beloved. It is God's unmerited love for us—a love that, rather than seeking to possess, seeks to improve, to bless, to grant happiness.

Some theologians, notably Paul Tillich and others profoundly influenced by *Platonism and *Neoplatonism, have sought to soften Nygren's contrast between *agapē* and *erōs*, claiming that there is a sense in which it is legitimate to desire the beloved and that certainly God desires to possess us, and claiming also that it is legitimate for Christians to love God because God is worthy, beautiful, and desirable.

Agnosticism   The term appears to have been coined by T. H. Huxley in 1869. Although in its popular use this word is synonymous with atheism, in the strict sense there are two important differences. First, the atheist is convinced that there is no God, while the agnostic does not know whether there is a God, and is convinced, not that there is no God, but that it is impossible to know one way or the other. Secondly, while atheism refers only to the nonexistence of God, agnosticism refers to the conviction that true knowledge is impossible in all matters beyond the reach of the senses and their experience—not only the existence of God, but also life after death, the freedom of the will, the meaning of life, and so on.

Albigensians   A *dualistic sect, also known as "cathars" or "pure," with possible historical connections with earlier *Manichaeism. It was imported from the East, apparently by returning Crusaders, and was particularly prevalent in the French town of Albi—hence the name "Albigensian." Like Manichaeans before them, the Albigensians distinguished between two levels of followers, the "perfect" and the "believers." They rejected all use of material elements in worship, and accused orthodox Christians of mixing the spiritual with the material. The movement expanded through Provence, and in 1208 Pope Innocent III promulgated a Crusade against them, resulting in thousands of deaths and apparently also in the total suppression of the movement.

Alexandrine Theology   The theology that developed in the city of Alexandria, beginning late in the second century. Alexandria was noted for its learning, its library, and its philosophers. It was also noted for the enriching and sometimes confusing encounter and mixture of religions and philosophies from various parts of the world. Even before the advent of Christianity, Alexandrine Judaism had engaged in an active dialogue with the philosophical currents of the city. Thus the Hebrew Bible was translated into Greek (in a version called the Septuagint); and, roughly at the same time when Jesus lived, Jewish philosopher Philo of Alexandria sought to interpret Judaism so as to make it compatible with the Platonic tradition (see *Platonism).

What Philo did for Judaism, Christian theologians in Alexandria tried to do for Christianity. The first great Christian teacher in Alexandria was Clement, who had come to the city on the Nile from Athens. He and his famous disciple Origen set the tone for much of Alexandrine theology. They tried to show that Christianity was compatible with the Platonic tradition by interpreting the Bible allegorically (see *Allegory). They preferred to speak of God in philosophical terms (immutable, impassible, infinite, etc.) rather than in the more *anthropomorphic language of Scripture. Like most of the Platonic tradition, the Alexandrine Christians valued spirit and mind over matter—and some of their early teachers believed that God intended only a spiritual creation, and that the material creation was a response to *sin. For them, an important element in the human predicament is that we forget who we are—spiritual beings created for the contemplation of the divine. For this reason they tended to stress the work of Christ as a teacher and an example, reminding us who we are and calling us to our true being.

It was in the context of the christological debates that exploded in the fifth century (see *Christology) that the contrast between Alexandrine theology and its *Antiochene counterpart came to the foreground. Since the Alexandrines focused on the Savior's role as a teacher and messenger from God, they tended to underscore the divinity of Jesus to the point that his humanity sometimes seemed to be compromised. The function of the humanity of Jesus was to make it possible for humans to receive his message, his teaching, and his illumination. This resulted in what theologians call a "unitive" Christology—one that stresses the union of the divine and the human in Jesus even if this compromises his full humanity—in contrast to the "disjunctive" Christology of the Antiochenes—one that seeks to preserve the full humanity of Jesus by establishing a clear distinction and sometimes even a separation between his divinity and his humanity. A fundamental principle of the unitive Christology of the Alexandrines was the doctrine of the *communicatio idiomatum*—the sharing of properties—according to which what is said of the humanity of Jesus may also be said of his divinity, and vice versa.

The result of all this was that some Alexandrines developed a "Logos-flesh" Christology—one in which the divine Logos is united, not to a full human being, but to a human body without a human rational soul (*see* *Apollinarianism). This was rejected by the Council of Constantinople in 381.

One of the champions of Alexandrine Christology in the fifth century was Cyril of Alexandria, who proposed the "anhypostasis," or *anhypostatic union, against the radically disjunctive Christology of Nestorius (*see* *Nestorianism). His views were affirmed by the Council of Ephesus in 431, which condemned Nestorius.

Shortly thereafter, the unitive Christology of the Alexandrines resulted in *monophysism—the theory according to which there is in Jesus only one nature, the divine, for the human has been absorbed by the divine. This was condemned by the Council of Chalcedon in 451, which is usually considered the ending point of these christological controversies.

The struggle, however, did not end. By then Alexandrine monophysite tendencies were conjoined with Egyptian and Syrian resentment against the central government in Constantinople. One result was a series of attempts at reconciliation in which the authorities in Constantinople proposed moderately Alexandrine compromises, all of which failed (*see* *Monotheletism; *Monergism). Another result was a series of schisms resulting in separate churches that subsist to this day, and which reject the decisions of Chalcedon as not paying sufficient honor to the divinity of Jesus —among them, the Coptic Church of Egypt, the Ethiopian Church, and the Syrian Jacobite Church.

Alienation   Separation or estrangement. This term became common in philosophy with the work of Hegel, and later of Feuerbach and Marx, and in theology in the writings of those most influenced by these philosophers. Today it is particularly common in the writings of theologians impacted by *existentialism. It most often refers to one's estrangement from oneself, from others, or from God. Self-alienation is both the distance that separates the self from its true being, and the inability of the self to accept itself for what it is. Quite often in contemporary theology alienation is used as a synonym for sin.

Allegory (Allegorical Interpretation)   A way of reading texts which sees in them, not their apparent literal meaning, but a symbolic one. Such interpretation was practiced even before the advent of Christianity by Hellenistic scholars who sought to vindicate Homer and other ancient writers by interpreting some of their most objectionable texts allegorically. It was also practiced by some Jews in their attempt to prove to their Hellenistic critics that Judaism was not a crude and primitive religion, but a philosophical truth at least as ancient as Greek philosophy. (Indeed, there were many Jews as well as Christians who argued that Moses was before Plato, and that Plato had learned his wisdom from the Hebrew Scriptures.)

With the advent of Christianity, which claimed to be the fulfillment of the promises made to Abraham, Christians found themselves with the need to interpret the Hebrew Scriptures in ways that were compatible with the Christian faith; and in their debates with their educated pagan critics they found a similar need to show that the Scriptures were not as crude as they sometimes seemed.

One way to respond to such needs was allegorical interpretation. Thus, if God ordered the children of Israel to destroy and kill everything and everyone in Jericho, what this means is that when God enters the soul we are to destroy every vestige of sin in it.

While such interpretation was fairly common among all Christians, it became a hallmark of *Alexandrine theology, and particularly of Origen and his followers. Origen claimed that every scriptural text has several meanings, and that behind the obvious literal meaning there is always a deeper, "spiritual" meaning that is to be found by means of allegorical interpretation. This was achieved by discovering the hidden, spiritual meaning of words and things, so that when one encounters such words or things in a passage one can read the passage "spiritually."

In the Middle Ages, such "spiritual" interpretation was quite common, and teachers became famous and respected precisely because they could draw profound teaching from the apparently most simple texts.

While this method of interpretation has the obvious advantage that it allows every text to be used for teaching and contemplation, and while there is no doubt that some passages are allegorical in nature—for instance, when Jesus calls himself a vine—it has been severely criticized because it puts the interpreter in absolute control of the text, which thus loses its "otherness."

Finally, allegorical interpretation is not to be confused with *typology, which also sees meaning beyond the obvious in texts—and particularly in events—but which does this on the basis of the literal, historical meaning of the text.

Amillennialism   The denial of the theory or of the expectation of the *mil-

lennium. While millennialists debate the order of events in Revelation 20:2–7, amillennialists simply declare that the thousand years mentioned there are not to be interpreted as a period of time, but rather as a metaphor for Christ's final victory over all evil. Thus, for most amillennialists the discussion about the millennium is of little interest, and it tends to be millennialists who dub them "amillennialists."

Anabaptism   The name given by its enemies to a movement that arose in the sixteenth century, whose followers held that baptism required faith, and that therefore the baptism of infants was not valid. The name "Anabaptist" means "rebaptizer," and therefore the Anabaptists themselves thought it was a misnomer, for they were not rebaptizing anybody, but only baptizing those whose supposed early baptism was invalid.

Anabaptism, however, was much more than a position regarding baptism. In general, Anabaptists proposed a radical return to the New Testament and its practices. They argued that in the New Testament people became Christians not by birth, but by personal decision, and that therefore the practice of taking for granted that all people born in a Christian society were Christians—a view that had been dominant since the times of Constantine—must be rejected.

This in turn means that there is a radical and discernible difference between the body of society and the body of believers. In some ways, this was what more traditional Christians found most upsetting, for it implied that governments and nations were not really Christian, and set the church apart as a smaller body of true believers in contrast to the larger mass of people simply born into the church and the state. For these reasons both Catholics and Protestants rejected and even persecuted Anabaptists, who were pushed into increasingly extreme positions. Some claimed that the final battle between good and evil was at hand, and became militant and even violent revolutionaries—which in turn led to even greater persecution and cruelty.

On the other hand, while some Anabaptists were becoming radical and violent revolutionaries others reclaimed the New Testament teaching of refusing to do evil to one's enemies, and thus embraced *pacifism (*see* *War). While this too was perceived as subversive by rulers menaced by Turkish threats of invasion, and consequently these pacifist Anabaptists were also persecuted, they persisted. This is the origin of the various *Mennonite bodies.

At a later time, a number of English dissenters, mostly of *Reformed or *Calvinistic traditions, were influenced by Anabaptism, and thus began the modern Baptist movement and the churches it now comprises.

Anakephalaiosis *See* *Recapitulation.

Analogy   Similarity among differing things, and the basis of much human language. A lion is strong; steel is strong; and an argument may be strong. In all these cases the word "strong" has different, yet similar, meanings. The theme of analogy as a way of speaking about God has been discussed by many theologians and philosophers. In the field of philosophy, the discussion goes as far back as Plato and Aristotle. In theology, although much used from the earliest times, analogy became a subject of study and discussion in *scholasticism, particularly with Thomas Aquinas and his interpreters (*see* *Thomism). (After Thomas's death, and as his theology became dominant, there was much discussion about the exact nature of Thomas's doctrine of analogy. Today it is generally agreed that Thomas's views evolved, and that this is the main reason for the divergent interpretations of his position.)

According to Thomas and other theologians, analogy is not simply a convenient and necessary way of speaking about God. If we can use analogy in order to speak about God, this is because there is a fundamental *analogia entis*—analogy of being—by which the creatures are analogous to the Creator. Thus, strictly speaking, the foundation for analogy is not that God is like creatures, but rather that creatures are like God.

The phrase "analogy of faith"—*analogia fidei*—appears often in patristic literature, usually referring to the relationship between the Old Testament and the New. Through this analogy of faith there is a continuity between promise and fulfillment.

In the twentieth century, Reformed theologian Karl Barth (1886–1968) began using the phrase *analogia fidei* as an alternative to *analogia entis*, which he saw as claiming a continuity between God and creation that he could not accept, and that to him was the essence of the contrast between Roman Catholicism and Protestantism. According to Barth, there is no "analogy of being," no ontological continuity nor even similarity between God and beings. There is only an analogy of faith, one that is produced by grace and communicated by revelation.

Anathema   A curse or prohibition. In the most common theological usage, a formal condemnation by the church or its authorities, usually involving *excommunication, and most commonly applied to those declared to be heretics. Sometimes, by implication, a thing to be avoided, as when a doctrine or theory is declared to be "anathema."

Angelology   That part of theology that deals with angels—which quite often includes not only "good" angels, but also demons and all such beings. Although angels and other similar beings appear repeatedly in Scripture, neither in the Old nor in the New Testament is there any attempt to explain what they are, or to classify them. They appear in the Old Testament at a relatively late date, simply as something whose existence is taken for granted—as it is also in the New Testament. The one point that is quite clear throughout

Scripture is that angels and all such beings are part of God's creation. They are creatures, and therefore not to be worshiped, as they were in much of the surrounding culture. Thus, the Bible simply accepts this element in the world vision in which it is set, but corrects it in terms of its own radical monotheism.

It was only in the early Middle Ages that Christians began developing an angelology in the strict sense. The two pioneers in this regard were, in the East, the *Neoplatonic Christian who wrote under the pseudonym of Dionysius the Areopagite; and, in the West, Gregory the Great (ca.540–604). Thus, Christian angelology dates generally from the sixth century. A common trait of this angelology was that it viewed angels as purely spiritual, incorporeal beings, and therefore superior to humans—this as a result of a Neoplatonic perspective, which considered spirit as intrinsically superior to matter. (In contrast, some earlier theologians, such as the author of Hebrews and Irenaeus, thought that angels were given as tutors for humans, who would eventually reign above angels.)

As angelology evolved, it combined an attempt to systematize all that the Bible says about angels with the hierarchical view of all reality proposed by Pseudo-Dionysius, who himself organized all angelic beings into a tripartite hierarchy, each with three choirs, for a total of nine choirs of angels. Even when the views of Pseudo-Dionysius were left behind, the main interest in much angelology has been to classify angelic beings, and to determine the relationship between angels, archangels, seraphim, and cherubim. In more recent times, there has been much popular speculation and fictional literature about angels, and this has prompted a number of theologians to revisit the subject, now trying to place it once again within the context of strict monotheism and a christocentric view of history and of creation.

Anglicanism   One of the main traditions stemming from the Reformation of the sixteenth century (*see also* *Lutheranism; *Reformed Tradition; *Anabaptism; *Tridentine). The Church of England, which originally separated from the Roman Church over the issue of the annulment of the marriage of Henry VIII with Catherine of Aragon, was profoundly influenced by Protestant theological views—particularly Reformed views. While this was a long and complex evolution, much of it may be traced back to those whose Protestant inclinations forced them into exile during the reign of Mary Tudor. Many of them were impacted by *Calvinism while on the Continent and then returned to their homeland during Elizabeth's reign. The influence of these repatriates gave the theology of the Church of England a decidedly Reformed tone. While some members of the Church of England became strict Calvinists, and their views prevailed briefly during the *Puritan Revolution, eventually the Church of England settled for a moderate Calvinism within which there was a great variety of positions—from strict Calvinists who insisted on *predestination, total *depravity, and the like, to *Arminians who rejected the more extreme forms of Calvinism. This attitude is often called the Anglican *via media*.

Within this great variety of opinions, what held the Church of England together, rather than adherence to a strictly defined orthodoxy, was its polity (its bishops), its connection with the nation and its government, and its liturgical practice, revolving around the Book of Common Prayer.

As the British colonial empire was dismantled, the Church of England in the newly founded nations also became independent, thus giving rise to a number of Anglican churches besides the original Church of England. To these were added churches resulting from missionary work beyond the former limits of the British Empire. All of these together constitute the Anglican Communion or Anglicanism. While they are independent, their leaders gather every ten years at the Lambeth Conference, presided over by the Archbishop of Canterbury. These conferences do not have legislative authority over the various churches that are part of the Anglican Communion.

Anhypostatic Union (Anhypostasis)

The theory, proposed mostly by Cyril of Alexandria (ca.375–444), according to which the divine and the human are so united in Jesus that, while there is a human nature as well as a divine nature, the former subsists in the *hypostasis of the latter. Thus, the humanity of Jesus has no hypostasis of its own, hence the name of "anhypostatic union" ("anhypostatic" meaning lacking a hypostasis).

The ambiguity of the word "hypostasis" makes it difficult to determine exactly what Cyril meant by this. Some interpreters have understood him to mean that in Jesus the divine nature took up human nature in general, and that therefore, as to his humanity, Jesus was not an individual. Most likely, what Cyril means is simply that the human nature of Jesus has no subsistence of its own, but subsists in its union with the divine.

For Cyril, this is the foundation of the *communicatio idiomatum*, which was the point of contention between him and the *Antiochene theologians (*see also* *Hypostatic Union).

Anomoeans

The extreme party within *Arianism. They held that the Son is so different from the Father that he is best described as "unlike"—in Greek, *anomoios*, hence their name—the Father. They held that the Son can only be called "God" because he shares in the power of God; but the Son is certainly a creature and a work of God. The chief theologian of this party was Eunomius, against whom several orthodox theologians wrote treatises.

Anthropology

Etymologically, the discipline that studies human beings. In a theological context, the term usually refers to the manner in which a theologian or a theological school understands human nature and human destiny. Although in matters of detail there are a number of different anthropological views in Scripture, there are some assertions that are basic to all biblical anthropology. Thus, it is clear in Scripture that humankind has its origin in God, its creator. It is also stated that humans bear the "*image of God," although the exact meaning of this is not altogether clear. This human being, created by God after the divine image, is to rule the rest of creation, and therefore is God's steward in the administration of creation. Thus, humans are part of creation and at the same time stand above the rest of creation. This is related to this creature's ability to transcend itself, to look at itself, as it were, from outside. Also, humans are intended to live in community— and the Bible speaks much more about peoples, tribes, families, and nations than about individuals. This creature, being free, has chosen to disobey God and to follow its own path—sin. In so doing, it has surrendered its freedom and its destiny to evil, and is therefore in need of redemption. Finally, by God's grace and thanks to Jesus Christ, this human creature is promised life abundant and eternal.

Starting from these premises, and often influenced by the culture around it, Christian anthropology has dealt with a number of issues. Some of them, such as the meaning of the divine image in humans, the tension between *freedom of the will and *predestination, and themes such as *sin and *salvation, have repeatedly been at the center of anthropological discourse.

An issue that has dominated much anthropological discourse, particularly in more conservative circles, is the question of the composition of the human. While the Bible rather consistently speaks of human beings as whole and indivisible entities, it is clear the humans are bodies, but are also bodies with particular attributes and capabilities that are not exhausted by their bodily reality. Thus, in the psalms "my soul" simply means "I," and so does "my body"— although with somewhat different emphases. Other words, such as "heart," "liver," and the like, are also used in the Bible to speak of a human being as a whole, but in each case with a particular emphasis. In Greek thought, on the other hand, the "soul" was often opposed to the body, as two constitutive and often warring parts of a human being. Thus, from a very early time there were among Christians—as there were also among pagan philosophers—discussions as to what were the constitutive parts of a human being, and how many they were. On the basis of different passing references in Scripture, some Christians have opted for the "dichotomous" position— humans are composed of body and soul—while others have preferred the "trichotomous"—body, soul, and spirit. (*See also* *Soul.)

Another subject that has sometimes become central to theological anthropology is the origin of the soul, with some holding that it is derived from one's parents (*see* *Traducianism) and others that each individual soul is a new creation by God (*see* *Creationism).

In more recent times, theological anthropology has once again tended to focus on the central issue of what it means to be authentically human, rather than on matters such as the composition of a human being or the origin of the soul.

Anthropomorphism   The tendency to depict God—or any gods—in human form. In Christianity, there have been those who have interpreted the *image of God in humans in this sense, and have thus come to the conclusion that God actually has a body like ours and looks very much as we do. By and large, Christian theologians have rejected such anthropomorphism.

There is, however, another dimension to this matter. We have no other language with which to speak about God than human language, and in that sense all speech about God is anthropomorphic. While theologians have always declared that such language is metaphorical or analogical (*Metaphor; *Analogy), some —particularly those most influenced by Greek philosophy, and later by various forms of *rationalism—have affirmed that more abstract language is more appropriate to speak about God, and have thus preferred to speak of God as "immutable," "impassible," for example (*Attributes [of God]). While there certainly is value to such language, which reminds us of the analogical nature of more clearly anthropomorphic language, it nevertheless remains anthropomorphic in the sense that it still is bound by the limits of human language and experience, except that in this case it is couched in more abstract terms—and therefore it is not necessarily better than more clearly anthropomorphic language, as when we say, for instance, that God loves.

Finally, in this discussion it is important to remember that the central claim of the Christian faith is that God became human—which is to say that in the *incarnation God became, so to speak, anthropomorphic.

Antichrist   A term that appears only five times in the New Testament—four in 1 John and a fifth time in 2 John—but which has been much discussed in Christian *eschatology. While the term itself appears only in the Johannine epistles, the concept of personal powers that oppose God appears repeatedly in Scripture. Since in the book of Revelation there is a final confrontation between God and the Lamb on the one hand, and the powers of evil—the dragon and the beast—on the other, the notion of the antichrist soon became associated with the leader of the forces of evil in this final struggle. As a result, throughout history Christians have repeatedly identified the antichrist with whatever power, institution, or individual opposed and persecuted them. Thus, already in the early church there were those who thought that the antichrist was Nero. The Reformers of the sixteenth century often equated the antichrist with the papacy, or with a particular pope. In more recent times, among American Christians, there were those who believed that the antichrist was communism. With regard to all this, it is important to point out that in the Johannine epistles the antichrist is not only the final enemy, but any who oppose the truth of God—which is why 1 John 2:18 declares that "now many antichrists have come." It is also important to point out that what makes this figure so evil is not that it blatantly opposes the true Christ, but rather that it passes for the Christ. It is Christlike, and in this lies the basis for its deceptive powers.

Antinomianism   From the Greek *anti*, against, and *nomos*, law. A term coined by Martin Luther in his controversies with Johann Agricola, who objected at first to the use of the *law of Israel—specifically, the *Decalogue—in instructing believers in their obligations, and later also to its use as a means to call sinners to repentance, arguing that the preaching of the gospel sufficed for that purpose. Luther responded with a treatise *Against the Antinomians*, in which he defended the use of the law in teaching and in preaching. Eventually, the Formula of Concord declared that the law has three uses: to show us our sin, to regulate the life of society, and to guide the lives of those whom God has saved by grace (*Law, Third Use of).

Although originally referring specifically to the position of Agricola and his followers, the term "antinomianism" has come to be applied by extension to all opposition to the value and use of the law in Christian life. In this sense, there have been antinomians at various points in the history of Christianity. In the early church, Paul's struggles with the law and its insufficiency for salvation led some to establish a radical opposition between law and gospel. Chief among them was *Marcion, who went so far as to teach that the law has been given by a lesser god than the Father of Jesus Christ, the God of love and of grace. Similar positions were held by a number of gnostics (*Gnosticism). In the Middle Ages, there were occasionally those who used Augustine's words, "Love God and do as you please" as an excuse for rejecting the law as a guide for Christian living. At the time of the Reformation, the controversy between Luther and Agricola was only one of several similar ones. Calvin wrote a treatise *Against the Fantastic and Furious Sect of the Libertines Who Call Themselves Spiritual*. Similar groups arose in England during the *Puritan revolution. In New England, the more traditional Puritans accused Anne Hutchinson of antinomianism. In more recent times, ethical theories that stress context or the principle of love above all others have also been dubbed antinomian.

Antiochene Theology   A school of theology that developed around the city of Antioch and in some sections of Asia Minor, and which contrasted radically with *Alexandrine theology. While the Alexandrines made free use of allegorical interpretation (*see* *Allegory), the Antiochenes preferred the literal, historical meaning of the text, and used allegory with greater moderation than the Alexandrines. And, while the Alexandrines felt that the human predicament was such that the chief work of Christ was as a messenger reminding humans of our spiritual reality, the Antiochenes believed that the human predicament was enslavement to sin and to the devil, and that therefore the chief work of Jesus was to head a new, free humanity by conquering the powers of evil through the incarnation, the cross, and the resurrection (*see* *Atonement). Thus, while the Alexandrines stressed the divinity of Jesus, the Antiochenes stressed his humanity, his being the "new Adam."

Although some of the earlier Antiochenes—such as Paul of Samosata (third century)—may have sought to safeguard the full humanity of Jesus by limiting his true divinity, such solutions were soon abandoned. Thus the Antiochenes developed a "disjunctive" Christology—one in which the full humanity of Jesus is preserved by radically distinguishing it, and sometimes isolating it, from the divinity. Hence the rejection by the earlier Antiochenes of the principle of the *communicatio idiomatum*, and the repeated attempts of the later Antiochenes to limit its implications.

Among the most famous teachers of Antiochene theology were Diodore of Tarsus (ca.330–ca.390) and Theodore of Mopsuestia (ca.350–428), as well as one of the greatest preachers of all times, John Chrysostom (ca.347–407). All of them were well known for their biblical studies and for their stress on the literal meaning of texts.

However, the most famous leader of the Antiochene school was Nestorius, the patriarch of Constantinople whose views were condemned by the Council of Ephesus in 431 (*see* *Nestorianism). Nestorius insisted—as eventually orthodox Christology came to hold—that in Christ there are two natures, a divine nature and a human nature. But he also insisted on the separate integrity of these two by declaring that in Christ there are two persons, one divine and one human. He rejected the *communicatio idiomatum*, insisting that there are some things that Christ does as human, and some that he does as divine. The point that led to a conflagration was his rejection of the title of *Theotokos*—bearer of God—for the Virgin Mary. Nestorius insisted that Christ is born of Mary, while God is not, and that therefore she should be called only *Christotokos*. His opponents, led by Cyril of Alexandria, countered that one could then say that Christ, and not God, walked in Galilee, and that Christ, and not God, suffered on the cross.

Although the teachings of Nestorius were rejected by the Council of Ephesus, this did not end the matter. Many of his followers became influential teachers in Persia, where most Christians came to

hold "Nestorian" views and to reject the Council of Ephesus. To this day, there are a small number of Christians whose roots go back to this schism. As for Nestorius, he was still alive when the Council of Chalcedon (451) moderated the extreme Alexandrine position of the Council of Ephesus, and he insisted that he agreed with the decisions of Chalcedon, which vindicated his views. But he was paid scant attention.

Apocalyptic (Apocalypticism)   In Greek, the term *apokalypsis* simply means "revelation," and it is in that sense that it is employed in the Revelation of John, which begins precisely with that word: "The revelation [*apokalypsis*] of Jesus Christ." However, precisely because of that use in Revelation, "apocalyptic" has come to have two meanings in modern language.

First, in its most common usage, it simply means catastrophic, as when commentators speak of "an apocalyptic view of the coming economic downturn."

More specifically, in theological discourse and in biblical studies, "apocalyptic" refers to a certain theological outlook and the literature emerging from it. In this sense, apocalypticism seems to have arisen first in Persia, among Zoroastrians, then to have been transmitted into Judaism during exilic times, and finally passed on from Judaism to some strands of early Christianity. The main feature of apocalypticism is a dualistic view of history, and the expectation that this dualism will be resolved in imminent eschatological times with the victory of good over evil. The dualistic view of history, in which the principle of good is opposed by the principle of evil, results in the division of humankind between those—usually the majority—who serve the powers of evil, and who therefore currently enjoy power and privilege, and an oppressed and persecuted minority who will share in the final victory of good, while the evil will be destroyed or cast into everlasting suffering. Given this outlook, it is not surprising that apocalypticism usually arises and flourishes within minorities that feel oppressed and persecuted—such as the early Christians, or the *Anabaptists in the sixteenth century.

Besides this fundamental outlook, apocalyptic literature also exhibits a number of common traits. Thus, it claims to be based on visions, and it tends to speak in symbolic terms, with strange beasts, much numerology, and cryptic language that often can be understood only by the initiated. Also, it is most often pseudonymous literature, claiming to have been written by a respected figure in the past—*Apocalypse of Abraham, Apocalypse of Elijah, Apocalypse of Peter*, for example.

Apocatastasis (or Apokatastasis)

A Greek word meaning healing, full restoration, a return to an original state. It is often used in this sense in the New Testament—for instance, in Acts 3:21. More specifically, in later theological usage it has come to mean the final restoration of all things to their original state. It was thus that Origen (ca.185–ca.254)—and later Gregory of Nyssa (ca.335–ca.394)—used the term. In this sense, the apocatastasis is the completion of the full circle of history: creation is restored to its original perfection. This contrasts with a view of history in which what begins in a garden, in Genesis, ends in a city, in Revelation.

Theories of the apocatastasis usually involve the expectation that in the end all, including the devil, will be saved (*see* *Universalism*), and therefore theologians tend to speak of all universalist positions as affirming a final apocatastasis. There is, however, an important distinction to be made, for it is possible to hold universalist views without believing that all of creation will return to its original state.

Apocrypha

The body of books not included in the *canon. Unfortunately, the word "apocryphal" means "hidden," and thus has given rise to the mistaken popular notion that all these books were hidden or forbidden—which is true of only a few of them. Furthermore, the term itself has very different meanings when applied to the Old Testament canon and when applied to the canon of the New Testament.

In the context of the Old Testament canon, the term "Apocrypha" was first employed by Jerome as a collective title for those writings included in the Septuagint (and also in his own Vulgate), but not in the Hebrew canon. He felt that these books, while good for edification and devotion, were not canonical in the strict sense, and therefore should not be used, as the rest of Scripture, to determine correct doctrine. However, since the early and medieval church did not normally use the Hebrew Bible, but rather the Vulgate and—in the case of Greek-speaking Christians—the Septuagint, and since both of these included the Apocrypha, Jerome's distinction was soon blurred and even forgotten.

At the time of the Reformation, Luther and others returned to Jerome's advice, declaring these books to be good, but not canonical nor authoritative. Luther himself put them all together at the end of his translation of the Old Testament. Other Protestant translations into other languages followed this example, often with an explanation as to the not quite canonical nature of these books. By the seventeenth century, Bibles began to be printed without the Apocrypha; and in the early nineteenth this became the policy of the British and the American Bible Societies.

In reaction to Luther and to other Protestants who questioned the full canonical authority of the Apocrypha, the Council of Trent (1545–63) declared that these books are fully inspired, and condemned as a heretic anyone who thought otherwise. However, as time passed, Roman Catholics began to acknowledge the particular status of these books by referring to them as "deuterocanonical," that is, forming a "second canon"—

which does not mean that they are not authoritative, but simply that they are not part of the Hebrew canon.

In the case of ancient Hebrew literature, those books which were never part of any canon, and which often claim to have been written by an Old Testament figure—for instance, the *Testaments of the Twelve Patriarchs*, the *Psalms of Solomon*, *Jubilees*, the *Apocalypse of Baruch*, and many others—are not called "apocrypha," but rather "pseudepigrapha."

The case is different with the New Testament, for the "Apocrypha of the New Testament" is not parallel to the Apocrypha of the Old. Most of these books were never considered canonical, except by the sects or movements that produced them; the most notable exception is the *Apocalypse of Peter*, which was considered canonical by some second-century Alexandrines. And the counterpart of this is also true: the books that at one time or another almost made their way into the Christian canon—such as the *Shepherd of Hermas*, the *Epistle of Barnabas*—are not generally part of the "Apocrypha of the New Testament."

The New Testament Apocrypha includes two sorts of books: some that were written in an attempt to expand on what is said in the New Testament, and some that were composed by a group or sect trying to put forward its own doctrine by means of a book, usually under the pseudonym of an apostle. The former include, for instance, a series of stories about Jesus as a child or a young man, and stories about the miracles and travels of some of the apostles. These were never suppressed, and many enjoyed wide popularity in medieval times. The latter include such writings as the *Gospel of Truth*, by the *gnostic Valentinus. These were generally suppressed, and have survived mostly in quotations from authors refuting them —or, as in the case of a series of papyri discovered in Egypt in the nineteenth century, in forgotten libraries that somehow survived the ravages of time.

Apollinarianism The christological doctrine of Apollinaris of Laodicea, rejected by the Council of Constantinople in 381, and thereafter by several other councils and church bodies. Apollinaris held that in Christ the divine nature took the place of the human rational soul. In other words, the humanity of Jesus was not a full, rational humanity. Jesus was human because he had a human body, and this body lived and functioned like any human body. But he was not human in the sense that he had a human mind, for in his case the *Logos, or *Word of God, took the place of the human mind. This is a typical expression of early *Alexandrine Christology, in which the Logos is united, not to a full human being, but to a human body.

The great objection to Apollinarianism came from those who held that Jesus had assumed human nature in order to save it. If such was the purpose of the incarnation, it follows that "what is not assumed by Christ is not saved." Thus, if Christ did not assume a human mind, the human mind is not saved. And yet, it is in the mind that sin proves most active and powerful. In order to save humans in their entirety, the Word of God has to become incarnate in a full human being.

Apologetics The rational defense of the Christian faith, its tenets and practices. From a very early time, the title of "apologist" was given to those who wrote in defense of Christianity, seeking to show that there was no reason for persecuting Christians, that Christianity was the "true philosophy," and that in fact Christian moral practices enhanced the whole of society. The earliest Christian apologists wrote in the second century, and, although some of their works have been lost, these apologists—most particularly Justin Martyr—were the first Christian theologians in the sense of offering a reasoned understanding of the faith. Several of the most outstanding Christian thinkers in the next generations, and until the end of the persecutions, also wrote apologetic works—Tertullian, Clement of Alexandria, Origen, Cyprian, and others.

Once Christianity became established as the official religion of the Roman Empire, and throughout the Middle Ages, there seemed to be much less need for apologetic theology. The two places where it was most practiced were in the encounter with the pagan tribes of the north, where missionaries sought to prove the truth of the faith to Saxons, Frisians, and others, and in the encounter in the south with Islam, where there were lively debates between Muslims and Christians as to the validity of their respective beliefs. Quite possibly, Thomas Aquinas's *Summa contra Gentiles* was initially conceived as a handbook for such debates.

With the growing rationalism and skepticism of the Renaissance and the centuries that followed, apologetic theology—or philosophical attempts to prove or to bolster Christian doctrine—once again became quite important. When the philosophy of Descartes (*Cartesianism) gained popularity, there were Catholics who tried to prove the rationality of their faith on Cartesian grounds; and the same was true of a number of Calvinists, particularly in the Netherlands, who believed they could prove the truth of strict *Calvinism. In England, under the aegis of Locke's *empiricism, a number of authors tried to prove that Christianity was eminently reasonable—and also the other side of the coin, that anything that could not be shown to be true by reason was not part of true religion. Such was the purpose, for instance, of John Toland's *Christianity not Mysterious* (1696), and of Matthew Tindal's *Christianity as Old as the Creation* (1730).

This tradition continued with Kant (1724–1804) who, after arguing that the main tenets of religion—the existence of God, the existence of the soul, and life after death—could not be proven by "pure reason," sought to prove precisely these points by means of what he called "practical reason." During the nine-

teenth century, when traditional Christian doctrines were repeatedly challenged by scientific discoveries, many theologians saw their task as defending the reasonableness of Christianity. Schleiermacher's first famous book, published just before the beginning of that century (1799), bears the apologetic title of *On Religion: Speeches to Its Cultured Despisers*. Slightly later, as Hegel's system became popular, there were a number of Hegelian reinterpretations of the Christian faith. In the twentieth century, the apologetic tradition continued in the work of Paul Tillich (1886–1965) and several other famous theologians.

On the other hand, there is also a long list of those who have felt that the apologetic task is misguided, because faith stands at the center of Christian belief, and faith cannot be produced by rational argument. This was the posture of Søren Kierkegaard (1813–55) in the nineteenth century, and of Karl Barth (1886–1968) in the twentieth.

Toward the end of the twentieth century and the beginning of the twenty-first, with the rise of *postmodernity, apologetics began taking a different direction, for now the very notions of objectivity and of universality, which had stood at the heart of modern philosophy, and therefore also of modern apologetics, were being doubted. In this context, probably the most that apologetics can do is to show that Christianity and its tenets are not absurd or irrational.

Apostasy   The act of abandoning the faith. From very early times, this was considered a very serious sin—to the point that some claimed that the three unforgivable sins were homicide, fornication, and apostasy, which included idolatry. Later, as rival churches and Christian traditions vied for the allegiance of the faithful, those who abandoned a particular church for another —for instance, Roman Catholics who became Protestants, and vice versa— were often considered apostates by the community they had abandoned. Sometimes "apostasy" is used also to refer to those who abandon a religious vow or commitment they had made—as when a priest decides to abandon the priesthood. This, however, is not the strict meaning of the term.

Apostolic Succession Originally an argument employed by those who sought to refute *gnostic and other teachers who claimed to have received secret teachings from Jesus or from the apostles. The argument was simply that, had there been any such secret teachings, they would have been passed to the same people to whom Jesus and the apostles entrusted the churches—that is, to the immediate successors of the apostles. These would in turn have done the same with their successors, and so on. At this time—that is, in the second century, when this argument was first used—there are a number of churches that can show an uninterrupted line of succession from the apostles. They all agree that there is no such secret tradition. Therefore, those who claim to have such a tradition are not to be believed.

At that time, this did not mean that those bishops and other leaders who could not claim direct apostolic succession were not valid bishops or leaders. If they agreed in doctrine with the bishops who could show such succession, this in itself validated them.

Slowly, however, the argument was expanded to mean that in order to be a true bishop one had to be part of that line of succession, consecrated by a bishop (or bishops) who was himself consecrated by a bishop within the succession, and so on, back to the apostles.

This has been the most common understanding of apostolic succession throughout the Middle Ages and to this day—an understanding held, not only by the Roman Catholic Church, but also by the various orthodox churches, by the *Anglican communion, and by many other Protestants.

In the eighteenth century John Wesley became convinced that in the early church a presbyter and a bishop were the same, and therefore when he found that the Church of England would not ordain ministers for America, he decided that, since he was a presbyter, he could transmit the succession to others, and proceeded to ordain two of his followers. This was part of a process begun at the time of the Reformation, in which apostolic succession, while still deemed important, was redefined in a number of ways—although still, in its most common usage, it retains its traditional meaning of an uninterrupted line of bishops going back to the apostles themselves.

Apostolicity A characteristic or mark that the church began claiming for itself in the fourth century by including it in a number of creeds, by which was meant that the church had been founded by the apostles, whose doctrines it still taught and whose successors the present leaders of the church were (*Apostolic Succession).

In other contexts this term simply means that something goes back to the time of the apostles, for instance in the phrase "the apostolicity of this doctrine cannot be denied."

More recently, in various parts of the world, but most particularly in Latin America, independent churches have begun to band together in what they call "apostolic networks," which give the title of "apostle" to some of their leaders and certify each other's "apostolicity." This is a new phenomenon, with little or no grounds in earlier Christian teaching and tradition.

Appropriations In Trinitarian theology, the principle whereby it is possible to affirm a particular relationship of one of the *persons of the *Trinity to one of its acts. For instance, it is the Second Person of the Trinity who has become flesh. This does not mean, however, that the other two persons are ever absent from the act appropriated to one. Thus, although only the Son is incarnate, the

Father and the Spirit are always present with the incarnate Son.

Arianism The doctrine of Arius, which led to the first great theological controversy after the end of the persecutions, and was rejected first at the Council of Nicaea (325), and then at the Council of Constantinople (381). Arius was a presbyter of the church in Alexandria who clashed with his bishop, Alexander, over the manner in which the divinity of Christ is to be understood. While Arius was willing to say that the Savior is divine, he insisted that this is not by nature, but by adoption. The Word who became incarnate in Jesus did not exist from all eternity with God, but is a creature—the first of all creatures, through whom God made the rest of creation, but still a creature. This view clashed with the teachings of Alexander, who insisted on the full and eternal divinity of the Son.

The debate became increasingly virulent. Arius was a popular preacher, and there soon were mobs in the street chanting Arian slogans such as "There was when he [the Son] was not." Alexander on his part employed his episcopal authority to discipline and to silence Arius, and eventually had Arius and his doctrine rejected by a synod of Egyptian bishops.

At that point Arius appealed to a circle of his friends whom he called his "fellow Lucianists," because they had been classmates under the famous theologian Lucian of Antioch. He then left Alexandria and found refuge with the most influential of his Lucianist friends, Eusebius of Nicomedia.

This widened the controversy, and eventually Emperor Constantine decided that it was time to convoke a great council of bishops of the entire church, to gather in the city of Nicaea in 325. After much debate, this council issued a creed which made it very clear that Arianism was not acceptable, by including phrases about the Son such as "only-begotten, that is, from the substance of the Father,

God from God, light from light, true God from true God, begotten not made, of one substance [*homoousion] with the Father." To this, the council added a series of anathemas against Arius and his teachings: "But as for those who say, There was when He was not, and, Before being born He was not, and that He came into existence out of nothing, or who assert that the Son of God is of a different *hypostasis or *substance, or is created, or is subject to alteration or change— these the Catholic Church anathematizes" (see *Anathema).

This, however, did not end the controversy. Many were concerned that the decisions of Nicaea tended to obliterate the distinction between the Father and the Son. Eusebius of Nicomedia and several others exerted their influence, and five years after the Council of Nicaea a reaction set in. Several of the bishops who had led the deliberations of that council were deposed. Others began seeking formulas that would not sound as extreme as those of Nicaea. After the death of Alexander of Alexandria, his successor, Athanasius (ca.293–373), became the champion of Nicene orthodoxy, and for that reason was repeatedly exiled.

As the controversy evolved, the term *homoousion* (meaning "of the same substance" as the Father) became the hallmark of the defenders of Nicaea. But other alternatives emerged. A very attractive one for many moderate bishops centered on the term *homoiousion (which by the mere inclusion of an *i* affirmed that the Son was "of a *similar* substance"). While these were not true Arians, but simply people concerned that the distinction between Father and Son be preserved, they were considered almost Arians—or "semiarians"—by the most staunch defenders of Nicaea. The true Arians, those who insisted that the Son was a creature, and not to be considered divine in the full sense, became known as the *anomoeans, for they insisted that the Son was *anomoios*, unlike, the Father. And then there were those who sought to stay on the fence by

declaring that the Son was "similar"—
homoios, hence their name of "homoeans"
—to the Father, without clarifying the
nature of that similarity.

In the course of that controversy, first
Athanasius and then the "great Cappadocians"—Basil of Caesarea, Gregory of
Nazianzus, and Gregory of Nyssa—clarified the meaning of several terms, and
thus gained the support of the vast majority of the leadership of the church. In
consequence, at the Council of Constantinople, in 381, the decisions at Nicaea
were reaffirmed. The creed resulting from
these controversies—usually called the
Nicene Creed, although it is not exactly
the creed agreed upon in that great
council—became the most widely used
throughout the church.

Although for all practical purposes
this ended the Arian controversy, Arianism did not die out. During the time of
its ascendancy, Arian missionaries had
gone to the Germanic tribes beyond the
borders of the Empire. Thus when those
tribes invaded the Empire, they were
already Christians, but Arian Christians.
In the West, where Arianism had never
gained a strong foothold, it was now
revived by the presence and the conquests of these Germanic peoples—
particularly the Vandals in North Africa
and the Goths in Italy and Spain. Eventually, however, it disappeared also in
the West.

Aristotelianism   The philosophical
tradition founded by Aristotle, in the
fourth century BCE. A disciple of Plato
(*Platonism), Aristotle wrote on a wide
variety of subjects: logics, *metaphysics,
*ethics, the *soul and its functions,
nature, and so on. He differed from his
master on the manner in which knowledge is attained (*see* *Epistemology).
While Plato felt that the senses and their
perceptions cannot lead to true knowledge, Aristotle believed that sense perception, while in itself not constituting
knowledge, is a source of knowledge,
and therefore should not be spurned in
favor of purely "intellectual" data. This

in itself contributed to Aristotle's interest in a wide variety of subjects, for in his
mind all of them led to true knowledge,
and none should be ignored or set aside
as irrelevant or as providing only the
temporary illusion of knowledge.

At the time of the advent of Christianity, the philosophy of Plato was
much more popular than that of Aristotle. Indeed, Aristotle's main influence
was mostly indirect, through his impact
on other philosophical schools such as
*Stoicism. Thus, in their *apologetic task
most early Christians tended to relate
Christianity with Platonism, and not
with Aristotelianism, and this in turn
resulted in an increasingly Platonic
understanding of Christianity and an
abandonment of Aristotle's insights.
During the *christological controversies
of the fourth and fifth centuries, most of
the participants used Platonic principles
to support their views. It was mostly the
*Antiochenes—and the most extreme
among them—who insisted on the value
of Aristotle's contribution as a means to
understand reality and as providing a
metaphysics that could be employed to
speak of the *incarnation. As a result,
when this particular Christology was
defeated in the Ecumenical Councils of
Ephesus (431) and Chalcedon (451), and
some of its proponents went into exile
beyond the borders of the Roman
Empire and into Persia, they took Aristotle's works with them. While in the
Byzantine East Aristotle was still fairly
well known, in the Latin-speaking West
he was practically forgotten. His logic
was employed during the renaissance of
the twelfth century by those who
defended the use of "*dialectics" in theology, such as Peter Abelard (1079–ca.1144),
but his metaphysics and his works of
nature and its knowledge were generally
unknown.

This situation changed when Latin
scholars began crossing into Muslim territories in Spain and formerly Muslim
Sicily, and there found the writings of
Aristotle as well as of his great Muslim
commentator, Averroës. The works of

Aristotle, which the Muslims had encountered and translated when they conquered the Persian Empire, now began making their way into Latin-speaking Europe, often joined with those of Averroës and other Muslim and Jewish writers. The result was a bitter debate among Western theologians, particularly in the University of Paris, regarding the value and the use of Aristotelianism in the field of theology. While the vast majority insisted on the traditional Platonic views, as reinterpreted and adapted in *Augustinianism, and others took the extreme position of accepting all of the new philosophy even at the risk of Christian doctrine (*Averroism), Thomas Aquinas (ca.1225–74) and his teacher Albert the Great (ca.1200–1280) took the bold step of employing Aristotelian philosophy for reinterpreting and rereading traditional theology—including Augustinianism. This was the genius of *Thomism, which eventually became the dominant theological tradition within Roman Catholicism.

Arminianism   The position of Jacobus Arminius (1560–1609) and his followers—often known as *Remonstrants —regarding *grace, *free will, *predestination, and the *perseverance of believers. Arminius was a Calvinist theologian in the Netherlands who, in those matters in which the *Reformed tradition differed from the Catholic or from the *Lutheran, always remained a Calvinist. It is important to remember this, because Arminianism is often depicted as the opposite of *Calvinism, when in fact Arminius and his followers were Calvinists in all points except the ones at issue. Also, it must be noted that the debate had much to do with the interest of one party to emphasize strict Calvinist doctrine in order to safeguard the recently acquired independence of the nation, while the other sought positions that would make it easier to conduct trade with nations not adhering to strict Calvinism. Partly for this reason, the strict Calvinists developed logical and

rational arguments based on Scripture and the principle of justification by grace alone, while the other party developed equally rational arguments based on commonly accepted principles of religion—by which they became forerunners of later *rationalism.

Arminius became involved in this debate when he determined to refute the position of those who rejected the strict Calvinist doctrine of predestination, but then became convinced that they were right, and became their champion. The strict Calvinists who opposed and eventually condemned Arminius were *supralapsarian. They held that God had first decreed the *election of some and the reprobation of others, and then decreed the *fall and its consequences, so that the initial decree of election and reprobation would come to fruition. They also held that the consequences of the fall are such that all human nature is totally depraved, and that the decree of predestination is such that Christ died only for the elect, and not for all humankind. At first, Arminius tried to respond to these views by adopting an *infralapsarian position; but he soon became convinced that even this was not enough. He criticized his opponents, arguing, first, that their discussion of the decrees of predestination was not sufficiently christocentric, for the great decree of predestination is the one "by which Christ is appointed by God to be the Savior, the Head, and the foundation of those who will be made heirs of salvation"; and, secondly, that God's predestination of the faithful is based on God's *foreknowledge of their future faith.

Since his opponents' doctrine of predestination was based on the primacy of grace, which is irresistible, Arminius responded by speaking of a "preventing" or "prevenient" grace, which is given by God to all, and which enables them to accept saving grace, if they so decide. And, since grace is not irresistible, this implies that it is quite possible for a believer, even after having received saving grace, to fall from it. It was against these proposals that the Synod of Dort (1618–19) affirmed the five central points of strict Calvinism: the total *depravity of humankind, unconditional election, the limited *atonement of Christ, irresistible grace, and the perseverance of the faithful.

The theories of Arminius were eventually adopted by a number of theologians of Reformed persuasion who were not willing to follow their Calvinism to the point where Dort took it. Most notable among them was John Wesley (1703–91). Among the English Baptists, those who accepted the Arminian position, insisting that Christ died for all, came to be known as "General Baptists," while those who insisted on limited atonement were called "Particular Baptists."

Ascension   Jesus' final act on earth, by which he ascended into heaven—and thereafter, as several creeds declare, "sitteth on the right hand of God the Father Almighty." The doctrine of the ascension has often been neglected in Christian theology, where it is sometimes seen simply as Jesus' exit from earth. Three crucial points that highlight its importance are listed in the Heidelberg Catechism (1562): First, it is the ascended Christ who is our advocate before the throne of God. Second, by his ascension and "session"—sitting—in heaven, Christ has taken humanity into heaven, from whence he draws us, as the body whose Head he is. Third, it is Christ sitting in heaven who sends the Holy Spirit, so that the Spirit is now present among us in a way that was not possible before the ascension.

Of these points, the second has often been the most neglected, but in some ways it has the most radical consequences. In it one sees echoes of Irenaeus's assertion that "God has become human so that humans may become godlike," and of similar views in the writings of Athanasius, Ambrose, and others (*Theopoiesis).

Asceticism   A discipline of renunciation for the sake of discipleship, often connected with the imitation of Christ as a norm for Christian living. At its best, it includes also the practice of Christian love—which is the reason why a number of pioneers in ascetic living came to the conclusion that true discipleship cannot be practiced in absolute solitude, and thus gave rise to cenobitic, or communal, monasticism. In the Middle Ages, asceticism became identified with monasticism, as a road to a Christian *perfection that was not required or expected of common believers. After the Reformation, many groups—particularly among the *holiness movement—have sought to revive ascetic practices as the common responsibility of all believers. In many cases, however, asceticism has reflected a negative attitude toward the body as evil, or at least as inclining the will toward evil, and has thus led to practices of punishing or "mortifying" the body with extreme fasting, uncomfortable positions, lashings, and the like.

Aseity   From the Latin *aseitas*, the characteristic of a being that is of, by, and from itself, without deriving its existence from any other being, or being in any way dependent from any other being. A term much used in medieval philosophy and theology to refer to God's absolute primacy over all other beings. A similar term, with slightly different connotations, is *perseity*, which refers to a being that exists of itself. Both of these terms are often used in traditional arguments for the existence of God (*see* *Cosmological Argument; *Ontological Argument).

Aspersion   Sprinkling. Sometimes used as a method for *baptism, when water is simply sprinkled over the head. Traditionally, most churches have frowned on this practice, and preferred either *infusion or *immersion.

Aspersion is traditionally practiced in connection with the renewal of baptismal vows—traditionally on Easter eve—when water is sprinkled on the congregation as a reminder of their baptism.

Assumption   Usually refers to the bodily assumption of Mary to heaven at the end of her earthly life, a dogma of the Roman Catholic Church proclaimed by Pius XII in 1950—but long held by many Catholic theologians and believers. The use of the term "assumption" (in contrast to "*ascension") means that, whereas Jesus "ascended" into heaven by his own power, Mary was taken up into heaven by the power of God. It was mostly in the fifth century and thereafter that the tradition became common that when Mary came to the end of her life, the apostles were miraculously summoned and brought to Jerusalem by angels, and as they placed her in the grave she was taken up into heaven. Beginning at that time, this tradition became increasingly popular. By the early eighth century, it was official tradition of the Byzantine Church, which celebrated the assumption of Mary on August 15. In the West, although not declared a dogma of the church, it was generally believed during the Middle Ages. Thus, the significance of the promulgation by Pius XII is that what up to that point was considered "probable," but not an article of faith, now became a dogma, and any who reject it are therefore to be considered heretics by Roman Catholic standards. In a way, the dogma of the assumption of Mary is a corollary of the dogma of her *immaculate conception, for if death is the consequence of sin, Mary should not be subject to it.

Assurance   The complete and absolute knowledge of one's salvation. Whether or not this is possible has been much debated, particularly since the time of the Reformation. The official Roman Catholic position on this regard, as determined by the Council of Trent (1545–63), is that such assurance is not to be expected, and that if any have such assurance it is only by a special revela-

tory act of God. For Luther, the doctrine of assurance was an expression of his own experience, eagerly seeking after salvation until he was assured that salvation was a matter of God's grace, which will not fail. Calvin held similar views. Particularly after the controversies regarding *Arminianism and the Synod of Dort, many strict *Calvinists came to regard such assurance as a matter of doctrine—one that follows from the principle of the *perseverance of the saints—although others insisted that, while it is true that the predestined cannot be lost, it is impossible to know in this life that one is actually among the elect. Most Arminians, as a consequence of their rejection of the doctrine of the perseverance of the saints, have also held that it is impossible to be assured of one's salvation, for a relapse—"backsliding"—is always possible. Wesley, in spite of his Arminian convictions, held that the internal witness of the Spirit, and a holy life, assure the believer of his or her own state of salvation.

Atonement   A word coined early in the sixteenth century by Matthew Tyndale, in order to convey the biblical notions of *reconciliation, *redemption, and *expiation. As such, it appears frequently in later English translations of the Bible in contexts such as "the day of atonement" and "making atonement." In theological discourse, it is presently used as a way to refer to the saving work of Jesus on the cross without necessarily opting for one of the various interpretations of that work. In such discourse, the two points most discussed have been (1) how it is that Christ saves us, often under the heading of "theories of the atonement," and (2) the extent of the atonement.

On the first of these questions, the dominant theory of atonement in the West has been "substitutionary atonement"—also called the "juridical" theory of atonement. According to this view, Christ saves us because in his death he took the punishment that was our due.

While elements of this theory appear much earlier, it was Anselm of Canterbury, in the eleventh century, who developed its classical expression in his book *Cur Deus homo? (Why Did God Become Human?)*. Anselm argued that all that humans can be and can do we already owe God, and that therefore once we have sinned we have nothing with which to pay for that sin—nothing that we do not already owe to God anyway. Furthermore, God being infinite, an affront to God is an infinite debt, which no finite being can pay. And yet, if it is to be paid, this must be done by a human being, for it is humans who have sinned. Thus, God becomes human in Jesus Christ, so that by his sufferings and his death he may make infinite payment—the traditional word is "*satisfaction*"—for the sins of all humankind.

Needless to say, this theory centers the *work of Christ on his sufferings, and particularly on the cross. The *incarnation becomes the means whereby Jesus gets to the cross, and his *resurrection is simply God's final vindication of Jesus. Thus, Christ is the victim in a cosmic act of sacrifice. In some cases, this theory has led believers to establish a contrast between a just and demanding Father and a loving Son, as if the Son had been forced to pay what the Father demanded.

In contrast to the substitutionary theory, others have proposed a "moral influence," or "subjective" view of atonement. According to this view, Jesus saves by setting an example of love such that by following it we become reconciled with God. In this case, although the cross and Jesus' attitude toward those who crucified him are the climax of the work of atonement, this takes place throughout his life, in his teachings and in his dealings with people around him. Although many had suggested such views before, it was Abelard, early in the twelfth century, who proposed it as an alternative to the substitutionary view—and in particular to the opinion that Satan had right of ownership over humankind, and that Jesus therefore

came to free us from that yoke. As *rationalism became increasingly common in the eighteenth century and thereafter, similar views of atonement were employed as a way to explain how it is that Jesus saves us, without having recourse to metaphors of debt and repayment. Thus, most *liberal theologians of the nineteenth century held to one version or another of this theory.

The main problem with this theory is that it comes very close to *Pelagianism, for it seems to imply that, given the proper example and inspiration, we are capable of working out our own salvation—that *sin is simply something we do, and, which we are able to leave behind if we simply decide to do so.

A third view of atonement sees the work of Christ as a victory over sin and evil. While this is the most common view in early Christian literature, it was Swedish theologian Gustav Aulén (1879–1977), whose epoch-making book *Den kristna försoningstanken*—published in English in 1931 in an abbreviated version as *Christus Victor*—brought this third option to the foreground. According to Aulén, the most common view of atonement in early patristic theology—which he calls the "dramatic theory" because it sees history as a great drama in which God and evil contend—was neither Anselm's nor Abelard's, but a third view in which Christ is the conqueror of the powers of evil that had held humankind in subjection. By opting for sin, humankind had become subject to Satan. What Jesus then does is to conquer Satan by entering his domain and breaking forth from it as a conqueror. This means that the work of redemption begins with the incarnation, and that what happens with the crucifixion, the resurrection, and the *ascension is that Christ breaks the power of evil and bonds that enslaved us.

In a variant of this theory, combining it with elements from the theory of substitutionary atonement, humankind belonged to Satan, who had the right of ownership over sinners, and the authority to use that right by torturing sinners. In his suffering, Jesus has paid a ransom to the devil, who no longer has a right of ownership over sinners.

Besides these theories, other views have appeared in Christian history. Thus, for instance, some have seen Jesus as the messenger from beyond who comes to call us to a different life. Others have seen in him the "exemplar"—in the *Platonic sense—after which a new creation is formed. And many have seen him as the "new Adam," the head of a new humanity whose body the church is, so that in his resurrection and ascension all those who are joined to him as members of his body are promised a share in his life and his victory. This latter view is often joined in early Christian literature with Aulén's "dramatic theory."

As to the extent of the atonement, the most common view throughout Christian history has been that Christ died for all. However, as a result of the debates between *Arminianism and strict *Calvinism, Calvinistic orthodoxy has come to the conclusion that Christ died only for the elect (*Atonement, Limited).

Atonement, Limited   One of the five central theological tenets defined by the Synod of Dort (1618–19), and therefore one of the pillars of *Calvinist orthodoxy. The question debated was whether Christ died for all, or only for the elect. The doctrines of predestination and of irresistible grace require the assertion that Christ died only for the elect, for to say that he died for all would imply that he died for those who were eternally destined for reprobation and who could not therefore receive the benefits of his death.

Attributes (of God)   Those characteristics or qualities that may be properly said of God—attributed to God. Traditionally, discussions on how it is possible to speak of God—to attribute any characteristic to God—have centered on three ways: the *via eminentiae*, the *via analogiae*, and the *via negativa*.

The *via eminentiae* is based on the presupposition that all that is good in the world has its origin in God—that all that is good is a vestige of the Creator in the creature. On this basis, one may claim that God possesses all good in the highest degree—eminently. Thus, if it is good to know, and the more knowledge the better, then God must be all-knowing—*omniscient. Likewise, if it is good to have power (provided one uses it properly), then God is all-powerful or almighty—*omnipotent. If being present is better than being absent, then God is everywhere—*omnipresent.

The *via negativa* has been understood in two different ways. In its strictest sense, it means that no human or creaturely attribute may be properly applied to God—that all we can say is that "God is not like . . ." Carried to its final consequences, this implies that no speech about God is possible—that all that is feasible before the divine presence is awe-stricken silence. This has been held by some mystics inspired by Pseudo-Dionysius.

In a more limited sense, however, the *via negativa* is simply the counterpart of the *via eminentiae*. If all good attributes may be eminently applied to God, all limitations must also be denied in God. Thus arises an entire series of attributes that are negative in character: God is infinite, having no end; God is *impassible, not being able to suffer the action of an exterior agent except through God's own will; God is unchanging, not subject to motion or variation; God is simple, not subject to division or inner contradiction. Along similar lines, since existing by virtue of another is an imperfection, God exists out of, and for, Godself (*Aseity).

On further reflection, however, some have pointed out that the human mind has a very limited idea of the meaning of "omni"—as in "omnipotent" or "omniscient." And one can also argue that the same is true of the negative attributes, for we cannot really conceive or understand infinity or absolute simplicity. This leads to the *via analogiae* (*Analogy), which claims that the relationship between Creator and creature is such that there is between the two, as a sort of link, an *analogia entis*—analogy of being. When we speak analogically, what we mean is that something is "like" something else—which in turn implies also that it is different. Thus, the way of analogy allows believers to speak of God using language already at hand (*see* *Anthropomorphism*), at once claiming the appropriateness of such language and its limitations. It is this that allows us to say, for instance, that God is loving, just, faithful, and so on. And one could even argue that, in the final analysis, all language about God is analogical—including those attributes that we reach through the *via eminentiae* and those reached through the *via negativa*.

Attrition The sort of compunction over sin that arises, not from true *contrition, from being sorry for sin itself, but rather from fear of punishment. During the Middle Ages, theologians long debated whether repentance limited to attrition suffices for forgiveness, or if true contrition is necessary. In more recent times, many have come to the conclusion that attrition may lead to contrition, and that in any case the two are often present and so entwined as to be indistinguishable.

Augustinianism The position of those who follow the teachings of Augustine of Hippo (354–430), most commonly known simply as "Augustine" or "St. Augustine." Since Augustine was without any doubt the theologian who most impacted Latin-speaking Christianity—with the exception of the apostle Paul—there is a sense in which practically all Western theology, Catholic as well as Protestant, is Augustinian. The term "Augustinianism," however, is usually reserved for those who prefer Augustine's positions on certain points at which they have been contested or debated.

Augustine himself went through a long process of conversion and theological maturation in which his theology was shaped by a series of controversies or of options that he rejected and refuted. In his youth he was attracted to *Manichaeism, which he eventually abandoned because it failed to fulfill its promise of solving some of the problems that Augustine found most baffling. One of these was the problem of the existence of evil (*see* *Theodicy), which Manichaeism explained by posing the existence of two eternal principles in constant opposition—a principle of good and a principle of evil. Although at first attracted to this position, Augustine soon began seeing difficulties in it, and sought further explanation from the most famous Manichaean teachers. When these failed, he found an answer in *Neoplatonism, which taught that evil has no existence in and of itself, but is rather the absence of the good. The more distant things are from the One, the less good they are. But they are still good, and not really evil. What we call "evil"—particularly moral evil—is what happens when a creature is more distant from the One than it ought to be, and so is less good than it ought to be. Given these views on the part of Augustine, sometimes "Augustinianism" refers to this understanding of evil as essentially not existing.

The nature of the soul also posed difficulties for Augustine, until through his studies of the Neoplatonists he came to the conclusion that the soul is incorporeal—a position by no means common among Christians at his time. Immediately after Augustine's death, "Augustinians" were generally those who held the soul to be incorporeal.

Then, Neoplatonism and the entire *Platonic tradition also attracted Augustine for their theory of knowledge. For Augustine, as for Plato and his followers, true knowledge cannot come through the senses, which only perceive passing and contingent reality. Plato explained knowledge as the memory that the soul has of a previous existence in the realm of pure and eternal ideas— a realm from which the soul has fallen into this material world. For a time, Augustine toyed with that explanation, which he eventually abandoned because it implied the *preexistence of souls. Eventually he settled for the theory of *illumination, claiming that the Word or *Logos of God illumines the soul so as to bring knowledge to it—a position that had been held earlier by other Platonist Christians such as Justin, Clement of Alexandria, and Origen, but which Augustine developed and refined.

In this context of the theory of knowledge, "Augustinianism" then refers to the position of those who affirm that knowledge comes through illumination. This became a controverted point in the thirteenth century, when the reintroduction of *Aristotle into Western Europe provided an alternative theory of knowledge in which the senses played a significant role. Those who rejected the newly introduced Aristotelian theories came to be known as "Augustinians," in contrast to the Aristotelians, who were often considered suspicious innovators. Since Thomas Aquinas (1225–74) was the most prominent and successful of those who sought to reinterpret Christian theology on the basis of Aristotelian philosophy, in this context "*Thomist" came to be the opposite of "Augustinian"—although, in all fairness, one must point out that Thomas himself sought to reconcile Augustine with Aristotle, and not to place one against the other.

As a bishop, Augustine was involved in two great controversies that also shaped his theology: one against the *Donatists, and one against the *Pelagians. The dispute with the Donatists had to do with the validity of *sacraments administered by unworthy persons, and with the nature of the church. In response to the Donatists, Augustine claimed that the validity of a sacrament came from God, not from the person administering it, and that therefore a sacrament is valid even when received from an unworthy minister, as well as when irregularly offered. As to the *church, Augustine had recourse to the distinction between the visible and the invisible church. In the visible church, the wheat and the chaff are mixed, and it is not possible for mortals to clear away all the chaff; but God knows where the wheat is and where the chaff, and the true church is therefore the invisible one, at present visible only to God, but to be revealed in the end. This does not mean, however, that the visible church is unnecessary or should be abandoned, for the only access we have to the invisible church is through the visible, in spite of all its imperfections.

In this context, "Augustinianism" usually refers to an *ecclesiology that, while distinguishing between the church visible and invisible, still insists on the necessity of the visible church. Also, when speaking of the sacraments, and particularly of Communion, some Protestants declare themselves to be "Augustinian," because there are passages in which Augustine speaks of a symbolic or "spiritual" presence of Christ in the *Eucharist—although there are other passages in which he speaks of the physical presence of the body of Christ in Communion.

Finally, Augustine's theology was profoundly shaped by the Pelagian controversy, particularly in matters having to do with *grace and *predestination. Augustine felt that Pelagius and his followers, by insisting on moral effort and on personal decision as the beginning of salvation, undercut the doctrine of grace (see *Freedom of the Will). Rather than placing the beginning of faith (*initium fidei) in human free will, Augustine declared it to be the result of a sovereign act of God by which some are foreordained to receive grace and thus be saved. In this context, many Protestants have claimed to be "Augustinians," for they too stress salvation by grace— although one should note that Augustine believed that salvation was attained by the *merits of *works performed with the cooperation of grace. Also other groups and movements that have underscored the primacy of grace in salvation, such as the *Jansenists, have called themselves "Augustinians."

Autonomy Apart from its political usage, a term found most often in moral discourse, where it refers to the ability to act out of one's own volition and integrity, rather than being led by random stimuli or by outside forces or regulations (*Heteronomy). In the work of Kant (1724–1804), and after him in most moral discourse, it usually does not refer to the absolute freedom to do as one pleases—which in fact is mere enslavement to stimuli, desires, and the like—but rather to the ability to follow universally valid rules of conduct, and to do so out of one's own volition, and not from coercion or fear of consequences.

Averroism The name given to the position of those, particularly in the thirteenth century, whose *Aristotelianism carried them much farther than the moderate Aristotelianism of Thomas Aquinas (see *Thomism), and who were accused of denying a number of tenets of the Christian faith. They were given the title of "Averroists" because many among their critics—including Aquinas —claimed that they were not in fact followers of Aristotle, but of his Muslim commentator Averroës.

It was mostly in the Faculty of Arts of the University of Paris that this "Latin Averroism" flourished. There, teachers such as Siger of Brabant (ca.1240–ca.82) and Boethius of Dacia insisted on the independence of philosophy, which should be free to pursue its course even if it reaches conclusions that are contradicted by theology. They were therefore accused of holding to a view of "double truth," whereby something that is true in philosophy could be false in theology. Apparently, such accusations were due

to an oversimplification of their position, for they did not claim that there could be two contradictory truths, but simply that philosophy ought to be free to pursue its own method, even if eventually some of its conclusions will have to be corrected by theology. In any case, such a position would seem to imply that at least some of the tenets of theology are contrary to reason, and this suffices to explain why the Averroists were repeatedly refuted and even suppressed by ecclesiastical and academic authorities.

The specific points of conflict between the Averroists and the theologians, beyond the fundamental issue of the freedom of philosophy, were several. First of all, the Averroists held that philosophical *reason led to the eternity of the world, or at least of matter—in opposition to the teaching of *creation ex nihilo, out of nothing. Then, they held that the movement of the heavenly bodies was also reflected in the movement of events on earth, and therefore proposed a cyclical view of history. Finally, the point that drew most opposition was their theory of the "unity of the active intellect," which meant that the rational *soul of all rational beings is one, and that therefore there is no individual life after death.

While Averroism was repeatedly condemned by bishops, synods, and leaders of the university, it persisted in Paris at least until the fourteenth century. By then a more extreme form of Averroism had developed in Italy, particularly in Padua. By the sixteenth century, some of these Italian Averroists were ready to reject Christian doctrine in the name of philosophy.

Axiology The discipline that studies the nature of values. In contrast to *ethics, axiology is concerned, not only with moral value, but also with aesthetic and practical values. Usually it does not deal with particular values, but with values in general—their formation, their explanation, their interrelation. Sometimes the term is used to refer to a value system —as when one speaks of someone's axiology.

Baptism   The traditional rite of initiation into Christianity. Its name is derived from a Greek verb meaning to bathe, to immerse, to dip, and sometimes to overwhelm—as a flood. Given the purifying function of water, it is not surprising that there are rites of purification involving water in many different religions. In the first century, one of the ceremonies by which Gentiles were admitted into Judaism was the "baptism of proselytes," which signaled the purification of the convert from all previous uncleanness. Thus, when John the Baptist calls Jews to be baptized he is implying that their sin is such that they have been defiled, and must now go through a repentance and purification similar to that required of Gentile converts.

From New Testament accounts, it is clear that baptism was practiced in the early church from its very beginnings—according to Acts, immediately after Pentecost. It is mentioned, discussed, or alluded to in almost every book of the New Testament—although little is said about how it is to be administered, and sometimes it is administered "in the name of Jesus" and sometimes in "the name of the Father, the Son, and the Holy Spirit."

The earliest discussion of baptism outside the New Testament occurs in the *Didache*, where believers are instructed to baptize in living—that is, running—water, with the provision that if such water is not available people may be baptized in water that is not running, and that if even this is not available, it is permissible to pour water over their heads three times in the name of the Father, the Son, and the Holy Spirit. (*See* *Immersion; *Aspersion; *Infusion.*)

After that time, references to baptism and instructions for its administration become more common—particularly in the writings of Tertullian (ca.155–ca.220) and Hippolytus (ca.170–ca.235)—and therefore it is possible to describe in some detail the rite of baptism as it was practiced toward the end of the second century, and perhaps before. At that time, it was customary for baptisms to take place in the Easter Vigil—the service Saturday night leading to the celebration of Easter. Catechumens (*see* *Catechesis) were baptized naked, the men apart from the women, apparently wading into water, kneeling in it, and then having water poured over them three times. According to the witness of Hippolytus, at least by that time the children of believers were also baptized. Baptism usually involved also an act of renunciation of "the Devil and all his works," a declaration of faith (the origins of what we now call the Apostles' Creed; *see* *Creeds), being clothed in a white robe, anointing with oil, and then joining the rest of the congregation for receiving *Communion for the first time—when they were given water to drink, as a sign of inner cleansing, and another chalice with milk and honey, as a sign of their having become heirs to the promised land.

The meaning of this act is multiple, and these various meanings are symbolized in the various shapes of baptistries and baptismal fonts. It is often understood as an act of witnessing to one's faith, and also as an act or a symbol of cleansing—in which case the shape of the baptistry is immaterial. It is also seen as the believer's dying and rising again with Christ—symbolized in baptistries in the shape of a coffin or a cross. It is also a sign of the new creation—often symbolized by an octagonal baptistry or font, pointing to the resurrection of Jesus as the first day of the new creation, after the seven days of the old. Then, a font or baptistry in the shape of a circle or a pear symbolizes a womb, and baptism is a sign of new birth. Finally, a common understanding of baptism, but one that is not easily signified in the shape of a font, is baptism as an act of grafting the person into the true vine, Jesus, thus becoming a member of his body, the church.

The practice of baptism has evolved through the centuries. Sometimes the notion that baptism washes away all previous sin, but has little to do with life thereafter, led people to postpone baptism as long as possible, until they had committed most of their sins—this, to the point that some waited to receive baptism until they were on their deathbeds. After the Roman Empire became Christian, it became customary to baptize practically every infant born within the Empire—except Jewish children, thus indicating that the church had become practically coextensive with society at large. Immersion, or at least walking into the water, was the usual form of baptism until the conversion of large numbers of people from northern and frigid climes led to the practice of pouring water over the head. At least until the eleventh century the church in Rome continued the practice of immersing infants, and the Eastern Orthodox churches continue that practice to this day. Most Protestant reformers—Lutheran, Reformed, and Anglican—changed little in the rites of baptism, with the exception of performing them in the language of the people. Luther did point out that baptism is valid, not only for the beginning of the Christian life, but throughout that life— much as an act of grafting is effective long after the act itself.

Although others had questioned the practice of baptizing children too young to believe, it was during the time of the Reformation that such questioning led to permanent divisions within the Christian church. The *Anabaptists held that baptism requires faith in the baptized, that for this reason only believers should be baptized, and that therefore those who had been baptized as children should be baptized anew. This principle of believers' baptism has since gained many adherents, not only among the original Anabaptist groups such as the Mennonites, but also as a foundational tenet of the many Baptist churches, the Disciples of Christ, some Pentecostal groups, and others.

Two recent developments in the practice of baptism should be noted. First, given the "post-Constantinian" context in which most of the older churches of Europe and America live, as well as the missionary contexts in which the church is growing at unprecedented rates, adult baptism has become more common, not only in denominations that traditionally have held to believers' baptism, but throughout the church at large. Theologically, this is connected with an increasing recognition of the difference between the church and the society in which it lives, and the ensuing refusal to baptize the children of parents who are not active participants in the life of the church. The result has been an increased emphasis on the preparation of adults for baptism, even in those churches that practice the baptism of infants.

A second change has to do with attempts to restore some of the practices of pre-Constantinian times as paradigms that may be valuable in an increasingly post-Constantinian age. This has led to the revision of many baptismal rites, and to the restoration of a number of ancient practices that had fallen into disuse— such as the renunciations before baptism and the yearly renewal of baptismal vows.

Barthianism   *See* *Neo-orthodoxy.

Beatific Vision   Literally, the "joyful vision." This is the vision of God, which according to much of Christian tradition is the goal of human life. Throughout history, there has been debate about its nature, its content, and its timing. Some have insisted that a full vision of God is not possible for the human intellect, even in paradise, for the finite cannot comprehend the infinite. Others have argued for a vision "in excess"—by which is meant a vision in which, rather than the intellect comprehending the divine, it is the divine that engulfs the human. As to the content of the beatific vision, the question is whether in heaven the intellect sees all things in God, or sees them directly. As to the timing, the question has been whether it is possible—in at least some exceptional cases—to attain such a vision during this life.

Beatification   The act of declaring a deceased believer "blessed," and therefore worthy of veneration. Although not in common usage, the title of "Blessed" or "Venerable"—as in Blessed John Duns Scotus and the Venerable Bede—has been understood as of lesser rank than that of "Saint." Since 1634, by action of Urban VIII, the process of beatification has been regulated by Rome, and has commonly become a step in the process of *canonization of saints.

Biblicism   Usually a term with pejorative connotations, applied to those who insist on the *inerrancy of Scripture, rejecting the findings of historical and literary criticism and often claiming that theirs is the only correct interpretation of Scripture.

Bishop   From the Greek *episkopos*, through the Latin *episcopus*. A title, meaning "overseer" or "supervisor," given to church leaders beginning in the late first century. At first, at least in some churches, the titles of "elder" and "bishop" seem to have been interchangeable. Possibly some churches had more than one such person—what historians call a "collegiate episcopacy"—but by the second century the usual practice was for the church in each city to have one bishop, a "monarchical episcopacy." Likewise, by the second century the traditional tripartite *hierarchy—bishop, presbyter, deacon—was fairly well established.

Bishops were normally elected by the congregation, but had to be confirmed in their appointment by other neighboring bishops—usually after receiving a written statement of belief—who then participated in the ceremony of their installation or consecration. Thus, the total episcopacy of the church was seen as a collegial community, which guarded and represented the unity of the church. For this reason, there was normally only one bishop in each city or town, and when the growth of the church required several separate meeting places in a single city, the presbyters would preside over *Communion in representation of the bishop. At least in Rome, a piece of bread—the *fragmentum*—from the Communion presided over by the bishop was taken to each separate venue where Communion was presided over by a presbyter.

With the rise of *heresies (*Gnosticism; *Marcionism; *Docetism) in the second century, bishops gained further prestige and importance as guardians of the faith of the apostles. The same challenge also gave impetus to the emphasis on *apostolic succession, claiming that those bishops who could trace their lineage back to the apostles were the authorized spokesmen and guardians of the true faith. At the same time, the witness of many bishops martyred during periods of persecution gave further prestige to the title.

When the Roman Empire became officially Christian, in the fourth century, the title of bishop became even more prestigious. Some bishops were among the advisers to emperors and other high officials. Although conflicts between the civil and religious authorities continued for centuries, now bishops and other clerics generally found themselves in a position of power and prestige—with the result that the church was increasingly viewed as a hierarchy in which *laity were relatively passive participants (*see* *Ecclesiology). During the same period, and in a process that took centuries, bishops were increasingly organized into their own hierarchy, so that bishops in provincial capitals came to have metropolitan authority over their colleagues in the province, and bishops in imperial capitals—Constantinople, Rome—came to have even wider jurisdiction.

At the time of the Reformation, *Anglicanism and much of *Lutheranism continued having bishops, while the more radical Reformers rejected the title altogether. In the *Reformed tradition, the emphasis on human *depravity as a result of *sin led to an unwillingness to trust any individual for the government of the church. Also, since in the Netherlands and in Great Britain bishops were generally supporters and agents of the crown, both the Dutch Reformed and the British Presbyterians—who eventually won the day in Scotland—were acutely suspicious of bishops. As a result, *Presbyterianism came to view the "presbytery"—the community of all the elders or presbyters—as a jointly held episcopacy.

In the eighteenth century in England, John Wesley (1703–91), pressed by difficult circumstances and petitions from America, where there was a shortage of ordained clergy, decided to ordain those who were to lead his movement in the recently created nation. As justification for this act, he claimed that since in the early church presbyters were also bishops, and he was a duly ordained presbyter of the Church of England, he was qualified—even though he did this reluctantly and as a last resort—to claim the episcopal function of ordination. Although Wesley still considered himself a faithful Anglican, this particular act, more than any other, sealed the breach between Anglicanism and emerging *Methodism.

Black Theology One of the most significant of the many *contextual theologies developed in the second half of the twentieth century, black theology is an articulation of the theological perspectives of persons of African descent enslaved in the Americas—particularly in the United States. While its formal articulation dates from the twentieth century, the emergence of black theology must be seen in the manner in which slaves interpreted the Christianity they had learned from their masters. Its most widespread expression during slavery was in the "Negro spirituals," which often referred to Moses as leading the people out of bondage, to God delivering Daniel and others, and to the "sweet chariot" leading people "home"—a veiled reference to the underground railroad and to the hope of freedom in the North. At times, this understanding of the faith as a call and a hope for freedom led to open revolt, as in the case of the famous preacher Nat Turner.

After emancipation, the African American religious perspective was always marked by the oppression of segregation and the longing for full citizenship and freedom. As is well known, the foremost spokesperson for these sentiments during the civil rights movement was Martin Luther King Jr.; but he was only the most famous of thousands of preachers and teachers who looked at Christianity from the perspective of oppression and exclusion.

The name most often associated with the formal emergence of black theology as a self-conscious attempt to look at traditional theology and correct it from an African American perspective is James Cone, whose book *Black Theology and Black Power*, published in 1969, marks the beginning of black theology as a formal enterprise. His later book *God of the Oppressed* (1975) applies the methodology and perspective of liberation to the doctrine of God, seeking to undo much of what had been done by traditional theology by way of depicting God as favoring the powerful.

Although originally an American development, as the notion of "negritude" and of black solidarity throughout the world gained more adherents, particularly in Africa and the Caribbean, new variants of black theology also developed in those regions.

African American women, conscious of their double oppression and exclusion as black and as female, and often disagreeing with the goals and perspectives of white *feminist theology, have developed their own form of black theology, *womanist theology.

Blasphemy Any word, gesture, action, or even thought that is purposively offensive to God—and, in some cases, to religion or to the church. In the Old Testament, it is punishable by stoning to death. Jesus was accused of blasphemy for speaking against the Temple —and so was Stephen. During the Middle Ages it was severely punished, often by death. After the Reformation, it was still considered a crime, not only in traditionally Roman Catholic nations, but in other lands where Protestant Christianity was the official religion, such as England and Scotland. As the lines of separation between church and state have become clearer, blasphemy is no longer punishable as a crime in most Christian lands— as it is in several Islamic countries. In several denominations it is punishable by *excommunication, shunning, or otherwise severing the guilty party from the community of believers.

Cabala A term derived from a Hebrew word meaning "tradition." It originally referred to all the Hebrew tradition beyond the Torah—both written and oral. Eventually, and particularly after the twelfth century, it came to mean a method of biblical interpretation that finds secret meanings in texts, mostly on the basis of numerology and mystical and *allegorical interpretation. Claiming to be a secret tradition dating back as far as Moses, it became quite widespread within late medieval and Renaissance Judaism. Some Christians were also profoundly impacted by it, and some employed the hermeneutical methods of the cabala as a means of finding in the Hebrew Scriptures such traditional Christian doctrines as the Trinity, the incarnation, and others.

Calvinism The theological tradition stemming from John Calvin (1509–64). As a Protestant, Calvin agreed with all the main tenets of Protestantism, such as *justification by faith, the primary authority of Scripture, the priesthood of all believers, and the sanctity of the common—that is, not monastic—life. He considered himself a faithful exponent of the teachings of Luther, who in turn spoke very favorably of Calvin's early theological work.

There were, however, a number of differences between Calvin and Luther, and these differences eventually gave rise to the Calvinist, or *Reformed, tradition. One of these differences may be seen in Calvin's emphasis on the process of sanctification as part of the Christian life and the goal of salvation—in contrast to Luther, who feared that too much talk of sanctification could lead back to justification by works. Also, Calvin insisted more than Luther on the value of the *law as guidance for the Christian even after having received the gospel, and not only as a means to lay bare our sinfulness. The law, which certainly condemns the sinner, also leads that sinner into a holier life. Thirdly, Calvin was much more inclined than was Luther to expect and demand that magistrates and government in general follow the law of God—which is one reason why revolution on religious grounds has been much more common in Calvinist than in Lutheran lands. Finally, there were differences between Calvin and Luther regarding the presence of Christ in the *Eucharist—both believing that Christ is really present in the sacrament, but Luther insisting on the physical presence of the body and blood of Christ in the elements, and Calvin declaring that the presence of Christ, although real, is spiritual, and that in Communion, by virtue of the power of the Holy Spirit, we are carried into the presence of Christ in heaven, rather than his body's having descended to the altar (*Virtualism).

These were the main differences between Lutheranism and Calvinism during the sixteenth century—differences that led some second- and third-generation strictly Lutheran theologians to attack Calvin and his teachings.

In the seventeenth century, however, other developments took place that led to a change in what is meant by "Calvinism." Both in the Netherlands and in Great Britain, divisions arose among Calvinists regarding *predestination and a series of related issues. In Great Britain, the Westminster Confession, and in the Netherlands the canons of the Synod of Dort (1618–19), issued against Arminius and his followers (see *Arminianism), now defined orthodox Calvinism much more narrowly than Calvin himself had done, and with greater emphasis on the doctrine of predestination and its ultimate consequences. Since that time, the term "Calvinism" has come to denote a position that agrees both with Calvin in his points of difference with Luther, as stated above, and with the orthodox Calvinism of the seventeenth century.

The main tenets of this orthodox Calvinism may well be summarized by the five main doctrinal canons of Dort: (1) the total *depravity of all humankind, so that as a result of the *fall there is no good in us capable of turning us toward God; (2) an unconditional election, so that God predestines some to salvation and others to perdition, not on the basis of anything they might do or believe, or that God foresaw they would do or believe, but simply by a sovereign divine decree (see *Predestination); (3) an *atonement, or *work of Christ, whose efficacy is limited to the elect; (4) the impossibility of resisting *grace, which is given to the elect and which they cannot reject; (5) the *perseverance of the saints, who—because they are predestined to salvation—cannot be ultimately lost.

In more recent times there have been currents within the Reformed tradition which, fully aware of the difference between Calvin himself and strictly orthodox Calvinism, are seeking a return to Calvin, and a new reading of his theology that is not dominated by the events and controversies of the seventeenth century.

Canon   A term of Greek origin meaning "rule" or "measuring rod." It is used in theological contexts with various meanings. The "canon of Scripture" is the list of books declared to be authoritative as part of Scripture. In matters of law and polity, "canon law" means the law of the church, as opposed to "civil law." In Roman Catholic liturgy, the "canon of the Mass" is the prayer of consecration. In Eastern liturgies, it refers to various series of hymns—usually nine, in acrostic form—prescribed to be sung in morning worship (matins). The list of approved saints is the "canon of the saints" (see *Canonization). As a title, a "canon" is usually a member of the chapter of a cathedral or collegiate church.

Canonization   In biblical studies, the process whereby a book or group of books became part of the *canon. In other contexts, the declaration by proper authority that a deceased Christian is worthy of veneration as a saint.

From a very early date Christians venerated the memory of their most outstanding saints, in particular the apostles and then the martyrs. The anniversary of their deaths was often celebrated as the day of their final victory, and when the person's tomb was readily accessible special services were held on that date at the place of their burial. Soon people also began collecting relics connected with particular saints, and placing them in special settings within the churches.

All of this took place spontaneously, so that in a certain locality the memory of a particular saint was venerated, and slowly the devotion to that saint spread to other regions, until it became a matter of general practice and acceptance.

In the Western church, by the late twelfth century the popes were claiming that no person should be canonized without proper endorsement from the Holy See. This principle eventually made its way into canon law, which now establishes the procedure through which a person who has previously been beatified (see *Beatification) is declared an official saint of the church. This process includes an adversarial process similar to a trial, in which an official of the church is charged with the task of raising all possible objections to the canonization of the person in question. In Eastern Orthodox circles, it is normally the Holy Synod or some such body that makes the determination.

Once canonized, the person joins the ranks of the official saints of the church, whose feast days are celebrations of the entire church, and after whom churches may be named.

Cartesianism   The philosophical system of René Descartes (1596–1650), whose Latin name was Cartesius; and, by extension, the system of his followers. The elements of Cartesianism that have most impacted Christian theology are its rationalism and its understanding of the relationship between body and soul. Descartes's rationalism, which took absolute doubt as its point of departure and was willing to accept as true only that which could in no way be conceived as false, drew much criticism from church authorities, who saw it as an attack on faith. Eventually, however, there were many theologians who valued Descartes's methods of inquiry and his proofs of the existence of God and of the soul, claiming that they were irrefutable and therefore a great aid to the church.

On the relationship between body and soul, he never offered a satisfactory explanation. His followers did offer a number of solutions, including *occasionalism, which claimed that God is the bridge between body and soul.

Casuistry   In its positive sense, the art and practice of applying general principles—particularly moral principles—to specific cases. This developed during the Middle Ages as pastors felt the need to apply *penance in responsible ways, and therefore many of the penitential manuals for confessors were in fact books of casuistry. In its pejorative, and now usual, sense, casuistry refers to

the practice of rationalizing the decision to follow a desired course of action by claiming that it is a particular case, and that therefore certain moral principles do not necessarily apply.

Catechesis   The process of instruction and preparation for *baptism. Those who are undergoing such a process are called "catechumens." In the early church, this process included both doctrinal and moral instruction, and often lasted as much as three years—with emphasis at first on moral matters, and on doctrinal issues only as the date of baptism approached.

After the Roman Empire embraced Christianity and the majority of the population were baptized as infants, catechesis became increasingly associated, no longer with preparation for baptism, but with the early instruction of children, usually preparing them for *confirmation. Instructions written to serve this purpose are called "catechisms."

In recent times, with the dechristianization of the West and the enormous growth of churches in former missionary territories, and with the consequent growth in the number of adult baptisms, many of the ancient practices of catechesis have been reinstated.

Cathars   See *Albigensians.

Catholicity   One of the *marks of the church, often understood as universality —the church is catholic because it is present at every place and time. Catholicity, however, may also have the connotation of a unity in which a variety of perspectives and contributions have a place—in contrast with universality, which often has the connotation of uniformity.

Causality   The relationship by which one event or thing results in another. Aristotle listed four forms of causality: material cause, formal cause, efficient cause, and final cause. The first two refer to the "stuff" of which things are made, and to that which gives them shape or structure. Tin is the material cause of a can, and its formal cause is its cylindrical shape, which turns the tin into a can. The third, efficient cause, is what we now commonly understand by "cause": one thing moves another, or one event leads to another, as when a billiard ball moves another or when prejudice leads to war. In such cases, we say that one event or reality has caused the other. The final, or teleological, cause is the purpose or goal that pulls things or events from their intended future. Things happen not only because their efficient causes "push" them, but also because their intended end "pulls" them.

Many of the traditional arguments seeking to prove the existence of *God proceed from the existence of things to their cause—usually in modern times their efficient cause, but also in earlier times their teleological cause. Thus, God is often spoken of as the "first cause" of all things—the primordial efficient cause—and as their "final cause"—the goal toward which they are being attracted.

The very notion of causality as an objective reality was severely questioned in modern times, first by David Hume (1711–76), and then by Immanuel Kant (1724–1804). As a result, arguments based on causality are often seen as convincing only within a certain set of presuppositions that are not self-evident.

Celibacy   The state of not being married, required in all Christian traditions of monks and nuns, in the Eastern Orthodox tradition of bishops, and in the Roman rite of the Roman Catholic Church of all clergy. In Eastern Orthodoxy, deacons and priests are allowed to marry, but only before ordination.

The call for celibacy has usually been based on four sorts of considerations, often intermingled. First, there has always been within the Christian church a strong tendency to devalue physical appetites, and particularly sexual appetites—with the corollary that sexual intercourse defiles, and that those practicing it should be kept from defiling worship by leading in it. Second, in some cases there has been the practical consideration that celibate workers and missionaries can take risks that married people with families cannot take, and that therefore a celibate clergy is a particularly useful tool for the mission of the church—as has been shown, for instance, in the missionary work of Franciscans, Dominicans, and Jesuits. Third, particularly during the Middle Ages, there was the consideration that the church owned vast properties, and that married bishops and other leaders would be more concerned with providing an inheritance for their children than in the interests of the church as an institution. Fourth, celibacy has often been inspired by eschatological expectation, as an effort to anticipate the life of heaven, where people are not married nor given in marriage. In some groups, an expectation of the imminent return of Jesus has also led to celibacy, on the basis that in the face of that imminent return all normal activities of life are to be set aside.

Although there are records of celibate bishops and pastors from very early dates, it was quite common for pastors and bishops to be married. As time went by, however, there was increasing pressure in favor of a celibate clergy. These pressures came to a climax during the reforms of Popes Leo IX (1048–54) and Gregory VII (1073–85), when many married clergy were forced to abandon their families. After that time, although with notable exceptions, a celibate clergy became the norm in the West. At the time of the Reformation, the Council of Trent insisted on clerical celibacy, and this has been the official position of the Roman Catholic Church since then.

Charity   In traditional theological texts, this term does not have the same meaning as in common usage. It is not the practice of giving alms or supporting the needy. It is, rather, Christian love, and comes from the Latin *caritas*, which is the most common translation of *agapē*. As such, it is the highest of the three traditional Christian *virtues—faith, hope, and charity.

Chiliasm   From the Greek word for "thousand," it is essentially the same as *millennialism—the expectation that Christ will come and rule on earth for a thousand years. Sometimes the term "millennialism" is reserved for modern eschatological speculation, often trying to determine the time of the millennium, or the order of the final events. In that case, "chiliasm" is used for the common view in early Christian theology of a reign of God on earth, with emphasis on its joy and its abundance rather than on its time or its duration. These views soon fell into disrepute as theologians more influenced by *Platonism declared them to be too materialistic, and not sufficiently spiritual.

Christology   The branch of theology that deals with Christ. Traditionally, it has been concerned with two central issues: the person of Christ—who he is—and his work—how he saves us. (For the latter, *see* *Atonement; also *Soteriology.)

From very early times, Christians have puzzled over how to understand and to express who this Jesus is who means so much for them. In the New Testament, he is called Son of Man, Messiah, Lord, Word of God, True Shepherd, Lamb of God, for example. It is also clear that our earliest records of Christian worship place Jesus at its center. Early in the second century, pagan writer Pliny attests to this, saying that Christians gathered "to sing hymns to Christ as to God."

Soon, however, what takes place in worship must also be expressed in theology and doctrine, and thus the question arises, Who is this Jesus? Is he divine? Is he human?

Some of the earliest answers were considered too simplistic, and were rejected by the church at large as denying an important aspect of the full truth. Thus, at one end of the spectrum there were those who believed that Jesus was a purely celestial being, an alien messenger from above who was human only in appearance. This view was called *Docetism, after a Greek word meaning "to seem." It was held by many *gnostics as well as others. We see echoes of its rejection in 1 John 4:2, where the test of orthodoxy is the affirmation that Jesus "has come in the flesh." The opposite extreme, often called *Ebionism, held that Jesus was a pure man, born like all men, whose purity was such that God gave him a special standing or role. This too was rejected by the church at large. Thus, from an early date it was clear that Christians wished to affirm that Jesus was both divine and human, but little thought seems to have been given to how to understand and to express this.

Very soon, partly on the basis of the Gospel of John, it became customary to declare that Jesus is the *Word of God made flesh—and it also became customary to refer to the Word as the Son. While this was helpful, it still left open a number of questions, particularly the question of how the Word, or Son, may be said to be divine. In the second century, Justin Martyr declared that the Word was a "second god"—an infelicitous expression that was soon abandoned. It was in the fourth century that this issue came to a head in *Arianism, and the process of refuting it and clarifying how the Word or Son is God led to the development and clarification of the doctrine of the *Trinity. Thus, by the second half of the fourth century, the general consensus was that Jesus is divine because he is the divine and eternal Word or Son of God made flesh.

It now remained to clarify how one is to speak of the relationship between that divine Word and the humanity of Jesus. Granted that Jesus, being God's Word or Son, is fully divine, is he also fully human? How is one to conceive of the relationship between the divinity and the humanity in Jesus? On this subject, there were two theological tendencies that clashed repeatedly. One, the *Alexandrine, emphasized the unity of the divine and the human to such a point that it might seem that the humanity was dissolved or engulfed in the divinity. If need be, the Alexandrines were willing to deny some aspect of the humanity of Christ in order to affirm the union of the divine and the human in him. This led to positions such as *Apollinarianism, which denied that Jesus had a rational human *soul, and which was rejected by the Council of Constantinople in 381.

The opposite theological school, the *Antiochene, was concerned over safeguarding the full humanity of Jesus, sometimes at the expense of its full union with the divine. This was the position of *Nestorius, who declared that in Jesus there are two natures and two persons, and that the union of the two is one of will rather than of nature or of person. His position was rejected by the Council of Ephesus in 431. As part of that rejection, his Alexandrine adversaries underlined the importance of the *communicatio idiomatum—the transferral of predicates from the human to the divine—in the person of Jesus Christ, so that whatever is said about him as human may also be said about him as divine.

In 451 the Council of Chalcedon finally arrived at the formula that eventually became generally accepted by most Christians, that in Christ there are "two natures in one person." While this did not solve the issue, it was simply stating that one must affirm Christ's full divinity, his full humanity, and the full union of the two.

Although most Christians eventually accepted the formula of Chalcedon, some rejected it. Those who followed the extreme Antiochene position, commonly known as *"Nestorians," took refuge in Persia, and to this day there is a small church that traces its origins to that schism. Others, who followed the extreme Alexandrine position, became known as *Monophysites—that is, hold-

ing to the doctrine of a single nature in Jesus. This is still the position of the Coptic Church, the Church of Ethiopia, the Syrian Jacobite Church, and others.

Although the Council of Chalcedon is generally said to mark the end of these debates, the truth is that the controversy lasted for centuries, and that its fires were fanned repeatedly as various theologians —and sometimes emperors seeking political aims—suggested solutions or compromises that were found wanting by the rest of the church. (See also *Monergism; *Monotheletism; *Hypostasis; *Hypostatic Union; *Enhypostatic Union; *Dyophysism; *Dyotheletism.)

The Protestant Reformers in general accepted the christological formula of Chalcedon and the decisions of the early councils on these matters, but were more concerned over the saving work of Jesus than over the question of how he can be both divine and human and still only one person. Among the major Reformers, Calvin tended to emphasize the distinction between the divine and the human in Jesus, much as the Antiochenes had done earlier. Luther inclined in the opposite direction, emphasizing the union of the divine and human—although he differed radically from the ancient Alexandrines in that he emphasized the reality of the humanity of Jesus, and insisted that we can see the divinity of Jesus only as it is revealed in his humanity, his weakness, and his sufferings.

In more recent times, many theologians have sought to leave these debates aside by concentrating on the work of Christ rather than on the metaphysical issues surrounding his person. (See *Atonement.)

Church   The English term "church" is derived from a Greek word meaning "that which belongs to the Lord." The Greek word most commonly used to refer to the church is ekklēsía, from which are derived the Latin ecclesia and similar words in Romance languages—iglesia, église, chiesa. For this reason things having to do with the church are often called "ecclesiastical," and the doctrine of the church is *ecclesiology.

While always referring to the community of the faithful, the term "church" has various meanings according to the context. It often refers to the local congregation—as in "the church in Ephesus," or "the church will gather this evening." At other times it includes all believers everywhere—as in Ephesians 3:10, or in "the church catholic." It is also used in the name of a particular denomination or faith community—as in The United Methodist Church, or the Roman Catholic Church. Sometimes it refers to the authoritative leadership of a particular community—as in "the church teaches that . . ." While these are different, there is also a relationship among them—and this is one of the themes that ecclesiology studies.

Circumincession   Derived from the Latin, circumincession is the equivalent of the Greek perichōrēsis, and refers to the interpenetration of the three divine *Persons of the *Trinity. Since perichōrēsis is very similar, though not the same, as a word that could be used for a choreographic dance, sometimes the image is used of the Trinity as a choreography in which all three Persons act together, yet distinctly, each as it were dancing around the other two. At any rate, the principle of circumincession, perichōrēsis, or interpenetration, is the basis for declaring that in every action of a person of the Trinity all three persons are present—in the classical Latin formula, opera Trinitatis ad extra indivisa sunt.

Communicatio idiomatum   Literally, the "sharing of the properties." This is a principle in classical *Christology by which whatever is predicated of the human nature of Christ may also be predicated of his divine nature—for instance, if the human nature of Jesus walked in Galilee, it may also be said that God walked in Galilee. It was stressed particularly by *Alexandrine theologians as a way of rejecting the "disjunctive" Christology of the *Antiochenes. It became particularly important in the debates surrounding *Nestorianism and the Council of Ephesus (431), for it was by virtue of the communicatio idiomatum that Nestorius's adversaries insisted that one must say that God was born out of Mary's womb, and that therefore Mary is *theotokos—bearer or mother of God.

Communion   See *Eucharist.

Communion of Saints   A phrase taken from the Apostles' *Creed (communio sanctorum), into which it was apparently incorporated in the fifth century. There is some debate as to its intended meaning when first added to the creed. There is no doubt that in this context communio still had its original meaning of sharing, common participation. The ambiguity is mostly in the meaning of sanctorum, which may refer to "the saints," as it is commonly translated, or "holy things." If the former, the phrase refers to the sharing that takes place among "saints," or believers—apparently both living and dead. If the latter, it refers to the sharing in "holy things," and may well have been introduced into the creed as an affirmation of unity of Christians in the *Eucharist and in other "holy things" such as ordination, against schismatics such as the *Donatists.

Given its common translation as the communion of saints, this phrase became important at the time of the Reformation, when Protestants often understood it as an explanation of the previous phrase, "the holy catholic church." In this case, what the creed says is that "the holy catholic church" that Christians confess, rather than a given institution subject to a single hierarchy, is the "communion of the saints."

Conciliarism   The claim that a council of the whole church is the supreme ecclesiastical authority, and is thus able to judge and depose popes. Although it had many precedents in earlier controversies, conciliarism became dominant toward the end of the Middle Ages, when the "Babylonian captivity" of the papacy in Avignon, the Great Western Schism—when there were two rival popes, and at times three—and the general corruption of the popes of the Renaissance led many to the conclusion that the only way to achieve a much-needed reformation was through the gathering of a council. Among the leaders of this movement were scholars such as Dietrich of Nieheim (or Niem) (1340–1418), Jean de Gerson (1363–1429), and Pierre d'Ailly (1350–1420). A series of councils (Pisa, 1409; Constance, 1414–18; Basle, 1431–49; Ferrara–Florence, 1438–45) managed to resolve the schism, but were unable to eliminate abuses and corruption in the church. Eventually, the conciliar movement itself was divided, so that there were now two councils and a single pope—which effectively put an end to the movement. However, even at the time of the Reformation there were several Reformers who insisted that the way to resolve the issues at hand was to call a general council of the church. When the Council of Trent (1545–63) first gathered, there were Protestants who attended its first session because they expected that the council would discuss and vindicate their views—which soon was revealed to be a false hope.

Concupiscence An inordinate desire in which temporal ends take the place of eternal ones, and in which the lower faculties—particularly the senses and their appetites—are not under the proper control of reason. Although commonly linked to sexual matters, concupiscence is much wider, and refers to all inordinate appetites. Augustine (354–430) explains the consequences of the *fall partially in terms of concupiscence, claiming that Adam and his descendants have lost the power to control the inordinate desires of the flesh by

the proper exercise of reason. According to medieval scholastic theology, concupiscence itself is not a *sin, but rather the consequence of *original sin—a view made official by the Council of Trent (1545–63). On the contrary, concupiscence is an opportunity for virtue, which is attained when the mind and the will resist the dictates of concupiscence. But concupiscence is also the occasion for sin. In Protestant theology—particularly in the theology of Protestant *orthodoxy—sin is not an action, but rather a state, and therefore the very presence of concupiscence is a sign of our sinful and corrupt nature.

Confession An affirmation or declaration, and therefore a term with two distinct meanings in theological discourse, for it is possible to confess sins as well as to confess the faith.

The confession of sins is a very ancient practice in the Christian church, still included in the worship services of most denominations, and playing a central role in the penitential system of the medieval church as well as in modern Roman Catholicism (*Penance; *Satisfaction).

A confession of faith is both an act by which the faith of the church is declared and the resulting document from such an act. Thus, the martyrs are said to have confessed their faith in the most difficult circumstances. Likewise, the title of "confessor" is usually given to those who confessed the faith even at the risk of their lives, or under torture or other duress.

When such acts of confessing the faith have resulted in a written document, that document is often called a "Confession." Such is the case of the Confession of Augsburg, presented by a group of noblemen in an act of confession of faith before Charles V, and since then the central document of the Lutheran tradition.

It is for both reasons that the segment of the church that opposed Hitler in

Germany received the name of "Confessing Church": because it produced the Barmen Declaration, and because it confessed the faith even at great risk and cost.

By extension, other documents expressing the faith of a particular church are also called confessions. Such are, for instance, the Westminster Confession, the First and Second Helvetic Confessions, and others. For this reason, the collection of fundamental doctrinal writings which the Presbyterian Church affirms is called the *Book of Confessions*.

Churches whose fundamental doctrines are stated in such documents—particularly the Lutheran and Reformed churches—are often called "confessional churches."

Confirmation   A rite—in the Roman Catholic Church, one of the seven *sacraments—administered after *baptism—in which a person is anointed and sealed in the faith. In the early baptismal rites, anointing the newly baptized was fairly common, often as a sign that the person was now part of the royal priesthood of God. As time went by, and particularly after the conversion of Constantine, baptism was increasingly conferred on infants shortly after their birth, as an almost automatic part of being born into a Christian society. It thus became necessary to provide an opportunity for these youngsters, after proper instruction, to be confirmed in the faith. In the West, the tradition developed that confirmation could be administered only by a bishop. The result was that the anointing that had earlier been joined to baptism now became a separate rite, usually several years after baptism.

The theological understanding of confirmation has never been clear. In the Eastern Orthodox churches the anointing or "chrismation" still takes place immediately after baptism, is performed by the priest, and is not a rite in which believers reaffirm their faith. In many Protestant churches that practice infant baptism, confirmation tends to be joined with the act or ceremony whereby a person previously baptized becomes a full voting member of the church.

Consubstantiation   A term often employed to express Luther's understanding of the presence of the body of Christ in Communion, but which Luther himself did not use. Its meaning is best understood in contrast to the Roman Catholic doctrine of *transubstantiation. Luther believed that the body of Christ was physically present in and with the eucharistic bread and wine. Yet he also believed that the bread did not cease to be bread, and the wine did not cease to be wine. This contrasts with the doctrine of transubstantiation, where the substance of the body of Christ takes the place of the substance of the bread, and thus led to the coining of the term "consubstantiation" in order to express the difference between Luther and his Roman Catholic opponents on this point.

Contextual Theologies   In the second half of the twentieth century, as the pool of those pursuing theological studies and reflection became increasingly diverse, it became apparent that every theologian's social and economic context leaves its mark on that person's theology. Thus arose a series of theologies that, rather than denying their contextuality, affirmed it, claiming that this provides new and valuable insights into the meaning of Scripture, of the gospel, and of doctrines in general. These various forms of theology are often called "contextual theologies," even though they claim that every theology is of necessity contextual, and that a theology that claims to be universal and free of every contextual bias is simply blind to its own contextuality.

Although often accused of relativizing truth, most contextual theologians claim that what they are doing is recognizing the manner in which context impacts perspective, and affirming it openly rather than obscuring it by unfounded claims of universality. Also, theologies that openly declare themselves to be contextual often draw parallels between their own situation and that of biblical writers, and thus claim to gain a particularly valuable insight into the meaning of the text.

Although there can be as many contextual theologies as there are human contexts, a number have made significant impact on theology at large, promoting dialogue with other contextual theologies as well as with more traditional forms. Among them one may mention *black theology, *Latin American theology, *feminist theology, *womanist theology, *mujerista theology, *minjung theology, and *Latino/ Hispanic theology.

Contingency A characteristic of every being—existent or not—whose existence is neither necessary nor impossible. Impossible beings are not contingent, for they simply cannot exist. A necessary being is that which must exist, whose nonexistence cannot be conceived, and whose existence does not depend on another—in other words, *God. Thus, of all possible beings, only God is not contingent. Another way in which theologians and philosophers have expressed this is by declaring that God is the only being whose essence implies existence. This identity of essence and existence is at the heart of Anselm's *ontological argument for the existence of God. On the other hand, the various *cosmological arguments begin with contingent beings, and from their existence move to the need for a noncontingent, necessary being that causes the rest to exist (see *Aseity).

Contrition The true, heartfelt pain for having sinned that is not based on fear of punishment or of discovery, but in true repentance. Medieval theologians often compared it to *attrition, and debated whether the latter was sufficient for forgiveness. It was commonly held that the difference between mere attrition and contrition is that the latter is based on love for God, which leads to a truly sorrowful heart. The Council of Trent (1545–63) stipulated that true contrition requires sorrow and detestation for the sin committed, and the sincere desire to sin no more.

Correlation, Method of A theological method often used in *apologetics, most clearly and consistently employed by twentieth-century theologian Paul Tillich (1886–1965). The method of correlation, as Tillich proposed it, consists in studying the deep existential questions posed by individuals and by a society, and then responding to them in terms of the gospel. Human existence is characterized by brokenness, incompleteness, and perplexity. We try to hide this from others as well as from ourselves. Sometimes we do this by asserting our self-sufficiency—what Tillich calls "*autonomy." At other times we try to find security and peace by grounding our existence on others, be they individuals or institutions—"*heteronomy." Both of these options fail; they produce an inauthentic life built on false ground. Therefore, says Tillich, our only real recourse is "*theonomy"—having the "ground of all being," God, as the foundation for existence. The gospel then responds to our deep and often unrecognized longing for theonomy, for an authentic existence properly resting on the ground of all being.

Cosmogony An explanation of the origin of the universe, usually mythical.

Cosmological Argument The name given to a series of arguments that seek to prove the existence of *God by looking at the world (cosmos), and moving from it to the existence of a Creator. This contrasts with arguments that try to prove the existence of God by showing that the very nature of God implies existence (*Ontological Argument). The most common and simple statement of the cosmological argument is exemplified by those who argue that if one finds a watch in a desert one concludes that someone has been there and left the watch behind; likewise, when one looks at this machinery that is the universe, one has to conclude that someone has created it.

The cosmological argument, however, may take various forms, as shown in Thomas Aquinas's (1225–74) classical "five ways"—which are in fact different statements of the same essential argument. The first way begins with movement, which requires a mover, and which eventually leads us back to the first "unmoved mover." The second way is based on efficient *causality: if all things are caused by another, there must be a first efficient cause. The third argues from the existence of contingent beings (*Contingency) to the existence of a necessary being. The fourth, from the degrees of perfection—one thing being better than another, but not as good as a third—to the perfect being from whom all perfection is measured. And, finally, the fifth way also begins with causality, but in this case final or teleological causality, arguing that things move according to an end or purpose—their "final" cause—and that there must be a final cause of all things, just as there is an efficient cause of all things.

Cosmology   An understanding of the universe, its structure and functioning. Early Christian cosmology, as was common at the time, saw the universe as essentially three-tiered, with earth between heaven and the "lower places." It was also deeply impacted by Platonic and Neoplatonic views, as well as by the Ptolemaic understanding of the solar system and the celestial spheres. As the accepted cosmology varies with time and with culture, the Christian faith has been expressed within the context of a variety of cosmologies (see *Culture).

Counsels of Perfection   According to medieval monastic theology, those guidelines or suggestions offered by God to those who wish to attain a higher

level of discipleship than merely obeying the commandments. The main biblical foundation for this distinction between commandments and counsels of perfection is in the story of the encounter between Jesus and the rich young ruler. There, once the young man declares that he has obeyed all the commandments, Jesus tells him that if he wishes to "be perfect" he is to sell all his possessions and give the money to the poor (Matt. 19:21). This is then interpreted to mean that obeying the commandments suffices for salvation, but that voluntary poverty is a counsel for those who wish to be perfect. Similarly, celibacy is said to be another such counsel on the basis of Paul's statement that it is good to marry, but it is better not to do so (1 Cor. 7:38).

Covenant   An oath or promise binding two or more parties together. These parties may be of unequal social standing, and in that case the covenant establishes the nature and terms of their future relationship. The notion of covenant is common in Scripture, where the covenant of God with Abraham and his descendants and "the new covenant in my blood" of the *Eucharist stand out among many. In earlier theology, the various covenants of God were often called *dispensations. Patristic and medieval theology frequently listed a series of covenants—with Adam, with Noah, with Abraham, and the covenant of grace or of the gospel, among others.

*Reformed theology—following the lead of Zwingli and Bullinger—has traditionally stressed the significance of the covenant as God's gracious act. The covenant is not an agreement between equals, but an act by which the sovereign God is freely bound to promises freely made. From this perspective, Reformed theologians have usually affirmed that every covenant is an act of grace—even though one may distinguish between the covenant with Adam, which may be described as a "covenant of works," and the "covenant of grace," which begins with Abraham.

This discussion about the covenant within the Reformed tradition led in the seventeenth century to the development of "covenant(al) theology," also known as "*federal theology."

Covenant(al) Theology *See* *Federal Theology.

Creation The doctrine that stands at the root of the Christian understanding of the relationship between God and the world. From a very early time Christianity, following the lead of Judaism, insisted that God is the creator of all that exists— a point expressed in the Apostles' Creed by the phrase "maker of heaven and earth," and in the Nicene by "maker of all things visible and invisible."

The doctrine of creation rejects two views that have repeatedly challenged it through the centuries: *dualism and *monism. The former holds that there are two principles of creation, usually God and something else. Sometimes this other principle opposes God. This view was quite common in the ancient world, and may be found in ancient religions such as Mazdaism, as well as in some strains of Greek philosophy, in *Gnosticism, and in *Manichaeism. Sometimes this other principle, while not opposing God, has an independent existence. Thus, in some ancient systems of thought there is a chaotic, primordial matter, from which God makes the world. At the other end of the spectrum, monism claims that since God—or the One—is the source of all things, there is no ontological distinction between creation and the creator. Such views were common in ancient times among some Platonists (*see* *Neoplatonism), who held that all that exists emanates from God, as a series of concentric circles in a pool, and that therefore everything is divine. Similarly, throughout history various forms of *pantheism have claimed that all is God.

Over against such views, Christians through the ages have affirmed that all that is owes its existence to God. There is no independent principle of existence— not the devil, nor matter, nor even chaos. Creation includes all things in heaven and on earth. The early church stressed this principle against those who claimed that God loves only spiritual reality, and that material creation—including the body—is therefore evil. During the Middle Ages, when a revival of the study of *Aristotelian philosophy led some to pose an eternally preexistent matter, the church insisted on creation *ex nihilo*—out of nothing.

In recent years and in some conservative Christian circles, the doctrine of creation has been proposed as a scientific hypothesis or explanation for the origin of the world—often in competition with the evolutionary hypothesis (*see* *Creationism). In much of that debate, the full meaning of the doctrine of creation is lost, and the stress lies on whether the Bible is to be taken literally or not, and on whether one of the two stories of creation in Genesis—or some combination of the two, obscuring the irreconcilable differences between them—is literally true.

The doctrine of creation, however, is much more than a matter of biblical *inerrancy, and does not stand or fall with the notion of six days of creation, or with the acceptance or rejection of some form of evolutionary theory (*Evolution).

Beyond all that, the doctrine of creation means, first, that all that exists is the result of God's will, and that therefore the physical world, as well as the spiritual—"all things visible and invisible"—is good.

Secondly, by affirming that things exist as a result of God's will—and not as an emanation of the divine essence—this doctrine affirms that there is an ontological difference between creator and creature, that the only necessary being is God, and that the entire creation is *contingent. This is why during the *Arian controversy the Arians insisted that the Word or Son is the result of God's will—and therefore a creature; and the Nicene Creed responded by declaring that the Son is "of one substance" with the Father—that is, not the result of God's will, as all of creation, but of the very essence of God.

Thirdly, again by affirming the contingency of creation, and its existence due to God's will, this doctrine claims that things have a purpose in God's mind, that they subsist by God's sustaining grace, and that they move toward God's intended ends (*see* *Providence; *Eschatology).

Finally, the notion that the entire universe is the product of a single and purposeful mind is the basis for the world's intelligibility. The universe may be studied and understood—within the limits of human knowledge—only because it is not created by many competing principles, nor does it result merely from the chance interaction of particles in a primal chaos.

Creationism   The response of some conservative Christians to the theory of *evolution, which they see as a threat to the Christian doctrine of creation. Creationism must be distinguished from the Christian doctrine of creation, which is not a scientific theory, nor an attempt to describe the origin of the species. According to creationists, the biblical story (actually, stories) of creation is scientifically defensible, and there is an irreconcilable difference between the Christian doctrine of creation and the scientific theory of evolution—with the consequence that teaching evolution in schools is ungodly.

In a different, more traditional context, "creationism" refers to the theory that each individual soul is the product of an act of divine creation, and is thus contrasted with *traducianism.

Creeds   Formulas in which the church seeks to encapsulate its teaching, particularly regarding items that are contro-

verted at the time. The origin of what we now call the Apostles' Creed is to be found in the ancient formula that scholars call the "Old Roman Symbol"—usually designated by the symbol "R." This was originally employed in baptisms, and this is the origin of its Trinitarian structure—"I believe in God the Father . . . , and in Jesus Christ our Lord . . . and in the Holy Spirit." At the time of their baptism, neophytes were invited to affirm their faith by responding to R, presented to them in interrogatory form: "Do you believe in God the Father . . . ?" Since at the time when this creed was first employed in Rome—the middle of the second century—Marcion and others were questioning the doctrine of creation, the real humanity of Jesus, and the final judgment, these items are stressed in R, and still are in the Apostles' Creed.

Neither the Old Roman Symbol (R) nor the Apostles' Creed was ever a creed of the entire church. Apparently other formulas were used in other cities and other areas. The most universally accepted creed in the entire church is the Nicene Creed, which was promulgated at the Council of Nicaea (325) and later modified at the Council of Constantinople (381). This was the creed commonly used both in the East and in the West until the ninth century, when the *Filioque controversy put the popes in the difficult position of having to take sides every time they recited the Nicene Creed. In order to avoid this, they reintroduced R, the old creed that had been used in Rome in previous centuries, claiming that it was the work of the apostles—hence the name "Apostles' Creed."

Many other creeds have been used by various churches at different times. (*See* *Rule of Faith.)

Culture   A system of symbols, attitudes, behaviors, relationships, beliefs, and responses to the environment shared by a particular human group in contrast to others. Since all humans live within such systems, all humans partake of at least one culture—and often of several overlapping cultural systems—and no one can claim to be free of cultural bias. Thus, Christianity—as well as any other religion—always exists in a given cultural context and reflects the impact of that culture in its life, doctrines, interpretation of texts, and so on. Therefore, the question of the relationship between Christianity and culture(s) is a crucial one that must always be asked anew, as cultural contexts shift.

The classical discussion of this issue is H. Richard Niebuhr's book *Christianity and Culture* (1951), where he develops a typology of five attitudes of Christians toward culture. He calls these five types: "Christ against culture," the "Christ of culture," "Christ above culture," "Christ and culture in paradox," and "Christ as the transformer of culture."

While this typology is worthy of consideration, the numerical explosion of Christianity in the non-Western world shortly after Niebuhr wrote his book shows how culturally conditioned the book itself is, for it hardly deals with the issue beyond the mainstream of Western civilization and the history of Christianity within it.

Not only in ancient times as it moved into the Hellenistic world, and in early medieval times when it was impacted by Germanic cultures, but throughout its history and all over the world Christianity has taken root in a variety of cultures, and these cultures have shaped its life and its doctrines. The missionary movement has long been aware of the need to present the gospel in terms that are understandable within a given cultural context, and has sought to do so while remaining faithful to its convictions (*see also* *Accommodation; *Acculturation). The growing awareness during the second half of the twentieth century of the impact of culture on Christianity is related to the rise of the various *contextual theologies. Beginning in the second half of the twentieth century, this has resulted in much missiological discussion on *inculturation—the process whereby the gospel becomes incarnate in a particular culture, and which is usually not so much the result of missionary reflection and adaptation as it is the result of the appropriation of the gospel by people in a particular culture.

Decalogue The Ten Commandments (from the Greek *deka*, ten, and *logos*, word). Their numbering differs. Jews and most Protestants count the commandment against other gods and the commandment against idols or graven images as two, while Roman Catholics and most Lutherans join them as one; in this case the number ten is reached by counting the list of prohibitions against coveting as two. In many churches the Decalogue is often read in worship, as a way of summarizing the law. Its placing, sometimes before the confession of sin, and sometimes as a response to the gospel, reflects different emphases on the function of the law—in the first case, the law as convicting the believer of sin, and in the latter case, the law as offering guidance for believers (*Law, Third Use of).

Decrees, Eternal The decrees—which some declare to be essentially one—by which God has eternally determined the outcome of creation, and particularly the salvation of some people and the reprobation of others. Although this issue was discussed earlier by the *scholastics, it has become characteristic of *Reformed theology, and particularly of orthodox *Calvinism, where there has also been much debate about the order of the divine decrees (*see* *Infralapsarianism; *Supralapsarianism; *Predestination). Some more recent Reformed theologians, following the lead of Karl Barth (1886–1968), declare that the eternal decree of God must be seen as that by which God graciously decreed salvation in Jesus Christ.

Deification   *See* *Theopoiesis.

Deism A movement, originating in England late in the seventeenth century and early in the eighteenth, whose main claim was that religion should be reduced to its most reasonable and universally accepted elements, and should be based on *reason rather than on *revelation. Its main forerunner was Lord Herbert of Cherbury (1583–1648), who argued that all religions have certain elements in common, such as the existence of God, the obligation of worship, the need for repentance, and an afterlife of reward and punishment, and that these are known, not by revelation, but by natural reason. Classical expressions of Deism are John Toland's (1670–1722) book *Christianity Not Mysterious* and Matthew Tindal's (1657–1733) *Christianity as Old as the Creation*, whose very titles suggest the nature of their contents.

Although originating in England, Deism influenced many of the philosophical and political leaders of other lands, such as Voltaire, Thomas Jefferson, and Benjamin Franklin.

Today, the term "deism" is often used in a more general sense, referring to the position that, while believing in the existence of God and perhaps also in creation, rejects the notion that God is still active in the world.

Demons   The term "demon" is of Greek origin, and in classical Greek literature does not necessarily have evil connotations. Thus, Socrates spoke of a "demon" that inspired him. In Greek Christian literature, however, the term is rather consistently reserved for evil supernatural forces or beings. Thus demons appear in the Synoptic Gospels, where illness is often described as "having a demon," and where Jesus repeatedly casts out demons. Later, as with the case of angels, there was much speculation as to the various orders of demons, their power, and so on.

Classical Christian theology usually discusses the origin of demons in the context of the origin of *Satan, who is often seen as the chief of demons. Although a number of explanations are given, orthodox Christianity has always insisted that, as part of creation, the devil and all demons also owe their existence to God, and are therefore originally good—the question then being the nature and origin of their evil, which is usually attributed to their ill use of the freedom God gave them.

Modern *empiricism, and scientific explanations of diseases as caused by germs, hormones, and the like, have led many to reject the notion of demons as the product of a bygone and ignorant age. However, in more recent times, others insist that such modern explanations do not dispel the mystery of *evil, but simply push it back, and that therefore the notion of demonic powers is not altogether misplaced.

Demythologization   The process, proposed mostly by Rudolf Bultmann (1884–1976), of reinterpreting the message of the New Testament for a time in which people no longer think in the mythological terms of the ancients (*see* *Myth), and the world is no longer conceived as the three-tiered structure of past times—with the earth in the middle, heaven above, and hell below. For Bultmann, the *existentialist philosophy of Martin Heidegger (1889–1976) provided the appropriate framework for understanding the gospel message for today. It may be argued, however, that Bultmann's project, rather than one of demythologization, was one of remythologization, reinterpreting the gospel within the context of the myths of *modernity.

Deontology   A system of ethics based, not on the ends that an action seeks, nor on rewards and punishments, but simply on what is right because it conforms to the will of God.

Depravity, Total   One of the principles of orthodox *Calvinism, particularly as defined by the Canons of Dort (1618–19) but having its roots in Augustine (354–430). According to this doctrine, the consequences of sin are such that all of humanity is depraved and capable of no purely good action, intention, or thought, for sin obscures and corrupts every human faculty. This does not mean that there is no good left in humans after sin, for the Synod of Dort still declared that there is still in the sinner "the vestiges of natural light, that allow for some knowledge of God, some understanding of natural reality, and some sense of the difference between good and evil."

Determinism   The view that all things and events are predetermined. Such views may be grounded on widely differing systems of thought. Most of the ancient *Stoics believed that history moved cyclically, that all events repeated themselves, and that they were therefore predetermined. In *modernity, a mechanicist view of the universe as a closed system of causes and effects has led many to embrace determinism. In some philosophical and theological systems, it is argued that God's knowledge of all things, including events still to come, requires determinism. Determinism is to be distinguished from *predestination, which does not claim that all things are preordained, but only the eternal destiny of the elect and the reprobate—even though there have been predestinarians who in their zeal to defend their position have fallen into determinism. (*See also* *Freedom of the Will.)

Deus absconditus   Literally, "hidden God." A phrase commonly used by theologians, such as Luther and Barth, as a way of emphasizing that even in revelation God remains sovereign, and is never fully known. Luther felt that God is best known in that which does not seem majestic, and particularly in the hiddenness of the cross. (*See* *Theologia crucis.*)

Deus ex machina   A phrase allusive to ancient pagan dramas, where the gods were brought in at appropriate times, sometimes by means of mechanical contraptions, and still used to refer to an unlikely resolution of a plot. In theological and philosophical discourse, it refers to the practice of bringing God in as an explanation or resource when everything else fails.

Deuterocanonical   *See* *Apocrypha.

Devil   *See* *Satan.

Dialectical Theology   A term often employed for the theology proposed early in the first half of the twentieth century by Karl Barth (1886–1968), Emil Brunner (1889–1966), Friedrich Gogarten (1887–1968), and others, and which soon developed into *neo-orthodox theology. It was called "dialectical," usually by those not participating in it, because it often spoke of God's relationship to the world—and to humankind—in contrasting terms, as both grace and judgment, "yes" and "no," veiling and unveiling. It was never "dialectical" in the *Hegelian sense of seeking or expecting a resolution of the tension into a new synthesis (*see* *Dialectics).

Dialectics   A term whose meaning has changed dramatically, and which therefore must always be understood within its proper context. In Greek philosophy, Plato wrote dialogues in which the truth was sought in a conversation, and therefore historians of philosophy speak of Plato's method as "dialectical." In the Middle Ages, the use of reason in theological inquiry was often called "dialectics," because reason proceeds in a sort of inner dialogue. Thus, for instance, St. Bernard (1090–1153) criticized and even persecuted Abelard (1079–ca.1144) because he dared use "dialectics" in religious matters. Shortly thereafter, following the example of Abelard's book *Sic et non* (*Yes and No*), the scholastics actually developed their theological discourse dialectically, offering an array of arguments for and against a given position, and then seeking a solution to the difficulties posed. In modern times, Hegel (1770–1831) developed a "dialectics" that was an entire philosophy of history as the unfolding of the thought of the universal mind. According to this dialectics, history moves, much as human thought does, from a "thesis" to an "antithesis" that negates it, and then to a "synthesis" that embraces both, only to become a new "thesis," and so forth. Somewhat later, Karl Marx (1818–83) rejected Hegel's idealism, but kept much of his dialectics, thus developing what he called "dialectical materialism" (*see* *Marxism). Early in the twentieth century, as *neo-orthodoxy was beginning to develop, some called it "dialectical theology"—although rather inexactly, for this was a theology of stark paradox rather than one in which the tensions were resolved in a higher synthesis.

Dispensation   The name sometimes given to the various covenants God establishes with humankind in Scripture. Irenaeus, for instance, speaks of four covenants: the covenant with Adam, lasting until the flood; the covenant with Noah, lasting until the exodus; the covenant of Moses, lasting until the incarnation; and the covenant of Christ, which will remain until the end of time. Although the notion of succeeding dispensations has been fairly common throughout the history of Christian theology, in the nineteenth century it developed into a specific scheme (or schemes) of history usually called *dispensationalism. Belief in dispensations, however, does not necessarily involve the acceptance of dispensationalist schemes.

Dispensationalism   A method of interpreting the Bible first developed in Great Britain by John Nelson Darby (1800–82), and popularized in the United States and elsewhere by the notes and interpretations of the Scofield Reference Bible, first published in 1909. Although there are several different dispensational schemes of history, they all agree that history is composed of a series of *dispensations in which God reveals something to humankind, and which humans

fail to fulfill, thus leading to a new dispensation and a new revelation. They also agree that much of Scripture—particularly Daniel and Revelation—is a prophetic announcement of future events, and that therefore by reading the prophecies correctly one can determine in what stage we are, and what events are still to come. In Darby's and Scofield's schemes, there are a total of seven dispensations, and we are currently in the sixth, or "dispensation of the church," which, like every other previous dispensation, is marked by a great *apostasy. This will come to an end with the return of Christ, which will mark the beginning of his earthly reign of a thousand years (*Millennialism), before moving on into the eternal kingdom of God.

While most biblical scholars dismiss dispensationalism as uninformed and as a misguided interpretation of Scripture, it has many adherents among the masses—witness the popularity of the *Left Behind* series, which is construed on dispensationalist assumptions. It should also be pointed out that, although many dispensationalists insist that the Jews are an apostate people, they also believe that Jesus will come when the state of Israel is fully restored to its biblical boundaries—hence the otherwise unexplainable phenomenon of conservative Christians who declare that God does not hear the prayers of Jews, but who still are strongly pro-Israel in their international pronouncements.

Divinization   *See* *Theopoiesis.

Docetism   A term derived from the Greek *dokein*, to seem, or to appear. Docetism is the claim that Jesus did not have a physical human body, but only the appearance of such. Such doctrines were quite popular in the early church, and often were joined to *dualistic views that only the purely spiritual can be good, while matter is evil. If matter is intrinsically evil, Jesus could not have had a human body, but only the appearance of one. Docetic doctrines seem to have circulated from a very early date, for 1 John 4:2 explicitly rejects them, and the many instances in the Gospels of Jesus' eating—even after the resurrection—seem to be an attempt to refute docetic tendencies. Such tendencies were common among the *gnostics, and were also held by Marcion, who apparently claimed that Jesus was not born, but simply appeared as a mature man during the reign of Tiberius (*see* *Marcionism). Much of the Old Roman Symbol, as of its later version, the Apostles' Creed (*see* *Creeds), seems to be devised as a barrier against docetic tendencies to deny the birth and the sufferings of Jesus—hence the affirmation that Jesus "was born of the Virgin Mary, suffered under Pontius Pilate, was crucified, dead, and buried."

Docetic tendencies have always been common in the Christian community, even though true Docetism has never gained a strong foothold in the church. By an extension of meaning, sometimes a doctrine that does not deny the physical reality of Jesus, but seems to diminish his full humanity, is called "docetic."

Doctrine   Literally, "teaching." The word "doctrine" has different levels of meaning according to its context. At its lowest meaning, it may mean simply someone's considered opinion and teaching about a given subject, and may be synonymous with "tenet"—as when one speaks, for instance, of Plato's "doctrine of the immortality of the soul." Sometimes it is used to refer to an entire heading of theological discourse—as when one speaks of "the doctrine of salvation," meaning *soteriology, or of "the doctrine of the church," meaning *ecclesiology. At a somewhat higher level, "doctrine" refers to those considered views and tenets that characterize a particular group within the church—as when one speaks of "the *Reformed doctrine of *predestination" or of "the *Wesleyan doctrine of *sanctification." Finally, a "doctrine" may be a teaching of such authority that rejecting it implies standing outside the bounds of orthodoxy. At this point, it becomes synonymous with dogma.

Even when the two are employed as synonyms, "doctrine" and "dogma" have different connotations. In order to be such, a dogma has to be promulgated by an official and authoritative body of the church. Thus, most Christian churches—Roman Catholic as well as Eastern Orthodox and Protestant—accept the doctrinal decisions of the first ecumenical councils (in some cases the first four councils, and in some the first seven) as a matter of dogma, while the Roman Catholic Church grants that status to a number of doctrinal decisions of later councils and popes. Therefore, "dogma" has an authoritarian connotation that most modern Protestants dislike, thus preferring to speak of the "official doctrines" of the church, rather than of its "dogmas."

While these "official doctrines" or "dogmas" of the church are not to be taken lightly, they are not to be considered full descriptions of the truth that lies behind them. The doctrine of the *Trinity, for instance is not a full description of God's inner being; it is rather a set of boundaries letting Christians know that they are to avoid a number of pitfalls when thinking about God—pitfalls such as tritheism, *subordinationism, *Arianism, and *modalism, for example.

Dogma   *See* *Doctrine.

Dogmatics   The discipline of theology, particularly when it views its task as studying the *doctrines or dogmas of the church, rather than constructing personal speculative systems. As a title, the term is often used as an abbreviated title for Karl Barth's (1886–1968) *Church Dogmatics*.

Donatism   A movement that arose in North Africa early in the fourth century, claiming that consecrations performed by bishops who had faltered in time of persecution were invalid, and therefore rejecting the authority of Caecilian, the bishop of Carthage at the time, who had allegedly been consecrated by one who had lapsed. This led to a schism that eventually was named after Donatus, one of its leaders. As the rest of the church and imperial authorities began opposing them, some of the more radical Donatists, known as "circumcellions," resorted to violence. Severely pressed by its enemies, and discredited by its more violent elements, the movement waned, but still subsisted until the Arab invasions four centuries later.

The theological issue raised by this schism—as well as by other, similar ones (*see* *Novatianism)—is the purity of the church and the validity of *sacraments and rites administered by unworthy persons. It was against the Donatists that Saint Augustine and others argued that the validity of a sacrament does not depend on the worthiness of the minister, but on the sacrament itself (*ex opere operato*). It was also against them that Augustine developed the distinction between the invisible church, which is the company of the elect, and the visible church, in which wheat and tares are still present. (*See* *Ecclesiology.)

Donum superadditum   In medieval theology, the "extra gift" that Adam and Eve were supposed to have had when created, and that they lost at the *fall. According to this theory, Adam and Eve had all that was needed to refrain from sin—in Augustine's terms, *posse non peccare*. In the view of some, the *donum superadditum* included also an excellence of intellectual and physical powers that have been lost as a consequence of sin.

Dualism   The notion that there are two sources of being. In its extreme cases, dualism sees these two principles as eternally opposed to each other. A classical expression of this sort of dualism is *Manichaeism, in which light and darkness have coexisted eternally, and the one can never destroy the other. According to this system, our present world is a mixture of the two, and the struggle of salvation is the process whereby they are being separated, and each confined to its own realm.

A milder form of dualism sees God as creating the world out of an eternally existing "unformed matter," or chaos. It was against this form of dualism, proposed by some during the revival of *Aristotelianism in the twelfth and thirteenth centuries, that the doctrine of *creation *ex nihilo was made a dogma of the church.

A third form of dualism, espoused by many *gnostics in the second century, begins with a single principle, but then claims that somehow error or evil crept into the equation, and that the result of this error or evil is the material world. This results in a dualistic view of the world, in which the spiritual is good and the material is evil.

Orthodox Christianity has had to walk a fine line on this subject, insisting that all that exists—including Satan and all the demons—is God's creation, and therefore originally good, but also affirming that the struggle with these powers of evil is real (*see* *Satan; *Evil).

Dyophysism   From Greek roots meaning "two natures." A term employed in *christological doctrine, and opposed to *monophysism. According to Christian *orthodoxy as defined by the Council of Chalcedon in 451, there are in the Savior two natures, one divine and one human, and these two exist in the *person of Jesus Christ, "without confusion, without change, without division, without separation." What this means is that Jesus is fully human and fully divine, and that his divinity in no way diminishes his humanity, or vice versa.

Dyotheletism (also dyothelism)   From Greek roots meaning "two wills." A term employed in *christological doctrine to refute *monotheletism. The Sixth Ecumenical Council, gathered in Constantinople in 681, rejected monotheletism and affirmed dyotheletism. This was simply an extension of the principle that Jesus must be fully human and fully divine, and that he must therefore have a human will as well as a divine will—even though the two coincide as to their contents.

Ebionism An early movement among Jewish Christians that is known only through the writings of some of its opponents, and whose actual teachings are not altogether clear. They derive their name from a Hebrew word for "poor," and apparently they lived in great simplicity. They were criticized mostly for their *Christology, for they apparently held that Jesus was a great prophet—the greatest of all prophets, but still only a prophet—whose faithfulness led to God's adopting him as Son (*Adoptionism). Later, the name of "Ebionite" has sometimes been used for anyone who holds a "low" Christology—that is, a Christology that does not declare Jesus to be fully divine.

Ecclesiology The theological discourse regarding the church and its nature. (In some circles, the same word is used for the art of designing and decorating church buildings.) The term "ecclesiology" is derived from the Greek *ekklēsia* and its Latin transliteration, *ecclesia*, which originally referred to a called assembly, as in the Athenian citizens' assembly, but in Christian circles was used to refer to the company of believers.

In the New Testament there is no ecclesiology as such; but there are many images used to describe the church, each of them stressing some of the various facets of the church itself—body of Christ, bride of Christ, people of God, ark of salvation, God's building, royal priesthood, the Lord's vineyard, for example. All these references, as well as the entire New Testament witness, indicate that the church is central to the Christian gospel, whose proclamation is incomplete if it does not invite people to join the body of believers.

In the early patristic period, the many theological controversies, and particularly the need to respond to the challenges of *Gnosticism and *Marcionism, led to a growing emphasis on the authority of the church. Hence the development of the doctrine of *apostolic succession, and the stress on *apostolicity, *unity and *catholicity as *marks of the church. Thus in the third century Cyprian declared that there is no salvation outside the church, and that one cannot have God as father without having the church as mother—statements that both Luther and Calvin quoted approvingly. Already at that time there were debates among Christians as to the purity of the church, and these debates grew stronger by the fourth century (*see* *Novatianism; *Donatism). As a result of these debates, *holiness was also defined and declared to be a mark of the church. Thus, while the original Creed of Nicaea simply declared faith "in the Holy Ghost," the text as amended at the Council of Constantinople in 381 adds "and in one holy catholic and apostolic church."

One of the enduring themes in ecclesiological discourse has been the relationship between the church as the body of believers in a particular place—as in "the church at Laodicea" or "First United Methodist Church"; the church as a national or international body—as in "the Church of England" or "The United Methodist Church"; and the church as the company of all believers—the "one holy catholic and apostolic" church. Clearly, the one, holy, catholic, and apostolic church exists on earth only as embodied in local congregations, in ecclesiastical organizations, denominations, and so on. Yet only a few of the more dogmatic and exclusivistic denominations claim that they, and they alone, are the church of Jesus Christ. How are these various "levels" or "embodiments" of the church related to the one church, the body of Christ?

A view that has been quite common since the time of Augustine (354–430), and which provides a partial answer to the question just posed, is the distinction between the visible and the invisible church. In this distinction, the invisible church—according to most theologians, known only to God—is the company of all those to be saved; the visible church is the earthly community in which the members of the invisible church are gathered by the Holy Spirit, but in which the wheat is still mixed with the tares. In Augustine himself, this distinction is not meant to diminish the importance of the visible church and its structures, but, on the contrary, to bolster its authority and importance even in the midst of its imperfections. Yet in later times others have used this distinction to argue that the visible church is of little or no consequence, and that they can abandon it without fear, for they are part of the invisible church.

Another point of disagreement in ecclesiological matters has been the relationship between the nature of the church and its government. From a very early date, leaders in the church were called *bishops, presbyters or elders (see *Priesthood), and deacons. Although it appears that for a time a presbyter was the same as a bishop, in the second century this tripartite hierarchy was generally established—bishops, presbyters, and deacons. However, this did not mean that the church was a hierarchy, but simply that it had this system of government. In the Middle Ages, a very hierarchical view of all of creation led also to a hierarchical view of the church, so that the church itself was seen as a *hierarchy. As in any hierarchy, the lower members derive their authority and even their being from the higher members. This view led to the point where it was common to speak of "the church" as the clergy, and particularly the higher echelons of the hierarchy, as if the laity were not the church. In the twentieth century, the extremes of this view were moderated by the Second Vatican Council, by speaking of the church as the pilgrim people of God and of the priesthood of all believers. Over against the hierarchical view of the church, oth-

ers have claimed that the church is the company of believers, and that it is in them that authority resides. This was the view behind late medieval *conciliarism, and has become prevalent in more recent times in many Protestant churches, where it is held that authority resides ultimately with the believers. In the sixteenth century, the Reformers—particularly Luther and Calvin—insisted that the church is not constituted by the hierarchy or by its members, but by the *Word of God—and by this Word preached in the sermon and enacted in the *sacraments. Hence Calvin's assertion that "wherever we see the Word of God purely preached and heard, and the sacraments administered according to Christ's institution, there, it is not to be doubted, a church of God exists."

Economic Trinity   The name usually given to the notion that the distinctions within the *Trinity have to do with God's activity in creation (*opera ad extra*), and are not intrinsic to the Godhead (do not exist *ad intra*). This view is commonly rejected by orthodox theologians, who insist that God is triune in Godself, and not only in outward relations—in other words, that there is an "immanent Trinity" in God. Within this latter context, the term "economic" is understood in its etymological sense as "management" or "administration," and what is meant by an "economic Trinity" is that the Trinity is a matter of God's outward management of creation, and not of God's very essence.

To complicate matters, some ancient theologians, when defending an immanent understanding of the Trinity, declare that God exists according to a divine "economy," and therefore seem to be proposing an economic or outward understanding of the Trinity, when what they in fact mean is that God's own inner ordering or management is triune—that God is triune because of that inner and eternal "economy" or "administration" within the Godhead.

Ecstasy An experience of prophets and mystics in which it appears that the person stands outside of the body, whose physical functions are normally suspended—hence the name "ecstasy," which means "to stand outside [oneself]." It varies according to individuals and traditions. Among Christian mystics, some hold that the ecstatic vision is the goal of life, to be attained only in the future life, and others claim to have had repeated ecstatic experiences along the way. Quite often the person coming out of an ecstasy remembers visions, instructions, or words of consolation received during the experience. At other times, the claim is made that the vision was such that it cannot be properly expressed in words. According to some, the final state of the soul in heaven is akin to a permanent ecstasy. (*See also* *Beatific Vision.*)

Ecumenism A term derived from the Greek *oikoumenē*, which means "the inhabited earth." Thus, "ecumenical" literally means simply "universal." It is in this sense that the early major councils of the church are called "Ecumenical *Councils"—for instance, the Council of Nicaea in 325. There is disagreement between the Eastern and the Roman churches as to how many of the councils are truly ecumenical, the East accepting only the first seven, ending with the Second Council of Nicaea in 787, and the Roman Catholic Church accepting twenty, up to the Second Vatican Council.

In more recent times, however, the terms "ecumenism" and "ecumenical" have been more closely associated with the attempt to bring the various churches all over the world into closer connection, and perhaps eventual unity. This modern ecumenical movement has several roots. One of them is to be found in what used to be called the "mission field," where missionaries soon discovered that the differences, divisions, and competition among various denominations were an obstacle in the evangelization of the world. Therefore, already in the early

nineteenth century William Carey called for a great international missionary conference that he hoped would meet in Capetown in 1810, in order to promote collaboration among the various Protestant missionary enterprises.

Other roots of the modern ecumenical movement are the renewed study of Scripture, which brought together scholars from different traditions; the need to respond jointly to such issues as totalitarianism, secularism, and world hunger; and the improved communications of the twentieth century, which made it easier for people from all over the world to meet and plan together.

This modern ecumenical movement, originating among Protestants and soon involving a number of Eastern churches, developed originally along three main lines of concern: "faith and order," "life and work," and missionary issues. The first sought to bring churches closer in matters pertaining to doctrine and polity. The second promoted collaboration in practical matters, charitable projects, and the like. These two gave rise to the World Council of Churches, organized in a worldwide assembly in Amsterdam, in 1948. Missionary concerns led to the first World Missionary Conference, in Edinburgh, in 1910—exactly a hundred years after Carey's projected conference—and crystallized in the International Missionary Council, organized in 1921. The International Missionary Council merged with the World Council of Churches at the New Delhi Assembly in 1961, and was succeeded by the Commission on World Mission and Evangelism of the World Council.

Among Protestants of evangelical leanings, many questioned the decisions, structures, and theology of the World Council of Churches and its related bodies. For some, the very word "ecumenical" was anathema, for it was understood as the willingness to forgo central items of doctrine for the sake of unity. Yet also among these groups there was a thrust toward greater unity and collaboration. This resulted in the Lausanne Movement—the Lausanne Committee for World Evangelization—launched at the 1974 Congress on World Evangelization.

Meanwhile, in 1962–65, the Second Vatican Council of the Roman Catholic Church had met. In calling for this council, Pope John XXIII had declared that this would be an "ecumenical" council. As the project evolved, it became evident that this council was expected to be ecumenical in both the traditional sense and the more modern sense. In the traditional sense, it was to be the twentieth in the series of ecumenical or universal councils of the Roman Church. In the modern sense, the council was to include the presence of representatives of Eastern and Protestant churches—although only as observers, not as full participants. At the same time, partly through the new openness brought in by John XXIII, the Roman Catholic Church became more involved in the modern ecumenical movement, and developed closer ties and collaboration with the World Council of Churches and similar bodies in various parts of the world.

Finally, as interreligious dialogue developed in the second half of the twentieth century, this was also called "ecumenism" in some quarters.

Election   The act or decree whereby God predestines some for salvation. (*See* *Predestination.)

Emanation   A particular understanding of the relationship between the One (God) and "the many"—the world. In this view, commonly held by many *gnostics and *Neoplatonists, the One radiates its own substance, as in a series of concentric circles from the center of a pool of water, or as heat from a fire. The closer a being is to the One, the better it is—thus, for instance, intellect is higher than matter, and formed matter better than chaotic diversity. Most Christian theologians reject this view, insisting that there is an ontological difference between God and creation, and that creation is not simply a lower level of the divine. One way to express this is to say that according to the theory of emanation the world is the result of God's essence, in which it shares, while in the doctrine of *creation the world is the result of God's will.

Although the theory of emanation has been generally rejected by Christian theologians, it did impact many medieval theologians who accepted the view that all of creation is ordered hierarchically (*Hierarchy), according to how close each being is to the divine. It also helped Augustine (354–430) develop his view of *evil, which he saw, not as a substance, but as a moving away from the One and toward the many.

Empiricism   A theory of knowledge (*Epistemology) that holds that all knowledge is derived from experience—be it sensory experience or inner experience—and which is therefore opposed to *idealism. Empiricism flourished particularly in Great Britain in the seventeenth and eighteenth centuries, under the leadership of John Locke (1632–1704). It found theological expression in *deism, and finally came to an impasse with the work of David Hume (1711–76), who argued that such fundamental notions as *causality and *substance are never really experienced and cannot be proved by experience. At a more popular level, "empiricism" is the attitude of those who say that they will only believe what they can see, or what can be proved by experimentation.

Enhypostatic Union   The *christological theory proposed by Leontius of Byzantium (sixth century), to defend the orthodox position that it is possible for two natures to unite in a single *hypostasis and still retain their distinction. Thus, the body and the soul unite in the single hypostasis of a human being, yet each could also exist separately. When they are united, they subsist in the single hypostasis, human being. When they are separated, each has its own hypostasis. In the case of the Savior, his human nature subsists in the hypostasis of the divine nature—even though normally a human nature would subsist in itself, with its own hypostasis—and the union is therefore "enhypostatic."

Enthusiasm   A term that originally meant being possessed by God or by the gods, and which generally had positive connotations in Christian theology until the seventeenth century, when it was applied to those who claimed to have a private communication with God, and who on the basis of such communication claimed to have received special instructions for themselves or for others. John Wesley (1703–91) was repeatedly accused of being an "enthusiast"—an accusation which he strongly and constantly rejected.

Epiclesis   The *eucharistic prayer, in which the presence of the Holy Spirit is invoked, usually to consecrate the bread and the wine, and sometimes also over the people, that they may receive the Spirit jointly with the consecrated elements. The epiclesis has always been an important element in all the Eastern liturgies for the celebration of the Eucharist. In the West, it fell into disuse during the Middle Ages, but has been reintroduced more recently by Protestants as well as by Roman Catholics. Traditionally, the Eastern churches have disagreed with the Roman Catholic Church, insisting that the consecration of the wine and the bread occur at the epiclesis, rather than when the priest pronounces the words of institution.

Episcopal   Pertaining or having to do with a *bishop—in Latin, *episcopus*—or bishops. Also part of the official name of the church that represents the Anglican Communion in the United States, the Episcopal Church.

Epistemology   The branch of philosophy that deals with the theory of knowledge. From ancient times, there was disagreement among Greek philosophers on how it is that the human mind acquires knowledge. Plato (*Platonism) felt that, since all that the senses perceive is passing and therefore not ultimately true, the senses cannot be the source of true knowledge. He therefore suggested the *preexistence of souls, claiming that it is in their previous existence that souls have been exposed to eternal ideas, and that all true knowledge in the present existence is a memory of that past knowledge. The function of a teacher, therefore, is not to instill new knowledge in the mind of a student, but rather to call forth the knowledge that is already there—much as a midwife helps a woman bear a child. Over against Plato, his disciple Aristotle proposed a theory in which knowledge begins with the data of the senses, from which the mind then distills the common essence behind things of the same species.

In early Christian theology, these two views vied with each other. In general, the *Alexandrine school of theology preferred Plato's option, and the *Antiochene leaned toward Aristotle. Eventually, however, Plato won out, and for centuries most Christian theologians subscribed to an essentially Platonic epistemology.

This required some adjustments, for fairly early Christian theologians rejected the notion of the preexistence of souls. This gave rise to the theory of *illumination, proposed by Augustine and others, which holds that, while the senses cannot be the origin of true knowledge, such knowledge comes to the intellect through an illumination from God's eternal Word or *Logos.

It was not until the thirteenth century, with the reintroduction of Aristotle's philosophy into Western Europe, that Christian theologians began considering anew the possibility that the senses may have a basic function in the knowledge of truth. This was one of the most significant contributions of Thomas Aquinas (see *Thomism), and in a way stands at the root of Western science, experimentation, and technology.

This emphasis on the senses and their experience reached its climax in British *empiricism in the seventeenth and eighteenth centuries, which claimed that all knowledge comes from the senses—either the outward five senses or the sense of inner experience—and which eventually culminated in *deism. Meanwhile, in continental Europe, Descartes (1596–1650) and his followers (see *Cartesianism) proposed a return to an epistemology not based on sense perception. Eventually, first in the work of David Hume (1711–76), and most definitively in the philosophy of Immanuel Kant (1724–1804), both British empiricism and Cartesian *idealism were replaced by the recognition that the structures of the mind play an important role in what is knowable, and how it is knowable, for knowledge is not a mere process of bringing things into the mind, but is an active process in which data are organized according to the capabilities and structures of the mind.

Erastianism A doctrine usually attributed to Thomas Erastus (1524–83), a Swiss-born professor of medicine at the University of Heidelberg who defended the power of civil authority in ecclesiastical matters. In a treatise on *excommunication published posthumously, he argued that the church had no power of excommunication, and that the punishment of sinners was the responsibility of the state. On the basis of this treatise, the view that the state is above the church, even in matters of church order and of ecclesiastical discipline, has been called "Erastianism."

Eschatology The doctrine of "last things"—from the Greek eschata, last things, and logos, treatise, doctrine, or word. Eschatology often deals with matters such as the *parousia of Jesus, the final *judgment, *eternal life, the *millennium, the *rapture, and the *resurrec-

tion of the dead. Since much idle speculation has been devoted to trying to determine the time and the order of such events (see *Dispensationalism, *Millennialism), and this has been so misused as a means of "scaring people into the faith," eschatology has often been neglected by theologians who feel that such matters are best left in the hands of God. Some have come to the conclusion that eschatological expectation is a metaphor relating to an individual's encounter with God—either in this life or after death.

There is another sense, however, in which eschatology is of fundamental importance for Christian theology. In this sense, eschatology, far from a matter of fear, is the basis of Christian hope and joy. Eschatology is the expectation and the assurance that in the end God and God's love will prevail. In this sense, eschatology, rather than being an appendix to the rest of theology, becomes one of the pillars on which theology is built (see *Hope, Theology of). Without an expectation of an end, all of history and all of life would be meaningless and hopeless.

On the other hand, much traditional speculation about the "end times" fails to take into account the fact that according to the witness of the New Testament there is a sense in which the end has already come. In the incarnation and resurrection of Jesus, the end of history has come into history. Repeatedly, the New Testament refers to the events of the life, death, and resurrection of Jesus, and to the outpouring of the Spirit at Pentecost, as "the last days." Thus, many theologians suggest that the best way to speak of Christian eschatology is by means of the paradox between the "already" and the "not yet." Jesus has already come; yet Jesus is to come. The kingdom of God is already among us; yet we pray daily for the coming of the kingdom.

Finally, it is important to point out that genuine eschatological hope has implications for the present life. Those who truly expect a certain outcome to their lives and to history will live according to that hope. Those who really expect their prayer to be answered, "Thy kingdom come," will live as those who indeed expect the kingdom to come. Thus, eschatological interpretation has an important ethical dimension that is often forgotten.

Essence   That which makes a thing be what it is, often in contrast to or in juxtaposition with that which makes a particular thing be, its *existence (*see* *Existentialism). Thus, one could say that the essence refers to what a thing is, its "whatness," while existence refers to the fact that it is, its "thatness." (*See* *Accident; *Substance; *Hypostasis.)

Eternal Life   A phrase that appears repeatedly in the New Testament, and one of the promises of the Christian faith. One could say that, strictly speaking, life after death, rather than "eternal," is everlasting, for *eternity belongs only to God. On the other hand, one could also interpret the phrase "eternal life" as referring not only to a life that goes on forever, but also to a life that is life in God, a sharing in the life of the Eternal One. At any rate, it is clear that Christianity, since its very inception and through its history, has held that there is life after death, and that this life is everlasting. On the other hand, such eternal or everlasting life in communion with God does not necessarily have to wait until death, and there is ample witness in the New Testament to an "eternal life" that begins during the present life. Finally, it should be noted that in early Christian *eschatology life after death is closely related to the expectation of a final *resurrection of the body, and that, in contrast with the Greek notion of the *immortality of the soul, such life after death is not something that belongs to us by nature, but is rather a gift of God's grace.

Eternity   A relatively ambiguous term, usually referring to that which is not bound by time. Augustine (354–430) argued that, strictly speaking, only God is eternal, for God created time, and everything that God has created God has placed within the framework of time. In a less restrictive sense, "eternal" is that which does not end, as in the phrase *"eternal life." In order to distinguish between these two meanings, medieval theologians sometimes referred to the first as "eternity," and to the second as "*sempiternity." Within the terms of this distinction, God is eternal, but the life of the believer is sempiternal.

Sometimes things that are not affected by time are called "eternal." This is particularly the case when speaking of "eternal truths"—such as mathematical truths, and in the case of some theologians, "theological truths." Strictly speaking, however, there is a question as to whether any such truth is indeed eternal, or is part of God's order for creation. (*See* *Potentia Dei absoluta.)

Finally, there is the question of whether eternity itself is conceivable. If, as Kant (1724–1804) argued, time itself is part of the structure of the mind, the mind cannot really conceive a reality without time.

Ethics   Sometimes a moral code or series of practices that are deemed morally acceptable—as in "professional ethics." Most often, in the context of theological discourse, the study of the principles, rules, and the like, by which Christian conduct is to be guided, and of their application to specific situations. Frequently, the study of principles and their application in specific areas of life—as in "social ethics," "sexual ethics."

Various systems of ethics may be classified according to the nature of their fundamental principles. Thus, an axiological ethical system bases decisions on a system of values (*Axiology); a deontological system (*Deontology) bases them on the will of God—which in turn may be understood as a series of laws, thus leading to legalism, or as the principle of *love, in which case such deontological ethics often becomes contextual ethics; and a teleological system (*Teleology) bases them on the ends for which those involved have been created. In spite of such classifications, rarely is an ethical system a pure example of one of these types. Thus, while Thomas Aquinas (1225–74) bases his ethics on the goal of human life, which is the *beatific vision, he also offers a series of rules or principles of conduct not derived from that teleological perspective, but from natural law. Likewise, the ethics of Luther is based on the dialectical relationship between *law and gospel, but also has a teleological and an axiological dimension. Contextual ethicists insist that laws and moral principles are employed in order to eschew moral responsibility and the burden of a free decision, and yet at times their application of the principle of love approaches *casuistry.

Ethics may also be classified on the basis of their main field of concern. Thus, sexual ethics has occupied much attention through the centuries—and still does, as issues such as homosexuality and birth control have come to the foreground. Social ethics has always been a concern of many Christians, and has centered mostly on issues political (for instance, is tyrannicide justifiable?) and economic (for instance, what to do about unemployment, the poor, the homeless, etc.). More recently, with the opening up of new medical possibilities—organ transplants, the artificial prolongation of life, cloning—the field of biomedical ethics has come to the foreground with great urgency.

In all these cases, it is clear that ethics never stands alone. Traditional Roman Catholic sexual ethics is grounded on certain views of sex and its function (*Sexuality). When those views change, the traditional system itself becomes unstable. Likewise, contemporary social ethics is profoundly impacted by new methods of social, political, and economic analysis and by new political systems such as secular democracy, and is closely related to the theological views behind it—for instance, theologies of *liberation.

Eucharist The most common name given to the shared meal that has traditionally been the center of Christian worship, also known as Communion, the Lord's Supper, the Holy Supper, or the Mass. The word itself, "eucharist," derives from the Greek word for "giving thanks," and is drawn from the New Testament accounts of the institution of this rite or *sacrament, where we are told that Jesus "gave thanks" over the bread. Its origin in the final meal of Jesus with his disciples before the crucifixion is told in the three *Synoptic Gospels as well as in First Corinthians. Although the Fourth Gospel does not speak of its institution, it does include eucharistic references. Also, the book of Acts declares that one of the regular activities of the very early church was to gather for the breaking of the bread. The same is attested by other early Christian documents such as the *Didache*, the epistles of Ignatius of Antioch, and Justin's first *Apology*.

From these and other documents it appears that the earliest Christian practice involved a full meal, but that even then the bread and the wine were the center of the rite itself. Soon, however, the meal was reduced to bread and wine—and these in such small quantities that they no longer constituted a full meal, but rather a symbol, or a reminder, of one. This meal was the high point of weekly worship, usually very early on Sunday morning, in celebration of the resurrection of Jesus. The service itself was clearly divided into two sections, the service of the Word and the service of the Table. During the first period, with all believers present—those already baptized as well as those preparing for baptism—Scripture was read, explained, and applied to the life of the church. Then those who would not participate in the Eucharist—either because they were not yet baptized, or because they were excluded from the meal by reason of their sins—were dismissed, and the service proceeded with the Eucharist.

As its very name indicates, the eucharistic service was joyful—hence the phrase "to celebrate the Eucharist." It was celebrating the presence and the victory of the Risen Lord, and an anticipation of the final banquet in the kingdom.

Since the Eucharist was the center of Christian worship, it is not surprising that it was held in high regard. Paul speaks of eating and drinking unworthily as not "discerning the body" of Christ—whether this means not realizing that the body of Christ is in the bread, or not realizing that the gathered community is the body of Christ, is subject to interpretation. Early in the second century, Ignatius of Antioch called the Eucharist "the flesh of Christ" as well as "the medicine of immortality and the antidote for death," and declared that those who withdraw from the Eucharist are actually withdrawing from Christ.

In spite of such statements, there is no unanimity among early Christian theologians about how Christ is present in Communion, or about the role of the bread and wine in that presence. There are numerous passages that focus on the bread and the wine, and that seem to indicate the belief that these have actually become the body and blood of Jesus. And there are also numerous passages that focus on the gathering of the community, and would seem to indicate that—while the bread and the wine are central to the rite—the presence of Christ is in the gathered community, and that the bread and the wine remain bread and wine. Likewise, some passages refer to the bread as "the body of Christ," while others refer to it as a symbol of that body.

After the conversion of Constantine, Christian services became increasingly elaborate, often imitating the pomp of the imperial court. Quite naturally, in the midst of such ceremonies the bread and the wine became the objects of great veneration and even superstition. (Saint Ambrose declares that his brother Satyrus was saved from drowning after being shipwrecked because he carried a piece of consecrated bread tied around his neck.) Still, the new liturgies were celebratory, focusing on the resurrection of Jesus and the believers' resurrection on the final day to eat with him.

It was in the early Middle Ages, as civil order seemed to collapse and death became a constant companion, that the Eucharist began taking the funereal overtones it retained at least until the twentieth century. The remembrance was no longer focused on Easter and on the final resurrection, but on Good Friday and the cross. While already in patristic times some spoke of the Eucharist as a sacrifice, now the view gained ground that the Eucharist was a repetition of the sacrifice on the cross, and that as such it gained merits for those who participated in it, and even for those in whose name it was celebrated. (Gregory the Great claims that after Masses were said for a dead monk for thirty days, one of the brothers had a vision in which the deceased told him that he was now free from *purgatory.)

By the ninth century, we have the first controversies as to whether the body of Christ present in the Eucharist is the same body that is in heaven, or whether the bread only represents that body. Similar controversies took place in the eleventh century. Finally, in the Fourth Lateran Council, in 1215, *transubstantiation was proclaimed to be the official doctrine of the church.

Progressively, the practice developed of withholding the cup from the laity, who received only the bread. One of the many reforms proposed by Jan Hus in the fifteenth century was returning the cup to the laity—Communion in both elements (*see* *Utraquists).

The Reformation reopened the debate, both about Communion in both elements and about the presence of Christ in the Eucharist. All major Reformers agreed that the cup should be restored to the laity, while the Roman Catholic Church continued resisting on this point until the twentieth century. It was on the manner of the presence of Christ in the Eucharist that the major Reformers disagreed. Luther insisted on the physical presence of the risen body of Christ in the bread (see *Ubiquity), although he disagreed with the Roman doctrine of transubstantiation, and declared that, while the body of Christ is physically present in it, the bread remains bread (*Consubstantiation). Zwingli held that the bread and wine are symbols of the body and blood of Christ. Calvin believed in the *real presence of Christ in the Eucharist, but held that this presence is spiritual, for the physical body of Christ is in heaven, and cannot be in several churches at the same time. He also declared that in the Eucharist, by virtue of the presence of the Spirit (see *Virtualism), believers are transported to the presence of Christ in heaven.

An unforeseen and unwanted consequence of the Protestant Reformation was the infrequency of Communion in many Protestant traditions. All the major Reformers believed that Communion was the highest act of Christian worship, and should be celebrated at least every Sunday. (In Calvin's Geneva, weekly Communion was discontinued; but this was the decision of the city government, against Calvin's wishes.) However, their stress on the importance of preaching, and their struggle to restore preaching to its proper place, eventually led other Protestants to regard preaching as the center of worship, and to relegate Communion to an infrequent celebration.

In the twentieth century, as part of the *liturgical renewal, the ancient celebratory nature of the Eucharist, and its focusing on the resurrection rather than on the cross, were recovered in the liturgies of many churches. Also, as a result of the same renewal, many Protestant churches are recovering the practice of frequent Communion.

Evangelicalism   A movement of ill-defined edges, cutting across Protestant denominational lines, emphasizing the authority of *Scripture; a personal experience of *regeneration or second birth; the work of Christ in *atonement as an *expiation on the cross for the sins of humankind; the need to preach the gospel to nonbelievers, particularly through international missions; and traditional moral views, particularly in the field of *sexuality. On the authority of Scripture, many evangelicals hold to *inerrancy, and all insist that the Bible is uniquely inspired by God. While salvation by the *grace of God, and not by *merits or *works, is a tenet of all evangelicals, and there is a strong Calvinistic influence on evangelicals, relatively few follow these views to the point of orthodox *Calvinism, while most evangelicals lean toward some form of *Arminianism—rejecting traditional Calvinism on points such as limited atonement, *predestination, and irresistible grace. Although evangelicalism is sometimes confused with *fundamentalism, there are different emphases in these two movements. Fundamentalism is more concerned with the letter of Scripture, and with doctrinal orthodoxy; evangelicalism, while also affirming these points, tends to stress the experience of the work of the Spirit in the believer through new birth, and the need to communicate the joy of the gospel to others.

On social and political issues, evangelicalism encompasses two diverse positions. While traditionally most evangelicals have been primarily concerned with issues of personal faith and morality, an increasing number of evangelicals insist that biblical faith requires that they be involved in the political and economic processes of society, working for justice and peace.

Evil   See *Theodicy.

Evolution   Most commonly, the name given to the theory of Charles Darwin (1809–82), that the species have evolved through a lengthy process in which small mutations and the survival of the fittest eventually lead to new species. Although Darwin himself was a Christian, and contributed significant financial resources to missionary work, his theory was seen by many as contradicting the biblical view of *creation. For this reason, as Protestant *fundamentalism emerged, creation in seven days was considered an essential point of Christian belief. For similar reasons, even as late as the twenty-first century there were those who considered *creationism opposed to evolution. There are, however, Christian theologians who have proposed their own versions of evolution. Most notable among them is Pierre Teilhard de Chardin (1881–1955), a noted paleontologist who accepted evolution as the process through which God creates, but insisted that the principle guiding evolution is not the survival of the fittest, but rather the "law of complexity-consciousness," whereby all reality evolves toward greater complexity and consciousness, and thus moves toward God.

Ex nihilo   Latin for "out of nothing." *Creation *ex nihilo* thus means creation out of nothing.

Ex opere operato   A phrase used to express the manner in which the *sacraments work in and of themselves, quite apart from the attitudes or thoughts of the person administering them. According to traditional Roman Catholic doctrine reaffirmed by the Council of Trent (1545–63), the sacraments confer grace *ex opere operato*—meaning, for instance, that a Eucharist or a marriage celebrated by an unworthy priest is still valid. Although the phrase itself does not appear until the late Middle Ages, already in late antiquity theologians had argued that the value of a sacrament cannot depend on the disposition of the celebrant, for in that case believers are left in constant doubt about the validity of the sacraments they receive.

Excommunication   The official act of barring a believer from participating in Communion. In Roman Catholic traditional practice, "major excommunication" implies not only exclusion from Communion, but also all other contact with the faithful, or attendance at any form of divine worship, while "minor excommunication" simply excludes the believer from celebrating or partaking of Communion. While often given other names, similar practices exist in some Protestant traditions, such as the "shunning" among *Anabaptists and the "placing under discipline" in some *Pentecostal churches.

Exegesis   The interpretation of a text, analyzing it in order to clarify its meaning. Given the importance of Scripture for the Christian faith, the exegetical task has always been paramount in theology. The word "exegesis" itself is sometimes used as a synonym for interpretation, and thus one finds writers speaking of an "*allegorical exegesis" or a "*typological exegesis." Common current usage, however, tends to limit "exegesis" to the task of grammatical, lexicographic, and structural analysis, and to speak of subsequent steps in the process of understanding a text and its relevance as "*interpretation" or "*hermeneutics."

Existence   In ancient and medieval philosophy, the actualization (*Act) of an *essence. Thus, existence is usually contrasted or compared with essence, so that while the latter refers to that which makes a thing be what it is—in the case of an apple, its "appleness"—existence refers to the fact that it actually is. In other words, while essence has to do with *what* something is, existence means *that* it is. In most classical philosophy—and theology—essence is seen as preceding existence, for ultimately all essences are eternally in the mind of God. Anselm's *ontological argument for the existence of God is ultimately based on the claim that in God essence and existence go together, so that the very essence of God includes existence—which is not true for any *contingent being.

More recently, particularly in *existentialism, existence has come to mean human life as a struggle and as a project —as in the phrase, "my existence." It is on this basis that existentialists often claim—in opposition to classical philosophy—that existence is prior to essence.

Existentialism A philosophical movement, begun by Søren Kierkegaard (1813–55) in the nineteenth century, but not generally recognized until the twentieth, which stresses the primacy of human *existence over abstract *essences. At a time when Hegel's philosophy was enthusiastically accepted, and everything, including theology, was being made to fit into that system, Kierkegaard protested that this system —in fact, any system—rather than explaining reality, obscures it, for it ignores the primacy of existence, the subjective reality in which all supposedly objective thought takes place. Furthermore, Kierkegaard felt that the Hegelian claim to a system that would explain everything was a usurpation of the sovereignty of God, and therefore erred not only philosophically, but also theologically. He insisted that the goal of human existence is not to know all truth, but rather to struggle constantly in the quest for truth. This set the tone for much of later existentialism, which insists that existence is never a given, but always a constant struggle for truth and authenticity.

As a philosophical approach, existentialism had many proponents in the twentieth century. Many of these were secular philosophers, such as Jean-Paul Sartre and Martin Heidegger. The most distinguished Jewish existentialist was Martin Buber (1878–1965). Among Christian philosophers, Nikolay Berdyayev (1874–1948), Karl Jaspers (1883–1969), and Gabriel-Honoré Marcel (1889–1973) were the most influential.

Among theologians, the impact of existentialism was almost universal. Karl Barth (1886–1968), who eventually rejected existentialism, had originally set out to develop an existentialist *dogmatics. Rudolf Bultmann (1884–1976) made use of the philosophy of Heidegger for his attempt to *demythologize the New Testament. Also impacted by existentialism were Paul Tillich (1886–1965) and Roman Catholic theologian Karl Rahner (1904–84).

Expiation The making up, or paying, for an offense either against God or against others by means of a sacrifice, punishment, payment, or other such action. The notion of expiation plays an important role in the "substitutionary" or "juridical" view of *atonement, which sees Jesus as making expiation for the sins of the world. It is also an important element in the penitential system of the medieval and modern Roman Catholic Church (see *Penance; *Satisfaction).

Extra calvinisticum The affirmation, common in traditional theology, that even at the time of the incarnation the divine Second Person of the Trinity, the Son or *Word of God, was not confined to the humanity of Jesus. The Word became flesh in Jesus, yes; but the Word also remained sovereign ruler of all things, and present everywhere. Such speculations, relatively common in the Middle Ages, came to the foreground in the debates between *Lutherans and *Calvinists regarding the presence of Jesus in the *Eucharist. While Lutherans insisted on the *ubiquity of the body of Jesus, as a result of the incarnation, their opponents declared that even at the time of the incarnation the Word was ubiquitous, and the body of Jesus was not. This claim that the Word was not circumscribed by the humanity in the incarnation was dubbed the *extra calvinisticum* by its Lutheran opponents—a term that eventually the Calvinists themselves accepted.

Faith   The term "faith" has various meanings, even in religious and theological contexts. Sometimes it means a body of belief—for instance, in phrases such as "the Christian faith holds that . . . ," or "the Reformed faith," "the Catholic faith." Most often it refers to an attitude on the part of the believer—as in the phrases "if you have faith," and "my faith is firm." But even in this latter sense, there has been much discussion as to the exact meaning of faith.

An often-forgotten scholastic distinction may be of help here. The scholastics spoke of faith, *fides*, as both the act of believing—*fides qua creditur*—and its contents, what is believed—*fides quae creditur*. In the first of these, what is most important is trust, turning oneself over to the one in whom one believes (**Fiducia*). In the second sense, faith involves the acceptance of what is to be believed. Clearly, the two go together, for trust requires an object, and what one believes that object to be determines the nature of one's trust. Yet at some points and in some theological circles the emphasis has fallen on one or the other of these two dimensions of faith.

In patristic theology, faith was usually considered within the context of the three theological *virtues—faith, hope, and love, with the highest being love, as the apostle Paul had declared. When so considered, faith is only one element of Christian life, and must lead to both hope and love. Thus the stress tends to fall on faith as assent to or acceptance of certain doctrines or beliefs—which is not to say that faith is mere intellectual assent, for the will plays a role in it, and it is not complete without hope and love.

Most medieval theologians followed this lead, and spoke of faith as assent. Since not all believers know all the doctrines of the church, the scholastics spoke of faith as both "explicit" and "implicit." The former exists when the believer actually knows and affirms what the church teaches. The latter is the faith of those who, even though they do not know all points of doctrine, are simply ready to believe whatever the church, in its divine authority, teaches.

Luther's experience, and his defense of *justification by faith, led him to emphasize faith as trust (*fiducia*), and to insist that the only proper object of faith is God. Faith is not assent to a doctrine or to a system of doctrine. It is not assent to the teachings of the church or of any other authority—not even to the teachings of the Bible. Faith is trust in God, and in God alone. Calvin agreed on this point, and saw faith as "a firm and certain knowledge" of God's love; but the very use of the word "knowledge" in this context shows that faith is not only a matter of the heart or of the will. Faith involves the whole person, and therefore includes the cognitive—knowing the God in whom one believes—and the affections, where faith is manifested in piety. On these views, most of the Reformers agreed.

The Protestant *scholastics of the seventeenth century tended to return to the view of faith as assent, and therefore stressed faith as an act of assenting to certain truths rather than as trust in God and in God alone—although the reason why such truths were to be accepted was that they had been revealed by God. Such views have continued well into the twenty-first century in some Protestant circles, where "faith" is accepting certain principles such as the *inerrancy of Scripture and substitutionary *atonement.

In the eighteenth century, with the growth of *rationalism and of *deism, many saw faith as the blind acceptance of that which *reason could not prove, or which reason actually contradicted. In that context, "faith" was often used as a synonym for *fideism, and quite often used pejoratively for those who would not follow the dictates of reason.

In reaction both to Protestant scholasticism and to the more rationalistic views of the deists, *Pietism sought to recover the affective dimensions of faith, and sometimes to stress faith as the experience of God's presence or of God's love. In this they were followed by much of the liberal theology of the nineteenth century (*see* *Liberalism), whose main leaders spoke of faith as "a feeling of absolute dependence" (Schleiermacher) or as the foundation of moral life (Ritschl), and even later by much *existentialist theology, which tends to speak of faith as "encounter," the "presence of the Other," and the like.

In the twentieth century, *neoorthodoxy returned to the Reformers' emphasis on faith as trust in God, but insisted —with Calvin—on the cognitive elements of such trust.

Faith and Reason   *See* *Reason and Faith.

Fall   The events described in Genesis 3, used in traditional Christian theology as the explanation—either literal or metaphorical—for the undeniable distance between God's will for *creation and for humankind, and the present state of both creation and humanity. In this sense, there is no doubt that ours is a "fallen" creation, in which violence and death hold sway, and in which therefore things are not as God intends.

On these points, there is general agreement among Christian theologians. Where disagreements are common is on the nature of the fall. First of all, there are those who insist on a literal fall, and on an actual time "before the fall," when creation was as God intended, while others declare that the fall—as well as the entire narrative regarding the original Eden—is a valuable metaphor to speak of the paradoxical truths that the world is God's good *creation, and yet is not what God intends. Then there are disagreements as to how the consequences of the fall are lived out in the existence of individuals (*see* *original sin), what has been lost in the fall (*see* *donum superadditum*), and the nature of the human predicament as a result of the fall (*see* *Alienation; *Anthropology; *Atonement; *Existence; *Existentialism; *Recapitulation; *Redemption).

Febronianism   An *ecclesiological position that derives its name from Justinus Febronius (pseudonym for Johann von Hontheim, 1701–90). According to Febronius, the pope derives his authority from the church, and not vice versa. Furthermore, the pope's jurisdiction does not extend beyond his own diocese, Rome, and his only privilege over other *bishops derives from his role as the guardian of the *canons of the church, which he executes as the representative of the entire episcopate. Finally, the pope has no authority over secular rulers— which made Febronianism quite popular among such rulers.

Federal Theology   Also called "covenantal theology." While the notion of covenant is central to the Bible, and the early Reformers repeatedly referred to it, it was Heinrich Bullinger (1504–75), Zwingli's successor in Zurich, who further developed the theme into an entire scheme of salvation history. According to Bullinger, the relationship of God with humankind is one of *covenant. From the very beginning, God made a covenant of salvation by grace with humankind. This covenant, however, is not to be understood in the sense that God and humankind entered into a bipartisan agreement. The initiative was and remains with God, the maker and warrantor of the covenant. At about the same time, Ursinus (1534–83) proposed a scheme with two covenants, one of works and one of grace. This was soon combined with Bullinger's covenantal history of salvation. According to this scheme, Adam was the "federal" head— hence the name of "federal theology"— of humankind, and his failure to meet the covenant of *works required the new covenant, of *grace, where the federal head of the new humanity is Christ (*see* *Recapitulation). This did not abolish the covenant of works, but supplemented it, and therefore believers and Christian societies are still bound to obey the first covenant even though they are saved by the covenant of grace and by being joined to Christ as their new federal head (*see* *Law, Third Use of*).

The impact of federal theology may be seen both in the polity of many *Reformed churches and in the political structures of societies and governments profoundly impacted by the Reformed tradition.

Feminist Theology The name commonly given to a variety of theologies that came to the foreground during the second half of the twentieth century, whose common characteristic is to reflect theologically while taking into account the experience of women—particularly, their experience of oppression in male-dominated societies and churches. Thus, feminist theologies are among the *contextual theologies that arose during the same period. They have developed in various parts of the world, as an expression of the worldwide feminist movements of the twentieth and twenty-first centuries.

While focusing on the experience of women, most feminist theologians are seeking the liberation, not only of women, but of all oppressed people—and, in a sense, also of their oppressors. Most particularly, they insist on liberating theology itself from the male dominance and male perspectives by which it has been bound through the centuries.

All feminist theologians are agreed that their experience as females in a church and a society dominated by males is significant. Like other contextual theologians, their method usually includes an actual commitment to liberative action (*Praxis) as well as reflection on that action and on its relationship to the central tenets and practices of the church and of society. On the other hand, Christian feminist theologians also belong to various Christian confessions and traditions, and these are often reflected in their work. Thus, Protestant feminist theologians tend to focus on the reinterpretation and recovery of Scripture—even while sometimes declaring some texts to be hopelessly male-oriented—while there are Roman Catholic feminist theologians for whom Scripture does not play such a dominant role—and even some for whom Scripture itself, and not just its interpretation, is part of the problem.

Then, women theologians also belong to other subgroups within society, and this has led some to the conclusion that most feminist theology has been too dominated by middle-class, North Atlantic, white women, with whom they must part company. This is true, for instance, of some African American theologians (*see* *Womanist Theology) and of some Latina theologians in the United States (*Mujerista Theology).

Fideism Most often used pejoratively. From the Latin *fides*, faith. The attitude of those who hold that the proper Christian attitude is to accept doctrines "by faith," without questioning their origin, significance, or rationality. (*See* *Reason and Faith.)

Fiducia Trust. In a theological context, trust in God. For Luther and for most of the Reformers, *fiducia* is the very essence of *faith, which is to trust in God and in God's promises.

Filiation Literally, being a son. This term is used in classical Trinitarian theology (particularly after a series of clarifications in the fourth century by the Cappadocians Basil of Caesarea, Gregory of Nyssa, and Gregory of Nazianzus) to refer to the eternal relationship between the First and the Second Persons of the *Trinity—precisely on the basis of their traditional nomenclature as Father and Son. This is what is meant by declaring that the Son is "eternally begotten" of the Father—in distinction to his being born of the Virgin Mary. Since the Son is "eternally begotten," the source of the Son's being is the Father, and yet the Son has no beginning. The Cappadocians also insisted that, while *creation is an act of God's will, and thus results in a reality that is not God, filiation is of the very essence of God, and therefore the Son is God. The counterpart of the Son's filiation is the Spirit's *spiration, by which the Spirit proceeds from the Father (and, in Western theology, from the Son—*Filioque).

Filioque Literally, "and from the Son." A phrase added in the West to the Nicene *Creed in the Middle Ages. When the Greek-speaking East protested against this unauthorized addition to the early creed, a long controversy ensued. The issues at stake were, first, the binding authority of the ancient councils, and, secondly, the orthodoxy of the addition itself. On this latter issue, the *Filioque* reflected a long-standing difference between the Western and the Eastern approaches to the doctrine of the *Trinity. In the East, there was a tradition of insisting that there is only one source in the Godhead, and that this is the Father. Thus, the Greeks would declare that the Spirit "proceeds from the Father, *through* the Son." In the West, on the other hand, since the time of Augustine it was customary to speak of the Spirit as the bond of love between the Father and the Son, and thus to say that the Spirit proceeds from the Father "and the Son"—*Filioque*. Each of the two branches of the church insisted on its position, and the disagreement regarding the *Filioque* was one of the reasons given for the final break between East and West in 1054.

Foreknowledge In classical theology that aspect of the *omniscience of God by which God knows events that have not yet taken place and things that do not yet exist. The concept itself has been the subject of much debate among theologians and philosophers, for if God knows all future contingent beings (*see* *Contingency), they seem no longer to be contingent, but necessary, and freedom (*Freedom of the Will) seems to be an illusion. Thomas Aquinas (1225–74) and others among the *scholastics devoted much thought precisely to this question—How can God know "future contingents" without making them necessary, and therefore not contingent? Some *Reformed theologians (notably Beza, Zanchi, and then the Reformed scholastics) have used God's foreknowledge as an argument for the doctrine of *predestination—with the consequence that predestination becomes *predeterminism.

Form and Matter A distinction dating back to Aristotle, who held that things consist of two elements: that of which they are made (matter), and that which makes them be what they are (form). This implies that form is the principle of individuation of matter; it is the form it receives that makes matter be, not only a certain sort of thing, but also this particular thing. There is, however, a hierarchy of forms, as may be seen in a classical example of a brick, whose matter is clay that has been "formed" into "brickness"; but the bricks themselves may then become the matter organized by the form "house"; and houses may be matter that is formed into a town; and so on. In Aristotelian philosophy, it is this *teleological drive that stands behind the movement from potency to *act—from possibility to reality.

During the revival of Aristotelian philosophy in the thirteenth century, one of the points debated was the *Averroist tenet of the preexistence of an absolutely "formless matter," out of which God created the world by giving it forms. It was against such views that most thirteenth-century theologians stressed the traditional doctrine of *creation *ex nihilo.

Another subject of theological debate, particularly in the thirteenth century, was whether purely rational beings —for instance, angels and souls—are composed of matter and form. This is technically called the "hylomorphic" (from the Greek *hylē*, matter, and *morphē*, form) composition of beings. In general, the *Augustinians affirmed it, while insisting on the distinction between "matter" in its philosophical sense, and body, while the *Thomists rejected such hylomorphic composition of intellectual beings.

Form Criticism   (In German, *Formgeschichte*.) A method for the study of documents, and in particular for the study of the Bible and the traditions behind various texts. Its basis is the notion that folk traditions are kept and transmitted following certain patterns or "forms"—patterns having to do mostly with their function within the community—and that these forms can still be discerned in documents that have incorporated them. By the study of such forms, the scholar can then determine the nature of the tradition behind a text, and the function of that particular tradition within the community transmitting and eventually incorporating it into a text.

Freedom of the Will   The ability of the human will to make decisions. For some theologians and philosophers, the absence of coercion suffices for such freedom. Thus, even though it is in the nature of a hungry dog to eat when offered food, its decision to eat is free, because it is not coerced. For others, true freedom exists only when the will is its own cause. Thus, insofar as one performs an act simply out of one's nature, such an act is not really free. True freedom requires choice and the ability to decide among various alternatives.

The freedom of the will is of concern for theologians mainly under two headings. First, Christian theologians are almost unanimously agreed that such freedom is crucial as the prerequisite for responsibility. In this sense, freedom of the will is opposed to *determinism, which holds that all things and all events are predetermined. Secondly, theologians have repeatedly debated the relationship between *predestination and the freedom of the will. In this context, it

is not a matter of all things being predetermined, but rather of the human will not being able to act for its own salvation, apart from *grace.

The classical discussion of the freedom of the will in Christian theology was developed by Augustine (354–430) in his debate against the *Manichaeans on the one hand and the *Pelagians on the other. Against the determinism of the Manicheans, Augustine argued for the freedom of the will as a good gift of God, but a good gift that, precisely because of its nature, may be used for evil. The Pelagian controversy forced him to clarify the sense in which the will is free, and he thus spoke of four different stages that set the limits for human freedom. In the first stage, in Eden before the *fall, humans had the freedom both to sin and to refrain from sinning (*posse peccare* and *posse non peccare*). However, as a result of the fall, we have all lost the freedom not to sin, and retained only the freedom to sin (*posse peccare*, but *non posse non peccare*). This does not mean that we have no freedom. It means rather that our alternatives are limited, and that they are all sinful in some degree. Redemption and sanctification restore in the believer the freedom not to sin (*posse non peccare*), while the possibility to sin (*posse peccare*) remains. Finally, in the future life, we shall still have freedom, but only not to sin (*posse non peccare*, but *non posse peccare*).

The point at which this scheme has led to debates is the passage from the second stage to the third—what is often called conversion. In Augustine's view, such passage is not possible for the will by itself, for the sinful will can only choose among sinful options, and conversion itself is not such an option. It is at this point that irresistible *grace and *predestination come into the picture, for it is God's grace that moves a sinner from one stage to the other, and such grace is given, not on the basis of anything that a person does or decides, but as the working out of God's free decree of *election. This is also the view of orthodox *Calvinism. Over against this position, *Arminianism, while agreeing that sinners do not have the ability in themselves to accept the gift of saving grace, seeks to avoid its predestinarian consequences and to preserve the role of the freedom of the will in salvation by declaring that there is a "prevenient grace," freely given to all, which allows them to accept saving grace if they so choose.

Fundamentalism Strictly speaking, a movement within North American Protestantism deriving its name from the five "fundamentals" of Christianity declared by the founders of the movement at a conference in Niagara Falls in 1895. These five points were the *inerrancy of Scripture, the virgin birth of Jesus, his death in substitution and payment for human sin, his physical resurrection, and his impending return. By extension, "fundamentalism" eventually came to mean any position insisting on the inerrancy of Scripture and rejecting much of the results of modern research on the history and development of Scripture. By a further extension, the same term is now applied to extremists in any other religion—as in the phrase "Islamic fundamentalism."

Gallicanism The position of those, particularly in France, who opposed absolute papal authority and the claims of the *ultramontanes. Since the times of the papacy in Avignon, the popes had made a number of concessions to the French church, its bishops, and its monarch. These, and other privileges added over the centuries, came to be known as the "Gallican liberties"—hence the name of "Gallicanism" for the movement that insisted on their preservation. After the Council of Trent in the sixteenth century, both the king of France and the French bishops resisted the promulgation of the Council's decrees in French territory, for the centralizing tendencies of Trent were opposed to the "Gallican liberties." Thereafter, the French crown

made use of Gallicanism to ensure its authority over the church, and thus Gallicanism took an increasingly secular bent.

Generation   See *Filiation.

Geschichte   See *Historie.

Gloria Patri The first words, and hence also the title, of an ancient doxological hymn, "Glory be to the Father. . . ." Although it existed in slightly different forms from an earlier date, its present form developed in the fourth century, when it was used as a guard against *Arianism. The main thrust of the hymn is that glory, which belongs only to God, has always belonged to the Father, the Son, and the Holy Spirit—"as it [the glory] was in the beginning, is now and ever shall be."

Glossolalia The name given since the nineteenth century to speaking in tongues. It appears in the New Testament in what are apparently two different forms. In the account of Pentecost in Acts, the disciples speak in the tongues of others who are present. In the Pauline epistles, speaking in tongues is certainly a gift of the Spirit, but here it seems to occur within the community of believers, even when no one can understand what is being said, and serves for the edification of the person speaking in tongues, rather than of others or of the community (1 Cor. 14:4). In such cases, Paul prefers "prophecy"—preaching—and suggests that any speech in tongues should be translated so that the church may be edified.

Both dimensions of glossolalia have been reported at various times in the history of the church. Thus in the sixteenth century it was said that St. Francis Xavier, as he preached in the Orient, was able to speak in the various languages he encountered. During the second century, glossolalia seems to have been fairly common, not only among *Montanists, but also in the church at large. While it tended to disappear in the Western church, it reappeared sporadically in the East, particularly in monastic communities. Among Protestants, there are few recorded cases of glossolalia until it became common in the *Pentecostal movement early in the twentieth century, and eventually spread to practically every other Christian communion.

A point of disagreement regarding glossolalia, even granting that it is a gift of the Spirit, is whether it is the necessary sign of the "baptism of the Spirit," or only one of many possible signs. On this point, the various Pentecostal movements are not in total agreement.

Gnosticism   The name jointly given to a variety of religious systems that flourished in the second century, whose common trait was that they promised salvation by means of a secret knowledge or *gnōsis*. While scholars debate about the exact origins of Gnosticism, it is apparently the result of the confluence of many diverse religious and philosophical traditions converging in the Mediterranean world at the beginning of the Christian era: Persian and Greek *dualism, Babylonian astrology, Jewish *apocalypticism, various *mystery religions, among others. Since Gnosticism was *syncretistic, many of its systems incorporated elements from Christianity—particularly the stories about Jesus—and thus gave rise to Christian Gnosticism, which for a time was a very serious competitor with the church at large.

Most gnostic systems explained the existence of the world and the human condition through an elaborate *cosmogony that usually included long series of purely spiritual realities or "eons," until one of these, either through an error or out of malice, created the physical world. Human *souls are part of the spiritual world that has somehow been entrapped in this physical world, and their salvation consists in ascending once again to the purely spiritual realm—usually called the "plenitude" or *plērōma*. In this ascent, the soul has to go through the various celestial spheres, and in some gnostic systems the secret knowledge of the initiate consisted precisely in the passwords allowing the soul to move through the various spheres.

Due to its understanding of physical matter and of the body as the result of error or of evil, Christian Gnosticism rejected the Christian doctrines of *creation, *incarnation, and the *resurrection of the body. Particularly on the subject of the incarnation, gnostics often held *docetic views, claiming that the body of Jesus was not real, or was made of a purely spiritual substance.

Although the church at large rejected it, Gnosticism has proved attractive at times when, for whatever reason, people are attracted to the esoteric and mysterious. During the nineteenth century, the rise of *transcendentalism and of Christian Science was an example of this. Likewise, in the last years of the twentieth and the beginning of the twenty-first century, interest in Gnosticism revived, and new forms of Gnosticism emerged—often claiming to be based on ancient secret lore.

God   The Christian doctrine of God evolved out of the Jewish doctrine as expressed in the Hebrew Scriptures. Thus, Christianity has always stressed the uniqueness of God (*monotheism), as well as God's holiness and love—requiring human response in love and in ethical conduct. In this context, even allowing for the limitations of human thought and language, God is seen as personal, and language about God tends to employ expressions drawn from human interpersonal relations—loving, faithful, compassionate, righteous, for example.

Thus, the very first thing to be said about God, according to Christian doctrine, is that God is one. Nonetheless, the most characteristically Christian doctrine regarding God is the *Trinity, that the one true and only God exists as three, and that these three, while distinct, are one God. The doctrine of the Trinity, although not formulated in its fuller form until the fourth century, appears in many early Christian documents, and from a very early date was associated with the act of *baptism, by which one was initiated into the Christian faith and joined to the body of Christ.

As Christianity spilled into the Hellenistic world, there were many who criticized its teachings as uncouth or irrational. Since Christians spoke of a God whom human eyes cannot see, and rejected the traditional gods, they were accused of being atheists. The very notion that there is only one God seemed strange, particularly in a world in which intercultural tensions had been partially relieved by the practice of accepting each other's gods.

Faced by such criticisms, some Christians had recourse to the Greek philosophical traditions that also spoke of a supreme being. In particular, they made use of the Eleatic and Platonic tradition, with its notion of a world of ideas above the sensory world, and the supreme idea of the good and the beautiful standing above every other idea. Sages such as Parmenides and Plato had spoken of a supreme being, Christians argued, and this supreme being is none other than the one, holy, and invisible God of Christianity.

While such arguments had great *apologetic value, they also introduced into Christian thinking about God a series of elements that are at odds with the more personal language about God. In this way of thinking, the *attributes of God were a denial of all limitation—God is infinite, impassible, unchanging; and a raising of positive elements such as power, knowledge, and others to the highest degree—God is omnipotent, omniscient, omnipresent. Once that step was taken, it became common for theologians to prefer the more abstract and apparently more rational language about God over the more personal and even *anthropomorphic images and metaphors—sometimes with the implication that it is more appropriate to speak of God as the philosophers do than as the Bible does. The interplay between these approaches to language about the Godhead has continued throughout Christian theology.

At some points, this tension has led to speculation about the extent of God's freedom and power. For instance, some late medieval theologians posed the question, Does God always do what is good? Or, Is whatever God does good? If the first, then it would seem that goodness is above God, for God is bound by it. If the latter, it would seem that goodness is a totally capricious matter, determined solely by the will of God. As a way out of these difficulties, some of these theologians proposed a distinction between the absolute power of God (*Potentia Dei absoluta), and God's ordained power, limited by God's sovereign decision to do so (potentia Dei ordinata). Thus, although God's absolute power determines what is good, God freely decides to limit Godself to that determination, and therefore it is true both that whatever God does is good and that God always does what is good.

While repudiating much of the late medieval speculation about the attributes of God, Luther and most of the Reformers underscored the sovereignty and the love of God. These two are to be held in tension, as seen in Luther's declaration that he could not love the sovereign God, who appeared to him as an awesome and implacable judge. To know God is to know God's love. To know God is to be overwhelmed by God's greatness. Following Luther, Calvin and much of the later Reformed tradition sought to keep these two in tension, and this tension is still one of the hallmarks of the *Reformed tradition—a tradition that at its best has also insisted that the purpose of religion is not one's own salvation, but the service and the glory of God.

Another major theme for Christian theology has been the manner in which humans attain the knowledge of God. Can God be known by means of human reasoning? Or can God be known only by means of *revelation? While a few theologians have held that human reasoning suffices for the true knowledge of God, some have held that, while *reason tells us that there is a God, it cannot tell us of God's gracious (see *Grace) disposition toward us, or of God's will for us.

Can God's existence be rationally proved? And if so, how? The most common arguments begin with the existence of the world, and from there move to the need for a first cause of all that exists (see *Cosmological Argument; *Causality). Others argue that the nature of God is such that the very idea of God includes existence, so that God cannot be thought of as not existing (see *Ontological Argument). Obviously, the preference for one or the other of these two sorts of arguments is closely bound with one's *epistemology. Then, some argue that even if these arguments were truly irrefutable, they would prove the existence only of a first cause or of a necessary being, but not necessarily of the loving God of Christian faith.

Gospel From the Anglo-Saxon *god-spel*, good story. The English equivalent of the Greek *euangelion*, good news. A word used to refer both to the books that tell the story of Jesus—the Gospel according to Matthew, the Gospel according to Mark, and so on—and to the good news of Jesus. Apparently it was used from a very early date to refer to the message of Jesus, for Paul employs it frequently, and Mark—most scholars consider his the earliest of the four Gospels—opens his book with the words "The beginning of the gospel of Jesus." Matthew follows Mark's usage of the term. Luke uses words derived from it, although less frequently. And John does not use the word at all.

When Mark wrote his book, he was using the term "gospel," not in the sense of a book, but rather as referring to the good news of Jesus. Mark, however, was also creating a new literary genre, and since the word "gospel" appeared at the

very beginning of his book, all subsequent books of the same genre came to be called "Gospels." This includes the four Gospels in the *canon of the New Testament as well as a number of other books, most of them much later—that also purported to tell the story of Jesus—books such as the *Gospel of Thomas*, the *Gospel of Truth*, and the *Gospel of the Hebrews*, among many others. The first three canonical Gospels, Matthew, Mark, and Luke, are called *Synoptic Gospels.

In its original sense, however, the gospel is the message of Jesus. In Matthew and Mark, Jesus repeatedly refers to his own message as the gospel, the good news—in Matthew, it is usually "the gospel of the kingdom." Traditionally, Christian theology has understood the gospel as the message of Jesus, not only in the sense that this is the message that Jesus proclaimed, but also in the sense that it is the message about Jesus. Jesus is not only the messenger, but also the content of the message. This has been disputed since the time of the Renaissance by those who claim that the original message of Jesus was not about himself, and that it was only later that the church focused on Jesus himself as the content of the good news. While there are still many who hold that the *historical Jesus did not consider himself part of the message, there are also many who insist that Jesus and his work are at the very heart of the gospel—that the good news that Jesus proclaimed was that in his person the kingdom of God had drawn near. Particularly after the work of Karl Barth (1886–1968) and his *neo-orthodox movement, Christian theologians have insisted that the gospel is the good news, not just of Jesus as the messenger, but also of Jesus as the message itself.

Government *See* *State.

Grace The unmerited love of God, which both forgives and transforms the sinner. It could be said that the "good news" of the *gospel is none other than the message of God's grace. While the word itself appears most frequently in the writings of Paul, it is a common thread throughout all of Scripture.

The first great debate concerning grace took place early in the fifth century between Augustine and Pelagius (*see* *Pelagianism). The latter was a British monk who was scandalized by Augustine's words, addressed to God in the *Confessions*, "Give what thou commandest, and command what thou wilt." As Pelagius read these words, they seemed to him a sort of *quietism, demanding nothing from the believer, who is simply to wait for the grace of God. As he learned more of the teachings of Augustine, he came to fear that they tended to destroy a sinner's sense of responsibility and desire to live justly. He therefore insisted that humans, even after the *fall, have never lost the freedom to refrain from sin—*posse non peccare* (*see* *Freedom of the Will). Individuals sin, not because of the fall, but out of their own freedom. As Augustine and the entire Christian tradition taught, Pelagius also believed that grace was necessary for salvation. But this was an "original grace" or "grace of creation," bestowed by God on all, and making it possible for sinners, out of their own free will, to repent and seek to undo the evil they have done. To those who follow such a course, God grants the "grace of pardon," by which they are saved.

Augustine would have none of that. He was convinced that sinners are incapable of making the decision to accept God's grace. The only freedom sinners retain is the freedom to sin—in Augustine's phrase, *posse peccare*. To move from that state to the next, where the freedom not to sin—*posse non peccare*—is restored, requires an intervention of divine grace that is in no way due to the will or the decision of the sinner. The converted sinner cannot claim any special virtue, act, or decision by which grace has been merited. Grace is always freely given—*gratia gratis data*. Thus, Augustine would

say that before we believe, grace operates in us so that we believe; and after we believe, grace cooperates with us for good works—hence the distinction, common in later theology, between "operating grace" and "cooperating grace." Furthermore, the will that cannot in and of itself accept grace also cannot reject it, for such a view would still imply a particular virtue on those who accept grace over those who do not. Therefore, grace is irresistible, and is granted only to the *elect, those whom God has *predestined for salvation.

While the church at large officially rejected the doctrines of Pelagius, and sided with Augustine, what in truth happened was that a mitigated form of Pelagianism persisted in much of Christian theology and piety (*see* *Semipelagianism). Very soon the notion prevailed that there is a "prevenient grace" given to all, and thus very similar to Pelagius's "grace of creation"—thus giving grounds for Luther's declaration that almost all medieval theologians had been Pelagians.

Most significantly, in the heat of the controversy between Augustine and Pelagius, there was an unnoticed shift on the common understanding of grace. Although Pelagius and Augustine disagreed on most points, they tacitly agreed that grace is a power given by God to humans. Grace, rather than being a way of speaking of God's unmerited and constant love, became something that God gave humans. For this reason, medieval theologians began distinguishing, and debating the difference, between "uncreated grace"—which is none other than God—and "created grace"—the power God graciously infuses in believers.

As Luther developed the theological implications of his doctrine of *justification by faith, he came to the conclusion that grace is not "something" that God infuses in the believer, but is rather God's attitude of love and forgiveness. He and the early Reformers rejected the understanding of grace as a created substance, or "infused grace." For both

Luther and Calvin, grace is none other than God acting on our behalf.

With the development of Protestant *scholasticism in the seventeenth century, there was a tendency to return to the understanding of grace as an infused power of God. Thus, when one reads the documents surrounding the Synod of Dort (1618–19), which defined orthodox *Calvinism, it is apparent that for many on both sides of the debate "grace" had once again become a power that God infuses in believers. Certainly, the *Arminian proposal of a universally bestowed "prevenient grace"—as well as much of the argument in favor of "irresistible grace" on the other side—implies that grace is something other than God or God's love.

In the twentieth century, the revival of *Reformed theology in *neo-orthodoxy, and of *Lutheran theology in the *Lundensian school, brought about a return to the view that grace is none other than God—and certainly not a substance or a power that God infuses in the soul.

Later in the same century, there was much debate among Protestant theologians about the relationship between grace and nature. Barth insisted that any sense of continuity between nature and grace was not truly Protestant, for the difference between Protestantism and Roman Catholicism hinges on the latter's claim, and the former's denial, that "grace does not destroy nature, but perfects it." On this point, Brunner and others parted company with Barth, claiming that there is still in nature a "point of contact" for grace, and that positing a radical discontinuity between nature and grace is a denial of the goodness of *creation. Tillich went even farther, declaring that there is a "grace of creation," which keeps all things in existence.

Habit In traditional *scholastic theology, and thereafter in much Roman Catholic *moral theology, an inclination for a faculty of the mind to act in a certain way. This includes both habits of the will—as when we tend to act a certain way—and habits of the intellect—as when we tend to think a certain way. As inclinations, habits do not destroy *freedom, but simply guide it in a particular direction. Thus, the theological notion of "habit" includes much of what in common language is usually understood by that term, and habits can therefore be good or bad, according to whether they incline the soul toward its proper end—the virtues—or away from it, as when habit becomes a vice. Such habits are usually defined as "acquired habits," in contrast to another sort of habit created by the action of *grace. The latter are also inclinations to act in a certain way, but cannot be produced by simple practice and repetition, for they require the supernatural intervention of grace. Properly developed, habits are then the foundation of the moral life, for good acquired habits lead to the practice of the cardinal virtues, and supernatural or infused habits lead to the theological virtues (*see* *Virtues).

Hades A Greek word that was originally the name of the god of the underworld. Eventually it became the term to refer to the underworld itself, and it is thus that it is employed in early Greek translations of the Hebrew Scriptures, to refer to the place of the dead. While originally the term "hades" did not necessarily imply a place of punishment, it progressively became the place where souls are imprisoned waiting for their redemption, or even the place of eternal punishment. Most Christian theologians have understood Hades (or hell) as a place of eternal torment, usually both physical and spiritual—although some, such as Calvin (1509–64), declared that the torment of hell is purely spiritual. Others—such as Origen (ca.185–ca.254) and, much more recently, Berkhof (1873–1957)—have held that it is a place where sins are purged. Still others—Berdyayev (1874–1948)—declare that there is no place of punishment, and that hell is a self-righteous, pious invention.

Heaven   In neither Hebrew nor Greek are there separate words to distinguish "heaven" from "sky." Thus, "the heavens" refers to all that is above earth—the atmosphere as well as the sun, the moon, and the stars. Likewise, in the New Testament and in early Christian literature "heaven and earth" means what today we would call the universe—thus the phrase "maker of heaven and earth" in the Apostles' *Creed. Also, given the reluctance in Judaism to speak the name of God, sometimes "heaven" is used as a substitute for "God." This is the case, for instance, in the Gospel of Matthew, where Mark's "kingdom of God" becomes the "kingdom of heaven."

The background of this vocabulary is to be found in the ancient view of the world as a tiered reality—usually three tiers, with the sky or heaven above, the earth in the middle, and the "lower places"—*infernus*, *hell—below. In this view, the "heavens" and their "spheres" are not always friendly places, and thus one reads of evil spirits in the heavens, and in many *gnostic systems the heavenly spheres were so many obstacles to be traversed by the soul in its return to its fullness.

Early Christian *hope for an afterlife (*see* *Eschatology) did not focus on "going to heaven," but rather on "a new heaven and a new earth" to be established at the end of the age. But, partly as a result of the *apologetic enterprise, and partly as a result of its contact with other religious views circulating in the Mediterranean at the time, it rapidly transmuted into the expectation of the immortal soul's going "up to heaven," and there living eternally (*see* *Immortality). Thus, "heaven" became the sum total of Christian hope, and the expectation of a "new earth" was generally left aside. Jointly with this development, heaven was conceived as a place where incorporeal souls floated around—sometimes in the clouds.

In summary, while "heaven" is a good metaphor for Christian hope, it should always be remembered that such hope includes the whole creation, physical as well as spiritual, and that therefore the metaphor of "heaven" has to be completed with other metaphors that reflect God's care and love for all of creation.

Hegelianism   The philosophical system of Georg W. F. Hegel (1770–1831). According to Hegel, the whole of history is the unfolding of the thought of the Universal Mind or Absolute Spirit. This thought moves dialectically, so that a thesis is posed, an antithesis opposes it, and the two are resolved into a synthesis. This synthesis in turn becomes a new thesis, opposed by a new antithesis, and so forth. Hegel himself showed this structure of thought—and therefore also of reality—in his own review of a number of historical developments. In particular, he claimed that Christianity was the highest religion, because in the *incarnation it brought together the apparently opposite divine and human. Likewise, the doctrine of the *Trinity shows that the dialectical process exists at the very heart of the Absolute.

The impact of Hegel was enormous. Many lesser figures devoted themselves to filling the gaps in his interpretation of history. Others sought to interpret various doctrines and their development in terms of Hegel's *dialectics. Kierkegaard (1813–55) mocked the popularity of Hegelianism, declaring that "now that the System is complete, or if not, will be complete by next Sunday...." Karl Marx (1818–83) recast Hegelian dialectics within a materialistic framework, thus developing "dialectical materialism" (*Marxism). In New Testament studies, the School of Tübingen developed a system claiming that Paul's theology was the antithesis of the Judaizing thesis of James and others in Jerusalem, and that the synthesis of the two resulted in much of the non-Pauline New Testament. While most of these instances of Hegel's influence have passed, one that remains in the twenty-first century is his emphasis on history as the realm in which truth is known and lived. (*See* *History; *Historie; *Heilsgeschichte.) Furthermore, his notion that history and the world evolve as the unfolding of Thought stands behind much contemporary *cosmology, as well as behind Darwin's theory of *evolution.

Heilsgeschichte A German term meaning "salvation history," and often contrasted with *Weltgeschichte*, or "world history." Beginning in the nineteenth century, but especially in the twentieth, many theologians and biblical scholars distinguished between these two sorts of history. In this they were reflecting long-standing educational practices, for in many schools it was customary to teach courses on the "history of salvation" quite apart from "universal history." In the view of the proponents of *Heilsgeschichte*, the Bible is to be read as the record of the "mighty acts" of God for the salvation of humankind—first in Israel, then in Jesus, and finally in the church. This history of salvation runs like a discernible thread through the rest of history, and gives meaning to the whole of history. Thus, the purpose of the study of *Heilsgeschichte* was to develop a biblical theology capable of interpreting both the Bible and history itself.

In more recent times, biblical scholars have questioned whether the notions of history that appear in the Bible are as different from other views of history as was claimed by the proponents of *Heilsgeschichte*. Also, among *liberation theologians several have argued that a sharp distinction between the history of salvation and the history of the world must be rejected, for it implies that history itself is of importance only as it leads to salvation—thus setting aside the significance of historical liberation.

Hell The most common English term for *Hades, derived from the Old English *helan*, which means to conceal. (While the traditional Latin word *infernus* has fallen into disuse in English, it still remains in the adjective "infernal," meaning hellish.)

Hell, Descent into An ancient Christian belief, already attested in the New Testament (Eph. 4:9; 1 Peter 3:19), that made its way into the present Apostles' Creed (*see* *Creeds) in the fourth century. It has been differently interpreted. The most common interpretation during the Middle Ages was that after his death Jesus went to a place where the ancient patriarchs awaited (*see* *Limbo), and freed them. Others claimed that Jesus had gone to *purgatory, to free the souls imprisoned there. Calvin spiritualized the phrase, declaring that it showed the depths of Jesus' pain and anguish. The most common view in ancient Christianity—a view that Luther also affirmed—was that Jesus went into the very abode of Satan, and there destroyed his power forever, freeing those whom Satan held captive. This is often called the "harrowing of hell."

Henotheism A term coined late in the nineteenth century to refer to religions that, while acknowledging a multiplicity of gods, serve and worship only a particular god. This is common, for instance, in some societies where each clan has its own deity. Many scholars believe that in its early stages the religion of Israel was henotheistic—Yahweh being the god of Israel, but not the sole existing deity.

Heresy A term that originally meant simply "party" or "sect," and that was used pejoratively even then. Very soon, however, it came to signify a doctrine against the central tenets of the Christian faith—or, more precisely, a doctrine that, while claiming to be Christian, threatens a fundamental aspect of Christianity. Thus, traditional heresies include Christian *Gnosticism, *Arianism, and the like. Traditionally, most Protestant theologians have restricted the use of the term to views that contradict such essential matters as the doctrines of *creation, *incarnation, and *Trinity. In contrast, in traditional Roman Catholic theology any contradiction or rejection of a *dogma defined by the church deserves the name of heresy. If the person holding such views does not know that they contradict the official doctrine of the church, this is a case of "material heresy," which may be corrected with proper teaching. If, on the other hand, the person knowingly rejects a matter of dogma, this is a case of "formal heresy," punishable by *excommunication. In the late-seventeenth-century Protestant *scholasticism, and in the nineteenth and twentieth centuries, a number of Protestant bodies of *fundamentalist persuasion came to accept this traditionally Roman Catholic understanding of heresy, and thus anyone within their ranks who did not agree with them in every point of doctrine was considered a heretic, and often tried as such.

Hermeneutics   The discipline that studies the rules of interpretation of a text—in the case of theological discourse, this usually refers to biblical interpretation. Early Christian theologians inherited the hermeneutical methods of both Hebrew and Greek antiquity. Thus, sometimes they interpreted texts literally, sometimes *allegorically—as was already customary among pagan interpreters of Homer and the ancient poets—and sometimes as *prophecy, as was often done in some Jewish circles. To this Christians often added a *typological, Christocentric method of interpretation which saw, not only the words of Scripture, but also the events told in it, as signs pointing to their fulfilment in Jesus Christ. Some also proposed a number of hermeneutical principles. Thus, Clement of Alexandria (ca.150–ca.215) insisted that no biblical text should be interpreted in such a way that it says something unworthy of God. For Clement, this meant that all *anthropomorphic language about *God should be interpreted in more philosophical terms. Origen (ca.185–ca.254) and others declared that every text has several layers of meaning, from the literal to the spiritual. Generally, the *Alexandrines preferred allegorical interpretation, while the *Antiochenes leaned toward literal and typological interpretations.

During the Middle Ages, it became customary to interpret the entire Bible christologically. This tendency was strengthened by the custom of reading Old Testament passages according to their suitability for various feasts and periods in the liturgical *year, whose structure is essentially christocentric—it celebrates the major events in the life of Jesus. Also, in the monastic reading of the Psalms, their setting lent itself to christocentric interpretations. This may be seen even in Luther, whose monastic experience led him to read the Psalms as referring to Jesus and his relationship with believers and with the church.

As *scholasticism became the dominant form of theology, its method of citing authorities for and against a particular position, often out of context, resulted in a literal interpretation of the texts cited, with little or no consideration given to their literary or historical context.

Luther's concentration on *justification by faith as a fundamental hermeneutical tool led him to question the value of the Epistle of James. His opposition to the papacy is often reflected in his interpretation of many of the most negative passages in Revelation. By insisting on the authority of Scripture, he and the other Reformers paved the way for new discussions on the principles and practices of hermeneutics. While declaring that tradition had no authority over that of Scripture, Calvin insisted on the traditional interpretation of the Song of Solomon as a love song between God and the soul, and considered Sebastian Castellio (1515–63) a heretic for declaring that it was an erotic song. Yet both Luther and Calvin understood the infallibility of Scripture as offering a sure path to the knowledge of the will of God, rather than as an *inerrancy in every detail.

Protestant scholasticism, as well as post-Tridentine Catholicism, reverted to the system of proof-texting—quoting short texts out of context, and sometimes connecting otherwise disconnected texts, in order to prove a point. This in turn required the inerrancy of Scripture, for any argument supported by such use of texts would only be valid if the texts themselves are inerrant—even out of context.

The counterpart of such use of Scripture was the development of modern historical and critical methods of research. Issues of dating, composition, and authorship now came to the foreground, often contradicting previous assumptions. Frequently, such issues so absorbed the interest of biblical scholars that there was very little discussion of what texts said or meant.

This situation began to change early in the twentieth century, when *neo-orthodoxy and other theological movements began returning to the question of what it is that Scripture actually says, while also taking into account the results of historical and literary criticism. Throughout the rest of the century, there was an increasing focus once again on the interpretation of texts and their significance for the life of the church and of the believer.

This, however, could no longer be a naive reading of the text, not only because the findings of critical scholars would not allow it, but also because as the twentieth century progressed it became increasingly obvious that interpretation is always a dialogue between the interpreter and the text, and that asking questions of a text from a particular perspective often leads to unexpected answers. The various *contextual theologies insisted on this point, and proved it with countless examples. Then, as *postmodernity advanced, this point became one of the main concerns of hermeneutical theory, in which the main debate was whether and how a text from the past, and from a different *culture, can be understood by readers in the twenty-first century. Do texts have an "otherness" that the interpreter cannot violate? What happens to that otherness when a text is read—and applied—in different circumstances? Does one ever really hear what the author meant? Does one even approach it? How do we know that we have approached it? Does the meaning of the text depend on the reader's response? These and other such questions have dominated hermeneutical discussion in the late twentieth and early twenty-first centuries.

Hesychasm   A *mystical and *ascetic practice common in Eastern Christianity since the eleventh century. Its name comes from Greek roots meaning "in silence," for hesychasts held that they could attain *ecstasy by sitting in silence, resting their chin on their chest, looking at their navels, and repeatedly praying, "Lord Jesus, have mercy on me." In their ecstasy, they also declared that they saw "the uncreated light" of God. This led to criticism from other Eastern theologians. Since most of these critics were also seeking a rapprochement with the West, the debate soon became entangled in those other issues. Finally, in 1351, the Byzantine Church officially accepted hesychasm, and one of its main proponents, Gregory Palamas (1296–1359), came to be regarded as a saint.

Heteronomy   A term derived from the Greek *heteros*, another, and *nomos*, law or principle, and thus meaning subjection to laws or principles outside of oneself. The term has been used particularly by Kant (1724–1804) in the field of philosophical ethics, and by Paul Tillich (1886–1965) in the field of theology. Kant proposed *autonomy, the rule of inner reason, as a form of ethics higher than heteronomy, in which one allows oneself to be governed by passions and desires, or by externally imposed laws. Tillich felt that both heteronomy and autonomy are to give way to *theonomy, in which autonomous reason is no longer grounded merely on itself, but on the ground of all being, God, and which therefore leads to authentic existence—a goal that is never attained, however, under the limitations of historical existence.

Hierarchy

An ordering in which a series of echelons connect the lower levels with the higher. In common ecclesiastical language, the "hierarchy" usually refers to the orders of the clergy—and particularly to its higher ranks, the bishops. During the Middle Ages, a hierarchical understanding of all reality was derived from *Neoplatonism, particularly through the work of an unknown author who wrote early in the sixth century under the pseudonym of Dionysius the Areopagite, and who thus was given great authority as a direct disciple of Paul.

For Pseudo-Dionysius, as generally for Neoplatonism, all of creation is organized as a great hierarchical pyramid, in which those beings that are closer to the One stand higher, and those that stand at a greater distance are lower. In particular, Pseudo-Dionysius developed a very elaborate system depicting both the celestial and the ecclesiastical hierarchies. In the celestial, there are three levels of angelic beings, each with three degrees, so that there are nine celestial choirs: at the higher level, seraphim, cherubim, and thrones; at the middle level, dominions, virtues, and powers; finally, at the lowest level, principalities, archangels, and angels. The ecclesiastical hierarchy comprises two basic levels, each with three degrees. First there is the priestly level, with the tripartite hierarchy of bishops, priests, and deacons. Then there is the laity, and they too are ranked in three groups: monastics, the faithful in general, and those believers who are excluded from Communion (catechumens, penitents, and energu-

mens—those who are thought to be possessed by demons and for whose liberation the church prays).

Although the scheme proposed by Pseudo-Dionysius lost credence as it became apparent that he was not actually Paul's disciple, the hierarchical view of the church prevailed in force until the Second Vatican Council (1962–65) began stressing the view of the church as the pilgrim people of God. At about the same time, however, various Protestant fundamentalists were proposing their own schemes for ordering the various ranks of angels and other celestial beings.

Historical Jesus

Often contrasted with "the Christ of faith," the phrase "historical Jesus" is somewhat ambiguous, for sometimes it refers to those things about Jesus that can be proved through rigorous historical research, and sometimes it simply means the historical figure of Jesus of Nazareth. The phrase itself, "historical Jesus," was popularized by the title of the English translation of a book by Albert Schweitzer, *The Quest of the Historical Jesus* (1910). In this book, Schweitzer reviewed a process, begun by Hermann S. Reimarus (1694–1768), which sought to discover the Jesus behind the Gospels by means of the newly developed tools of historical research. After reviewing this quest of almost two centuries, Schweitzer concluded that what each of the scholars involved had discovered was not in fact Jesus of Nazareth as he lived in the first century, but rather a modern image of Jesus, as much informed by modern bourgeois perspectives as by historical research itself.

Although it is generally asserted that Schweitzer's book put an end to the quest for the historical Jesus, that quest has not been entirely abandoned. What has been generally discarded is the notion that historical research can yield a view of Jesus as he was in the first century. Clearly, the earliest documents that tell us about Jesus—the Gospels and other Christian literature—are not "historical" documents in the sense that they simply chronicle events. They are written for the instruction and devotion of believers, and are therefore books of faith. They refer to Jesus as a historical figure, but they are not historical documents in the technical sense—and it is impossible to go behind them to discover the historical data from which they evolved. Thus, more recent historical studies have tended to be minimalist, not really trying to discover who Jesus was, but what are the bare facts that can be affirmed about him and his teachings.

Historicism   A term with two very distinct meanings. Sometimes it refers to the reductionist view that all reality can be explained in terms of a sequence of historical events and circumstances. In this sense, it often has a pejorative connotation. More recently, "historicism" has come to mean the view that all thought is historically conditioned, reflecting the conditions in which it takes place. Such is the case, for instance, of the sociology of knowledge, which explores the manner in which historical social circumstances impact knowledge and the interpretation of reality. In theology, historicism in this sense implies that "eternal truths" are never known as such, but only in particular historical contexts. (*See* *Contextual theologies.)

Historie   One of two German terms for *history—the other being *Geschichte*. These two terms have been used by theologians, both in Germany and elsewhere, in order to distinguish history as a series of verifiable events (*Historie*) from history as a meaningful narrative (*Geschichte*)—usually one whose meaning is not derived from the events themselves, and which therefore is not subject to the sort of objective verification that *Historie* requires. This distinction has receded in importance as *postmodernity has argued that even the supposedly objective events of history are always seen and interpreted from the subjectivity of the observer.

History   Besides its common meaning as the study of past events, in theological usage "history" often means the sphere of earthly and temporal existence in which human life takes place, and in which God relates to humans. It thus includes the past as well as the present and the future. In much contemporary theology, history is seen as the only locus where eternity can be known and experienced in this life. Thus, when one says, for instance, that the *incarnation is a historical event, this does not mean that it can be objectively ascertained by means of historical methods, but rather that it took place at a certain time and date, that it is connected with all of God's dealings with history, and that it is known to us through a sequence of historical witnesses linked to each other in the form of a *tradition—a tradition that certainly is grounded and attested in the New Testament, but that includes also a chain of witnesses connecting the New Testament with later generations. In this sense, one of the marks of theology in the twentieth and twenty-first centuries has been the rediscovery of the centrality of history for Christian faith. This may be seen as partly the result of *Hegelianism—which, even though eventually rejected by most, left a legacy of focusing on history—as well as of the availability of new methods of historical research and, in the field of theology, of the impact of *neo-orthodoxy, the *Lundensian school, the theology of *hope, *contextual and *liberation theologies, and others that stress the significance of history as the realm of God's activity.

As to the discipline of church history, it too has been impacted by the *historicism of recent decades, so that now there is a common awareness that history itself has a history. The *Church History* of Eusebius of Caesarea (fourth century) is not just a compilation of data, but a compilation that has been selected and organized according to a certain agenda. In the sixteenth century a group of Protestants, the "Centuriators" of Magdeburg, undertook the task of writing an entire history of the church from a Protestant perspective, and Cardinal Baronius (1538–1607) responded with his voluminous *Ecclesiastical Annals*. Late in the twentieth century, it became obvious that Christianity had become much more than a Western religion, and this reality, jointly with the *ecumenical movement, led to new attempts to write the history of the church from new perspectives that are more inclusive of various cultural and theological traditions.

Holiness Movement   A movement stemming from John Wesley's emphasis on "spreading holiness throughout the land," and on "scriptural holiness." Wesley (1703–91), like Calvin, stressed the significance of *sanctification, but, in contrast to Calvin, insisted that "entire sanctification" was possible in this life—even though rarely attained—and should be preached as the goal of Christian life. Late in the nineteenth century, and during the first half of the twentieth, several groups within Methodism felt that the emphasis on holy living was being lost, and this gave rise to churches within the Wesleyan tradition that stressed holiness as the goal of Christian life, often listing some of the characteristics of such holiness as abstaining from "worldly" activities such as gambling, consuming alcoholic beverages, or attending frivolous entertainment. Among these denominational offshoots from traditional Methodism are the Salvation Army, the Church of the Nazarene, the Wesleyan Church, and several others. Many of these movements spoke of sanctification as a "second blessing" after conversion—although they did not always agree as to whether this second blessing is instantaneous or not, how common it is, or what its signs are. Early in the twentieth century, it was within some of these holiness communities that people began having experiences of speaking in tongues, and came to associate the "sec-

ond blessing" with the outpouring of the Spirit, and the latter with *glossolalia, thus giving rise to the modern *Pentecostal movement.

Holy   The English equivalent of the Latin *sanctus* and the Greek *hagios*, the holy is difficult to define. In Scripture God is repeatedly declared to be holy, and in a somewhat derivative sense objects and even people closely related to God are also called "holy"—the Temple, the ark, the Sabbath, the "holy people" of God; or called to be holy—"Be ye holy." In some Christian traditions, people who have been particularly close to God are called "holy," or "saints"—St. Paul, for instance.

For some, holiness is one of the "moral attributes" of God. This, however, tends to limit the "holy" to the field of morality or behavior, while it is clear that God's holiness includes also a dimension of awe. This was made clear in the very influential book by Rudolf Otto (1869–1937), *The Idea of the Holy* (1917), in which he explored the "holy," not only in the Judeo-Christian tradition, but in religious experience in general, and concluded that the idea of the holy is common to all religions, and that it expresses human awe before the overwhelming mystery—*mysterium tremendum et fascinans*—of the "wholly Other" that cannot be understood or approached face to face.

Thus, while God's holiness certainly includes moral purity, and in turn demands moral purity of God's followers (*see* *Holiness Movement), it is also God's mysterious otherness, which no one can see and still live.

Holy Spirit   *See* *Spirit, Holy.

Homoiousion   (From the Greek *homoios*, similar, and *ousia*, substance. Also, in other grammatical contexts, *homoiousios*.) A formula proposed in the second half of the fourth century by some who, while not holding to *Arianism, were fearful that the decision at

Nicaea (see *Creeds) summarized in the formula *homoousion tō Patri—"of the same substance as the Father"—could be so interpreted as to favor *Sabellianism. Their alternative, homoiousion tō Patri—"of a similar substance to the Father"—sought to preserve the divinity of the Son, while still retaining the distinction between Father and Son. For this reason, those suggesting this formula have been called "semi-Arians," although such a label is not warranted. Later in the century, in part through the work of the Cappadocians and of Athanasius, most homoiousians came to accept the Nicene homoousios.

Homoousion (From the Greek homos the same, and ousia, substance. Also, in other grammatical contexts, homoousios.) A formula included in the Nicene *Creed as a clear declaration of the full divinity of the Son. The full phrase in the creed is homoousion tō Patri—"of the same substance as the Father." It is one of many phrases in the creed whose purpose is to reject *Arianism—"from the substance of the Father . . . God from God, light from light, true God from true God, begotten not made." Yet it became the touchstone in the subsequent controversies, for in declaring that the Son is of the same substance as the Father it seemed to leave the way open for *Sabellianism. One of the points of contention in that subsequent controversy was whether the Second Person of the Trinity—the Son—is the result of God's will, as are all creatures, or is of the very substance of God, which is to say that he is fully divine. Thus, the homoousion formula encapsulated the issues being debated.

Hope, Theology of A school of theology closely connected with German theologian Jürgen Moltmann (1926–), who in 1964 published Theology of Hope. Theologically, Moltmann had been profoundly influenced by Barth and the entire *neo-orthodox revival of theology. Philosophically, he was impacted by *Marxist philosopher Ernst Bloch, whose book The Hope Principle led Moltmann to consider the degree to which Christian theology had abandoned a theme that ought to have been at its very center. This led him to a recovery of *eschatology as central to Christian faith—yet eschatology not as merely "the doctrine of the last things," but rather as the hope by which the church lives. Christian hope being the certainty of God's future for creation, it frees believers from the need for self-redemption, and thus makes self-expenditure possible. This self-expenditure, however, is not that of traditional *mysticism or *asceticism, for it has a definite political dimension. Since the promise of the kingdom stands at the very heart of Christian hope, politics and participation in it are a necessary part of a truly eschatological faith. In a later book, The Crucified God, Moltmann made it very clear, however, that this is not the political triumphalism of the Crusades, or the sentimental contemplation of the cross of much traditional piety, but full engagement in a world in which there is injustice, and in which Christ's death is the result and the sign of the power of political sin. The cross implies that Christian political involvement must find God in those places in history that bear the sign of the cross, such as among the oppressed, the dispossessed, and the afflicted.

Given its rejection of various sorts of oppression based on gender, race, and class, for example, the theology of hope has influenced many *contextual and *liberation theologies. This has been particularly true of *Latin American theology, where Rubem Alves's A Theology of Human Hope (1969) was influential.

Humanism A movement that developed during the Renaissance, first in Italy and later in northern Europe. It was deeply suspicious of medieval scholasticism and of the educational methods of the Middle Ages, and proposed curricula that emphasized the languages and literature of antiquity, as well as the power of the human intellect to seek truth and beauty. Deeply aware of the degree to which the medieval tradition had impacted the interpretation of both classical and Christian antiquity, the humanists sought a return to the sources of antiquity—as they said, going *ad fontes*, to the sources. Much effort was devoted to restoring ancient texts by eliminating the additions and variations that had accrued over centuries of manuscript copying and recopying. Among Christian scholars, this meant producing critical editions of Scripture as well as of ancient Christian writers. Foremost in this task was Erasmus (1466?–1536), whose text of the Greek New Testament was deeply influential on the Reformation. In Spain, Cardinal Francisco Jiménez de Cisneros (1436–1517) produced an even greater work, the *Complutensian Polyglot Bible*.

Several of the leaders of the Reformation, including Zwingli, Melanchthon, and Calvin, were humanists. While Luther himself was not a humanist, his insistence on the need to return to biblical faith was parallel to the *ad fontes* of the humanists, and was influenced by it.

More recently, particularly late in the twentieth century, the term "humanism" has been used in a very different sense, referring to a system of thought that places humankind and human potential and achievement at the heart of philosophy, ethics, and politics. At that time, the term was used favorably by *Thomists, who argued that there are humanistic dimensions in the thought of Thomas Aquinas (1225–74), inasmuch as he argues for a positive role for human reason in the quest for knowledge, and for a natural law through which all humans have a notion of God's will. More recently, some *fundamentalists use this term pejoratively, applying it to any who do not agree with their views.

Hussites   The followers of Jan Hus (John Huss) (ca.1372–1415). After his death, his followers divided into several groups. Some took up arms to defend

themselves when a Catholic Crusade was called against them, and although thousands died, their resistance was such that eventually they gained a number of concessions—at which point many were reconciled with the Catholic Church. Others remained staunchly opposed to Roman Catholicism, and organized themselves into the *Unitas Fratrum*—Unity of Brethren. A number of them settled in Moravia and came to be known as Moravians. Thanks to the impact of *Pietism among the Moravians, particularly through the influence of Count Zinzendorf (1700–60), they became a strongly missionary movement, and thus spread throughout the world.

Hybris   (Also hubris.) Pride that carries one beyond the confines of one's limits, attempting to be what one cannot be. According to some theologians, the very essence of sin.

Hypostasis   Literally, substance. A word that played a very important role in both the Trinitarian and the christological controversies. In the Trinitarian controversies, it was used at first as a synonym for *ousia*. Thus, in the *anathemas that were originally appended to the *Creed of Nicaea, the doctrine was rejected that the Father and the Son are different "in *ousia*, or in hypostasis." This caused much confusion, particularly since in the West the vocabulary was different. In the West, since the time of Tertullian, God was declared to be "three persons in one substance." When Greek-speaking theologians translated this, a literal translation would be "three *prosōpa* in one hypostasis." The Greek *prosōpon* (plural, *prosōpa*) could mean "person," but it could also mean "mask" or "character," as in the theater. This led many Greek theologians to believe that the Latin-speaking theologians were referring to God as a single substance having three faces or playing three roles, which they considered *Sabellianism.

On the other hand, when Latin-speaking theologians heard the Greeks speaking of three hypostases, they understood this in the sense of three substances, and therefore three gods. It took an entire generation, and the foundational work of the Cappadocians, Athanasius, and others, to bridge the gap between the Greek East and the Latin West, and to come to the conclusion that the Latin formula, "three Persons in one substance," was equivalent to the Greek "three hypostases in one *ousia*."

The notion of hypostasis then played a role in the christological controversies, particularly in the fifth century, in the debates surrounding the Councils of Ephesus (431) and Chalcedon (451), whose final outcome was to define christological orthodoxy in terms of the *hypostatic union.

Hypostatic Union   A term apparently coined by Cyril of Alexandria (ca.375–444) in his debates against *Nestorianism. Nestorius held that in Christ there were two natures, each with its own subsistence or hypostasis. If it were not so, he claimed, the two elements of the union in Christ—his divinity and his humanity—would have resulted in a third reality, neither human nor divine, and it would no longer be correct to speak of a "union," but only of the result of that union. It was for this reason that he insisted on Christ's having two natures—the divine and the human—and two hypostases on which those natures subsist. It was also for that reason that he rejected the principle of *communicatio idiomatum*, for predicates always apply to the substance, to the hypostasis.

In response to Nestorius and his followers, Cyril declared that the union in Christ is such that both his divinity and his humanity subsist in the one hypostasis, the Second Person of the Trinity. Thus, Christ's humanity has no hypostasis of its own (*Anhypostatic Union). While he is both divine and human, he is both in a single person. Therefore, all that is said about Christ is said about his person, and hence Cyril's insistence on the *communicatio idiomatum*.

This view was adopted by the Council of Chalcedon (451), which declared that Christ is both divine and human, and these two "concurring into one Person and one hypostasis."

Iconoclasm   A movement that appeared in the Eastern church in the eighth century, opposing the use of images in worship. Its causes were many—among them, the desire to respond to the accusation by Muslims and Jews that Christians were idolaters, and also the desire of officials in government to curtail the power of the church. By extension, an "iconoclast" has become anyone who seems to delight in destroying cherished notions.

The iconoclastic controversy began in 725, when Byzantine Emperor Leo III the Isaurian ordered the destruction of an image of Christ that supposedly had miraculous powers. This was soon followed by a series of imperial edicts against the use of images (or icons) in worship. The patriarch of Constantinople, who was opposed to imperial policy, was deposed by the emperor, and this resulted in a break between Constantinople and Rome. A long succession of Byzantine emperors continued the iconoclastic policy of Leo, and were opposed by the defenders of images, who were called "iconodules"—that is, servants of images.

The iconodule party, although out of power, was staunchly supported by the majority of the laity, who were accustomed to the use of images in worship and even to their veneration, and whose opposition to imperial policy was encouraged by many monastics as well as by a number of church leaders who had to flee from the Byzantine government. Finally Empress Irene, regent for her son Leo IV, reversed imperial policy and, jointly with Pope Hadrian I, called for an ecumenical council that gathered in Nicaea in 787 and decreed the restoration of the images, or icons. In its theological justification for the use of images, the council resorted to the earlier arguments of Patriarch German of Constantinople, who had declared that worship in the strict sense, *latreia*, is due only to God; but that other objects, such as images, were worthy of a veneration, *proskynēsis*, and a service, *douleia*, precisely because they were close to God and pointed to God.

Although this seemed to have put the matter to rest, early in the ninth century Emperor Leo V reinstated the iconoclastic policies of his predecessors, and therefore the controversy continued until the final restoration of images by another regent, Empress Theodora, on March 11, 842—a date still celebrated by the entire Eastern church as the "Feast of Orthodoxy."

Theologically, there were many defenders as well as opponents of images. Outstanding among the former was John of Damascus (ca.675–749), who was free from imperial pressures because he lived under Muslim rule, whose *Exposition of the Orthodox Faith* included a strong defense of images. According to him, images are to be used, first of all, because God made humans after the divine image, and thus the first to make an image and to show that the divine can be mirrored in an image was God. Secondly, in the *incarnation God has taken human form, and has therefore made the divine accessible to humankind in human forms and images. Finally, the icons are the books of the unlettered, who learn of God and of Christian living through them.

Iconodules   *See* *Iconoclasm.

Idealism   Besides its common usage, in the sense of being guided by ideals, in philosophical discourse "idealism" refers to any theory or worldview that regards reality as consisting primarily of mind or of intellectual processes. Thus, the term encompasses a wide variety of philosophical systems, such as *Platonism, *Cartesianism, and *Hegelianism.

Ideology   Many contemporary *contextual and *liberation theologians use the term "ideology," not in its more common, neutral sense of a system of ideas, but rather in the *Marxist sense of a system of ideas devised—usually unconsciously—to bolster a particular social or economic agenda. In this context, an "ideology" is often seen as an oppressive misconception that has to be unmasked.

Illumination   A basic tenet of Augustine's *epistemology, that all true knowledge is based on the activity of God, illumining the mind. As a follower of the *Platonic tradition, Augustine (354–430) did not believe that the knowledge of eternal truth—which is the only knowledge worthy of the name—can result from the activity of the senses, which are mutable and *contingent, or even of the human mind, which is also mutable and contingent. On the other hand, he could not accept Plato's theory of the *preexistence of the souls—although he did flirt with it—as the basis for human knowledge of eternal ideas. He thus had resort to the theory of illumination, claiming that knowledge is the result of the divine light acting on the mind. Although at times Augustine appears to be saying that God illumines truth so that the mind can perceive it, the general thrust of his thought seems to be in the direction that God's *Logos infuses knowledge into the human mind. This theory of knowledge dominated the Middle Ages until the reintroduction of *Aristotle into Western Europe resulted in the *Thomistic alternative. At that point, it became a hallmark of *Augustinianism, particularly in the thought of Franciscan writers such as Bonaventure (ca.1217–74).

Image of God   (In Latin, *imago Dei.*) According to Genesis 1:26, the principle or pattern by which God created humankind. This has been variously interpreted. Some have understood it to mean that humans are physically like God, and that it is because of this resemblance that *anthropomorphic language about God is acceptable. Others have seen the image in terms of dominion: just as God is the ruler of all, God gives the human creature dominion over the rest of creation. Similarly, some have interpreted the image of God in humans in terms of freedom, of ethical responsibility, or of the intellectual gift of being able to conceive what does not yet exist and bring it into existence. A common theme in patristic theology is that God made humans "after" or "according to" the Word incarnate, Jesus Christ, who is "the image of the invisible God" (Col. 1:15). According to this view, the *incarnation was always part of God's purpose for humankind, and therefore God created humans following the pattern of God incarnate. Similar views were held by Teilhard de Chardin (1881–1955), who spoke of Christ as the *homo futurus* toward which history is moving. Another common theme in patristic theology, particularly after Augustine, is that the image of God in humans is in the "vestiges of the *Trinity"—*vestigia Trinitatis*—found in humans, where intellect, will, and memory, while being distinct, are a single mind. Finally, also basing their views on the doctrine of the Trinity, some hold that the image of God in humans lies in their being by nature social, called to a community patterned after the community of Father, Son, and Holy Spirit.

Another point that has been debated, particularly in patristic and medieval times is whether the "image" and the "likeness" of Genesis 1:26 are two ways of expressing the same reality, or are in fact two different dimensions of human relationship to God. According to some, while the likeness was lost with the *fall, the image remained.

Images, Use of in Worship *See* *Iconoclasm.

Imago Dei *See* *Image of God.

Immaculate Conception The official Roman Catholic doctrine that the Virgin *Mary, through a special dispensation of God's grace, was preserved from *original sin from her conception. Already a common belief in popular piety during the Middle Ages, the immaculate conception was denied by many distinguished theologians, including Thomas Aquinas (1225–74), who felt that this doctrine diminished the universal saving power of Jesus. It was strongly defended by others, particularly Franciscans such as John Duns Scotus (1266?–1308). It was made a *dogma of the Roman Catholic Church in 1854 by Pope Pius IX's bull *Ineffabilis Deus*. This was the first dogma of the church ever defined by a pope on his own authority, without the concurrence of an ecumenical council.

Immanence One of the traditional attributes of *God, often contrasted, and kept in polar tension with, *transcendence. It refers to God's presence in and within creation, permeating and sustaining all that exists. An extreme doctrine of immanence, without a balancing transcendence, would lead to *pantheism, while the opposite—denying or diminishing God's immanence—is characteristic of *deism.

Immensity Literally, immeasurability. Traditionally said of God, who cannot be measured by anything outside of Godself. Since it implies that God is not bound by space or time, it is sometimes used to indicate that all of God—and not just part of God—is present everywhere and at all times. (*See* *Omnipresence.)

Immersion The method of baptism in which the candidate enters the water, and either is submerged or kneels in the water and has water poured over the head (*Infusion). It is the most ancient method of Christian baptism, although from a very early date other methods were allowed in special circumstances. It was progressively abandoned in the West after the twelfth century, and later reinstated by the *Anabaptists and others following their lead. It has remained the common form of baptism in the Eastern churches, and is becoming increasingly common in the Roman Catholic Church as well as in other Western traditions.

Immortality The quality of being incapable of death. Frequently said of God, as one of the divine attributes. Also frequently predicated of the *soul. Many of the ancient peoples of the Mediterranean basin believed in the immortality of the soul. So when Christians entered the Gentile world preaching life after death, they found fertile soil ready to receive their preaching, especially if they related it to the teachings of respected philosophers such as Plato. The result was that soon most Christians came to view the Christian doctrine of *eternal life, and of life after death, in terms of the immortality of the soul. Many, however, saw two important differences between Christian doctrine and the commonly held notion of the immortality of the soul. First, according to Christian doctrine the soul is mortal. If it lives, it is only because God grants it continued life, not because of some inherent characteristic of the soul itself. Second, Christians held that the soul without a body is not a complete human being, and thus insisted on the *resurrection of the body—a "spiritual" body, true, but still a body.

Impassibility One of the traditional *attributes of God, resulting from the philosophical notion that being changed by another—or being capable of such a change—is an imperfection. Strictly, it does not mean that God is incapable of passion or compassion, but rather that God is never the passive object of action by another. Clearly, the God of Scripture suffers with the pain of creation, and therefore many theologians have claimed

that impassibility is not a proper divine attribute. Others respond that God suffers the pains, and shares the joys, of creation, not because creatures have the intrinsic power to affect God, but because God has determined to share in that pain and those joys. Thus, even when being compassionate toward creation, God is not the passive object of creaturely activity.

Imputed Justice See *Justice, Imputed.

Incarnation God's act of "taking flesh" (from the Latin *in*, and *caro, carnis*, flesh) in Jesus Christ. The incarnation is a central tenet of the Christian faith, and one of the main points distinguishing it from other monotheistic religions.

From a very early date, Christians were convinced that God was present in a special way in Jesus. Paul spoke of him as "Lord"—the term that in the Septuagint, the Greek translation of the Hebrew Bible that Paul quoted in his letters, was used to refer to Yahweh. Matthew depicts him as speaking on a mountain, and there setting principles of conduct for his followers, just as God had spoken to Moses and to the children of Israel on Mount Sinai. John depicts him claiming a unique unity with the Father. Early in the second century, Ignatius of Antioch, referring to the passion of Christ, calls it "the sufferings of my God." Thus, while debates about the exact meaning and mode of the incarnation would continue for centuries, the unique presence of God in Christ was settled quite early in the nascent Christian community.

How this presence took place, however, was not clear. At one end of the spectrum were those who believed that Jesus was a unique prophet, but still only a man whom God had inspired as the prophets had been inspired earlier, or one whom God adopted into sonship at some point during his life—according to some, at his baptism, when God declared him to be God's beloved Son (*see* *Ebionism; *Adoptionism). At the other end of the spectrum, there were those who claimed that he was not truly human, that he was a celestial being who only seemed to have a body (*Docetism; *Gnosticism; *Marcionism). Both of these positions were soon rejected by the church at large. Of the two, it was the latter that people found most attractive, and that posed a threat to Christian orthodoxy for a longer time.

Between those two extremes, there was a wide gamut of views regarding the presence of God in Jesus—all agreeing that he is both divine and human, but disagreeing as to how best to interpret and to speak of this fact. In the West, Tertullian used legal language to declare that in Jesus there were "two substances"—the divine and the human—in one person. Apparently in this context he understood the terms "substance" and "person" as Roman law understood them—the substance being the property or office that determines the character and status of an individual, and the person being the one holding such property or office. Although Tertullian's writing on this subject was not employed in the course of the controversies of the next two centuries, it is significant that eventually Christian orthodoxy was defined as holding that in Christ there are two "natures"—the divine and the human—in one person.

In the East, there were two basic schools of thought. One, often called the *Alexandrine school, tended to emphasize the union of the divine and the human, sometimes to the point that the human seemed to be absorbed or eclipsed by the divine. The other, the *Antiochene tendency, took the opposite tack, insisting on the need to affirm the full humanity of Jesus, even though this might require limiting his divinity, or limiting the union, so that his divinity would not obscure or overwhelm Jesus' humanity. Scholars often refer to the former as a "unitive," and to the latter as a "disjunctive" *Christology.

The unitive Christology of the Alexandrines was early expressed in what scholars call a "Logos-sarx" (that is, logos-flesh) Christology, in which what God assumed in Jesus, rather than a full human being, was a human body or flesh. This was the position of the *Apollinarists, who held that in Jesus the *Logos or Word of God has taken up a human body, so that there is in Jesus no human "rational soul"—that is, in modern terms, no human mind—for the place of the rational soul is taken by the Logos. This view was soon declared to be unacceptable, for it made Jesus something less than human.

The Antiochene, disjunctive Christology became the center of debate when *Nestorius proposed speaking of Jesus as having "two natures" in "two persons," and these two joined in what he called a "moral union," so that it was possible to say that Jesus did some things as human, and some others as God. Thus, for instance, Jesus the man was born of Mary; but God was not—which was why the term *Theotokos became the crux of the controversy. This position too the church rejected—at the Council of Ephesus, in 431.

In opposition to Nestorius, Cyril of Alexandria (died 444) insisted on the need to understand the union in such a way that whatever is said of Jesus is said about both his humanity and his divinity, for the subject of such predication is neither the divine nor the human, but the one person of God incarnate (*Communicatio idiomatum). This Cyril called a *hypostatic union, meaning that in Jesus two natures—the divine and the human —exist in only one *hypostasis, one person, the Second Person of the *Trinity. Others in the Alexandrine school went farther, claiming that once the union has taken place it is no longer possible to speak of a human nature of Christ, but only of a divine nature that has absorbed the human. These received the name of *Monophysites—that is, persons holding to one nature—and their teaching was also rejected by the church at large in 451, when the Council of Chalcedon declared that in Christ there are two natures and one person, or hypostasis.

As a result of these controversies, the first permanent rifts in the Christian church appeared, so that today there are still Christians—mostly in the former territories of the Persian Empire—who follow the lead of Nestorius, and many more—in Egypt, Ethiopia, Syria, and even India—who are said to be "monophysites," although the matter of their supposed heterodoxy is subject to debate.

Even then, the controversy did not end. Embroiled in political considerations, it continued around new formulations such as *monergism and *monotheletism. Also, even though accepting the decisions of Chalcedon, there are differences of emphasis among theologians. Thus, it has frequently been said that while Luther leans toward a unitive Christology, Calvin's inclinations are more toward a disjunctive one.

In more recent times, *liberalism resurrected the notion of Jesus as an exceptional teacher, a holy man, or a prophet, but not God incarnate. While this view of Jesus has become widespread in secular society, Bonhoeffer's (1906–45) comment is worth considering: that such views, even though apparently more rational than the traditional doctrine of the incarnation, actually turn Jesus into a superhuman phenomenon, and are thus less credible than ancient docetism.

The various opinions on the mode of the incarnation are closely related to different views regarding its purpose. The most commonly held view on the purpose of the incarnation is that Jesus was incarnate for our salvation; but even here there are several options open (see *Atonement; *Expiation). In the West, the most commonly held understanding of the atonement is that Jesus pays for human sin on the cross. In the classic essay on this subject, Anselm of Canterbury (ca.1033–1109) holds that this requires that Jesus be human, for it is

humanity that has sinned, and that he be divine, for his payment must be infinite. Such views see little redemptive significance in the incarnation itself, which is simply a means toward the cross. If, on the other hand, what humans need is not someone to pay for their sin, but rather someone to show them the way to God, then the humanity of Jesus is merely an instrument through which his divinity speaks to us, and this is perfectly compatible with a Christology along the Alexandrine lines. If the purpose of the incarnation is to open the way so that humans can join God (*Theopoiesis), to lift humankind to communion with God, then it is of great importance that Jesus be fully human, as the Antiochenes insisted, and the incarnation itself—and not only the cross—is a redemptive act.

Furthermore, throughout the centuries there have been theologians—among others, Irenaeus in the second century, Alexander of Hales in the thirteenth, and Teilhard de Chardin in the twentieth—who have seen the incarnation, not primarily as God's response to and solution for human sin, but as the very purpose of God in creating humankind. In that case, rather than beginning, as does most traditional Christology, from the contrast and the distance between humanity and divinity, it is possible to develop a Christology that sees the two as essentially compatible.

Inculturation   A term that became common in missiological theory during the second half of the twentieth century, to refer to the process whereby Christianity develops roots within a *culture. It is often contrasted with *acculturation and with *accommodation, the method by which missionaries adapt their preaching, teaching, and practices to various cultures, for rather than being a missionary method it is the result of the actual practice of Christian living within a culture. In other words, the agents of inculturation are not missionaries or others from outside the culture looking for "points of contact," but rather Christians within the culture who, sometimes quite unconsciously, interpret and live out the gospel according to their cultural traditions and patterns. In its content, it is much wider than acculturation, for the latter deals with the receptor culture only in terms of those points at which there is a possible bridge, while those who are part of the culture have to deal with it as a whole as it relates to Christianity.

Some missiologists use the model of the *incarnation as a paradigm for inculturation, arguing that the only way to know the Christian faith is through its incarnation in a culture, and that every attempt to separate an eternal and unchanging set of doctrines from the culture is doomed to fail—just as *christological orthodoxy has long held that the divinity of Christ cannot be separated from his humanity. In inculturation, not only is the culture Christianized, but the gospel is also "culturalized"—interpreted and lived in a particular way appropriate to that particular culture. This means that the missionary process, rather than being a mere expansion of Christianity, is a constant reinvention of Christianity.

Indulgences Acts by which the church remits temporal penalties for sin. In this context, "temporal" refers specifically to the time that the *soul has to spend in *purgatory as it atones for its sins, or is cleansed from them, before passing on to heaven. Thus, indulgences do not free a soul from *hell or from eternal damnation. The practice of indulgences developed out of the medieval penitential system (see *Penance), and from those cases in which a sinner could not perform the prescribed penance and was allowed to substitute another for it—for instance, someone who could not go on a pilgrimage for reasons of health could send someone else instead. At the time of the Crusades, "plenary" indulgences were granted to participants in the enterprise meaning that all their sins were forgiven, and all their temporal

punishment canceled. Other "partial" indulgences were also common for acts such as going on pilgrimage. Eventually, the practice developed of offering money as an act of penance, and thereby obtaining an indulgence. Since the church had at its disposal the merits of Christ and the *treasury of merits, these merits could be applied to sinners in the form of indulgences. This was the origin of the sale of indulgences, which toward the end of the Middle Ages became a scandalous affair, and in a way precipitated the Protestant Reformation. The Roman Catholic Church still holds to the doctrine behind indulgences, but these are now more carefully regulated than in earlier times.

Inerrancy The claim, made by many *fundamentalists, that the Bible is absolutely true, and contains no error, not only in matters of faith and doctrine, but also in matters of history or the physical sciences. This refers only to the original, autograph texts of Scripture, and therefore there may be errors in all present manuscripts, copies, or translations. It also refers to the final truth, to be discovered only at the end times. Thus, if the Bible says that the sun moves around the earth, one cannot say that science proves this to be wrong, for all the facts are not in, and in the end we shall discover that what the Bible says was in fact true, no matter how unscientific or inexact it might appear at present.

Infallibility The capacity to teach, and particularly to define doctrine, without the possibility of error. Some Christians claim that the Bible is infallible, not only in matters of faith, but in all matters (*Inerrancy). At various times, others have held that the dogmatic declarations of ecumenical councils are infallible (see *Conciliarism)—although there has been much debate as to which councils fulfill the necessary requirements to be considered ecumenical. Since the promulgation of the dogma of papal infallibility by the First Vatican Council in

1870, the Roman Catholic Church holds that the pope is infallible when he speaks *ex cathedra*—that is, out of his own office and authority as pope. Late in the twentieth century, a series of debates emerged within Roman Catholicism as to when it is that the pope actually speaks *ex cathedra*, and therefore about what papal infallibility really means. These debates have continued into the twenty-first century.

Infralapsarianism In the debates regarding *predestination that developed in Protestant *scholasticism, the position of those who held that, in the order of the divine decrees, the decree concerning predestination follows, and does not precede, the decree concerning the *fall. In other words, God first decreed the fall, and then decreed the election of some and the reprobation of others. In later usage, the term "infralapsarianism" has become ambiguous, for some apply it to the claim that God decreed election on the basis of God's foreknowledge of the fall—in the case of some theologians, after the event of the fall. (*See* *Supralapsarianism.)

Infusion (Also affusion.) The method of *baptism in which water is poured over the head. Sometimes confused with *aspersion, which consists in sprinkling water on the head of the baptized. (*See also* *Immersion.)

Initium fidei Literally, the "beginning of faith." The first step toward salvation, that of accepting *grace. This played an important role in the controversies regarding Augustine's doctrine of grace, both during his lifetime and immediately thereafter (*see* *Pelagianism; *Semipelagianism). Augustine and his followers insisted that the *initium fidei* is in God's grace, which is irresistible and which is given according to God's sovereign decision of *predestination. Their opponents held that sinners are capable in and of themselves to accept the grace that God offers—that is, to take the first step toward salvation. In 529, the Council of Orange declared that the *initium fidei* is not in human nature, but in divine grace—normally received at baptism.

Inspiration A term most commonly used in connection with the authority of *Scripture. Etymologically, it derives from the Latin for "breathing," and is the common way of translating the assertion in 2 Tim. 3:16, that "all scripture is breathed [inspired] by God" (in Greek, *theopneustos*). Throughout history, most Christians have agreed that Scripture is inspired by God, even though there have been different ways of understanding such inspiration. At one end of the spectrum, many *fundamentalists claim that the Holy Spirit so possessed those who wrote Scripture that the process was tantamount to dictation, and that therefore there is neither error nor variation in the books of the Bible (*Inerrancy). Others hold that divine inspiration did not erase the personalities and style of particular authors, but used them in order to convey God's truths. At the other end of the spectrum, some have claimed that the Bible is inspired in the sense in which any work of genius is inspired, and that—as in any other piece of literature—readers must search in it for those truths that are significant for them. Still, the vast majority of Christians have always held that Scripture is inspired by God, and that God speaks to them in the Bible or through it.

At various times, there have been other issues regarding inspiration. One issue has to do with the inspiration of translations and of the process of transmitting the text. Although today very few Christians would argue that a particular version of the Bible is divinely inspired, in recent times there have been those who have claimed that they were guided by the Spirit in the process of translation, and that therefore their version has divine authority. Similar claims were made even before the advent of Christianity for the common Greek translation of the Hebrew Scriptures into Greek known as the Septuagint, based on the legend that a number of scholars, all working independently, produced identical translations. During the period of Protestant *scholasticism, there were those who claimed that the system of punctuation in the Masoretic Text of the Hebrew Bible, even though developed by Jewish scholars long after the advent of Christianity, was divinely inspired and therefore infallible.

A much more difficult question regarding inspiration has to do with the formation of the *canon. Scripture is a collection of individual writings that have been declared to be authoritative, some first by the people of Israel and eventually all by the church. Did the Holy Spirit inspire those who made the selection? How does such inspiration relate to the inspiration of the writers themselves? Does this mean that the church can claim an authoritative inspiration by the Spirit? Such questions go beyond the authority of Scripture and into the issue of the authority of the church vis-à-vis Scripture, and therefore have been hotly debated between Catholics and Protestants.

Finally, there is the question of the action of the Spirit in the current reading of Scripture. Does it suffice to say that Scripture was inspired when it was written, or must one add that a proper reading of Scripture requires the active inspiration of the reading community by the Spirit? On this score, one could point out that in Genesis, God "breathed" into the man "the breath of life." If God's inspiration (breath) is what gives life to an otherwise inanimate body, can a parallel be drawn, saying that God shaped Scripture (through divine inspiration of the writers), and now breathes into it breath of life (through the divine inspiration of the reading community)?

Interpretation *See* *Hermeneutics.

Jansenism A movement named after Dutch Roman Catholic theologian Cornelius Jansenius (1585–1638), who opposed *Molinism on the basis of a radically *Augustinian doctrine of *grace and *predestination. According to Jansenius, *original sin has so marred human *freedom of the will that after the *fall we have no freedom or power to resist sin or to perform any truly good action. In such condition, even those who outwardly obey the commandments of God are not truly obedient, for the foundation of obedience is love, and apart from the irresistible grace of God we are completely incapable of loving God. Jansenius and his followers were repeatedly accused of being secret *Calvinists. The Inquisition banned Jansenius's main work, *Augustinus*, in 1641; but the University of Louvain, and a growing portion of the faculty in the Sorbonne, in Paris, refused to abide by this decree. In 1643 Pope Urban VIII added his authority to that of the Inquisition, once again condemning the *Augustinus*. Ten years later Innocent X condemned five Jansenist propositions; but the Jansenists claimed that these propositions were not actually what Jansenius had taught, and that they could therefore ignore the pope's condemnation.

A French Jansenist, Antoine Arnauld (1612–94), gave the movement a more practical bent by applying its principles, first to the practice of frequent Communion, and then to an entire gamut of ecclesiastical practices and policies. Thus the movement made a turn toward politics, both secular and ecclesiastical, and eventually the issues of grace and predestination were eclipsed by matters of authority and order. In France, the influential abbey of Port-Royal, inspired by Arnauld, refused to submit to the papal condemnations of Jansenism. Although Arnauld had to flee into exile, the torch was taken up by Blaise Pascal (1623–62). Louis XIV agreed with Rome on the condemnation of the movement, which in turn became further politicized and radicalized. Clement XI reiterated its condemnation in 1713. Jansenism joined forces with *Gallicanism, and eventually contributed to the more radical elements within the French Revolution.

Joachimism A movement of *apocalyptic inclinations named after Joachim of Fiore (or of Flora, ca.1132–ca.1202), a Calabrian mystic who devoted the latter years of his life to the study of the book of Revelation. On the basis of this study, he concluded that history was unfolding in three stages: from Adam to Christ, from Christ to the year 1260, and from that date to the end. These three stages he related to the three persons of the *Trinity, so that the first is the age of the Father, the second is the age of the Son, and the third is the age of the Spirit. The date for the transition between the second and the third ages was determined by a mathematical calculation, on the basis that each age should have the same number of generations. Since between Adam and Jesus there were forty-two generations, there will also be forty-two between the time of Christ and the age of the Spirit. The perfection of the age of the Son requires that these generations be of equal length. At thirty years per generation, one arrives at the date 1260. Just as John the Baptist was a forerunner before the beginning of the second age, there will also be a forerunner before the dawning of the age of the Spirit. According to Joachim, the entire monastic community at its best was such a forerunner, and therefore an announcement of the dawning of the new age.

The Fourth Lateran Council (1215) condemned Joachim's views on the Trinity, which made it appear that the Father, Son, and Holy Spirit were three phases of the divine. However, it is quite possible that the condemnation was also a reaction to the increasingly subversive tones of the Joachimist movement. This subversive dimension came to the foreground in the radical Franciscans who claimed that the Order at large had betrayed St. Francis's principles, particularly on the matter of radical poverty. Eventually Joachimism became a radical critique of the papacy and of the entire church, claiming that the new age was dawning, that its forerunner was St. Francis, and that the church and its authorities were a matter of the dying past age.

Judgment Through the centuries, Christianity—as well as Judaism and many other religious traditions—has held that God not only loves, but also judges—or, perhaps more exactly, that God's love includes judgment. This was one of the main points of contention against *Marcionism, and the reason why the return of Jesus to judge "the quick and the dead" was incorporated into what eventually became the Apostles' *Creed. While the Bible certainly speaks of a final judgment, this does not deny the possibility and the experience of judgment within history. This is seen, for instance, in the repeated instances in the book of Judges, where God punished the people's unfaithfulness by delivering them into the hands of oppressors. Christians continued this tradition by writing, for instance, of the death of persecutors as God's punishment upon them. Yet, it is also clear that any such judgment is at best partial, and that in history the good do not always prosper, nor do the evil always perish.

It is at this point that the notion of a final judgment becomes important. God judges, not only within history, but also beyond it, so that evil will be completely destroyed, and good will prevail. In Christian theology, this final judgment has long been associated with the *Parousia or return of Jesus. While traditionally most Christians have believed that this judgment includes both eternal salvation and eternal damnation, there have been many who have held that the love of God is such that eventually all will be saved (*Universalism), and who therefore see judgment on evildoers as followed, not by an eternal *hell, but rather by a process of painful purification (*see* *Purgatory).

Justice An attribute of God to be reflected in all creation—particularly in humankind—and eventually realized in the *kingdom of God. To say that God is "just" does not mean only that God is fair, but also that God is righteous and dependable, and that God demands a similar righteousness from humans. Thus, the term "justice" is often used in discussions of the relationship between humans and God (*see* *Justification; *Justice, Imputed).

In *Aristotelian philosophy, and in much Christian theology derived from it, justice is one of the four cardinal *virtues, and it includes both one's relationships with others and one's own personal rectitude. In contemporary theological discourse, justice is considered both in its retributive aspects—as punishing evil and rewarding good—and in its distributive dimension—justice requires a proper distribution of resources and power. Retributive justice tends to be emphasized by those who also underscore the personal dimensions of *sin, while distributive justice is often the counterpart of a stress on the societal manifestations of sin, such as hunger or oppression.

Theologians at various times have explored the difference between justice and love. Ambrose, in the fourth century, felt that justice consists in giving all their due, and that one can only practice love—for instance, in giving alms—after one has practiced justice. Some contemporary ethicists feel that, while the principle of love is crucial in interpersonal relationships, the principle of justice serves as a guide for the concrete practice of love in a world of conflict and unjust relationships.

Justice, Forensic See *Justice, Imputed.

Justice, Imputed The view of justification, typical of much of the *Lutheran tradition, that holds that in *justification God does not make sinners objectively just, but declares them to be so—in the case of most theologians hold-ing to this doctrine, by imputing the justice of Christ to sinners. Sometimes called "forensic justice," because God's action of justification is akin to that of a judge declaring the accused innocent. This view is often summarized in the phrase *simul justus et peccator*, at the same time just and a sinner—meaning that, even after justification, sinners remain such.

Justification A term that has its origins in courts of law, where it means to render verdict in favor of an accused, who is thereby declared to be blameless. One of the principles of the Protestant Reformation is "justification by faith"—or, more properly, by grace through faith in Christ. What the Reformers meant by this is that what makes a sinner just is not good *works—"works of righteousness" —but a divine act of *grace. Although in the heat of the debate some Roman Catholic theologians came close to declaring that justification is the result of good works, and this was certainly the popular understanding of matters in the sixteenth century, in fact most Roman Catholic theologians have agreed that justification is an act of God's grace. The difference lay in that for Luther and the main Protestant theologians justification was God's gracious act of declaring a sinner just, even in spite of the continued presence of sin, while Roman Catholics saw justification as God's act of infusing *grace into the sinner, who can then perform acts of justice—good works—and thus become just. Luther's emphasis on imputed justice (*see* *Justice, Imputed), as well as his experience of having sought to justify himself through works, led him to view with suspicion any attempt to speak of justification in connection with good works, and thus not to stress *sanctification, as did Calvin and the *Reformed tradition in general (*see* *Calvinism; *Methodism; *Sanctification).

Kairos In ancient Greek, there were two main terms to refer to time: *kairos,* and *chronos.* The latter meant time in its measurable dimension, such as years, weeks, hours. *Chronos* has a certain repetitive or circular dimension, as year follows year, and hour follows hour. In contrast, *kairos* refers to time as a significant moment, certainly within *chronos*, but with implications beyond it—much as today we say "your time has come." In the New Testament, the central *kairos* is the advent of Jesus Christ. On this basis, *kairos* is often used of a present occasion whose implications go beyond those of ordinary time. Sometimes in modern usage the term is turned into an adjective, as in the phrase "this is a kairotic event."

Kenosis   A term derived from the Greek word for emptying, as found in Phil. 2:7, "he . . . emptied himself." In the eighteenth century, and particularly in the nineteenth, that passage in Philippians was the basis of a *christological view that sought to explain the possibility of the *incarnation by claiming that the eternal Word, or *Logos, of God divested himself of the divine attributes that are incompatible with being human —omnipotence, omniscience, and so on—in order to make the incarnation possible.

Kerygma   A Greek noun meaning "preaching," and used to refer both to the event and to the content of preaching. The term became particularly popular in the first half of the twentieth century, when C. H. Dodd (1884–1973) argued that it was possible to discover, behind the various writings of the New Testament, the essential *kerygma* of the apostles. There is another series of words that can also be translated as "preaching," all related to the verb "to prophesy." These are usually applied to speaking within the community of believers, explaining Scripture and applying it to their lives (*Prophecy). This is closely related to *didachē*, teaching. In contrast, *kērygma* is both the proclamation of the great deeds of God—particu-

larly in Jesus Christ—and the content of that proclamation. It is not just a narration of events, nor even their interpretation, but also a call to the listener, who is invited to belief and to new life.

Kingdom of God   In recent theological literature, often called the "reign of God," both in order to avoid the gender-specific connotation of "kingdom" and in order to stress that the phrase does not refer to a new or different place, but rather to a new and different order.

The Gospels repeatedly tell us that at least part, if not the very heart, of the preaching and teachings of Jesus had to do with the kingdom of God. The notion of the kingdom of God has deep roots in the religion of Israel, even though the words themselves do not appear until fairly late in Hebrew literature. When it appears, sometimes it refers to the eternal rule and power of God over all things, sometimes it has to do with Israel's acceptance of God's rule, and sometimes it has an eschatological dimension, referring to the final consummation and the subjection of all things to the will of God.

While all these strains of thought may also be found in the teachings of Jesus, it is clear that he stressed the eschatological dimension of the kingdom. The kingdom is about to come—or has already come in his own person, and is about to break forth. This is the subject of many parables where Jesus speaks of the return of a master, a householder, an owner, or a king.

In the teachings of Jesus, the eschatological dimension of the kingdom is closely related to a radical overturning of the present order, as may be seen in his declaration that the last shall be first; that sinners and harlots go into the kingdom ahead of the religious; that the wayward prodigal son is received with feasting, while the obedient brother stays out of the feast.

In the Gospel of Matthew, the phrase "kingdom of heaven" is often substituted for "kingdom of God." This probably reflects the pious Jewish custom of avoiding speech about God, and sometimes using "heaven" as a way of speaking of God without mentioning the name. It does not seem to mean, as many understood later, that the kingdom of God is somewhere "up there," in a different place called *"heaven," and has nothing to do with earth. For Matthew, just as much as for Mark or for Luke, the fullness of the kingdom lies, not in some celestial sphere, but rather in the future.

As early Christianity moved into the Hellenistic world, the notion of a coming kingdom of God was both alien and subversive. It was subversive because its very proclamation implied a criticism of the existing order, of the "kingdom" of Caesar. It was alien because most Hellenistic thought conceived of the golden age of happiness, not as in the future, but rather in the long-lost past, and also because it implied a view of history that contradicted much of the cyclical views of *Stoicism and other dominant philosophies.

At this juncture, Christian *apologists found some support in the *Platonic notion of a higher and more perfect world of ideas, of which the present world is but an imperfect reflection, and began speaking of the kingdom of God as if it were similar to what Plato had said about such a purely spiritual world. Since Matthew had Jesus proclaiming a "kingdom of heaven," it was relatively easy to interpret these words as referring to a sphere of reality different from—or "above"—this present, physical world. Thus the eschatological dimension of the preaching of the kingdom was eclipsed, and the emphasis was shifted to the place where souls go after death (*see* *Immortality).

In more recent times, the biblical studies of the nineteenth century, particularly on the subject of the *eschatology of the New Testament, and the various *liberation theologies of the twentieth, have sought to reinstate both the escha-

tological and the radical dimensions of Jesus' teachings on the kingdom.

Knowledge, Theory of   *See* *Epistemology.

Koinonia   A Greek word usually translated as "fellowship," but whose meaning is much deeper than the mere good feeling among friends or companions. *Koinōnia* was also the equivalent of our modern "corporation," where two or more people hold a property in common. Its parallel verb, *koinōnein*, appears frequently in the New Testament and in secular literature in the sense of "sharing." And the plural noun, *koinōnoi*, means "partners." Thus, a phrase such as "the *koinōnia* [communion] of the Spirit" may mean any or all of the following: (1) the companionship of the Spirit with the believer; (2) the fellowship or corporation that has the Spirit as its common possession or inheritance (i.e., the church); (3) the sharing of goods and love that is the result of the presence of the Spirit.

Laity   A term derived from the Greek *laos*, people. In the Septuagint, the people of Israel are often spoken of as the *laos* of God. In the first chapters of Acts, there is a clear contrast between the "people" (*laos*) and their leaders, so that while the "people" are sympathetic toward the nascent church, it is their leaders who oppose it. Thus, the term "people" was often used in the sense of "common folk," and it is from that usage that the traditional Christian practice arose of referring to believers at large as "laity," as opposed to the leadership, or "clergy." This distinction appears as early as the end of the first century, in Clement's letter to the Corinthians. Therefore, in its most common use the term "laity" refers to those who are not ordained.

Although in its origins the monastic movement involved a protest against the professionalization of the faith in the hands of the clergy, and was therefore strictly speaking a lay movement, it eventually became associated with the clergy, so that in some cases the "laity" refers to all who are not ordained, including monastics, and sometimes it refers to those who are neither ordained nor in monastic orders.

From this latter meaning evolved the common contemporary usage of "layman" or "laywoman" as a synonym for "not professional," or even "not very well informed"—as in the phrase "in my layman's opinion."

From the contrast between an ordained clergy and a laity that is not ordained came the use of the adjective "lay" as "secular," or at least as not under the control of the ecclesiastical hierarchy—as in the phrase "lay state," meaning a state whose government and goals are not determined by the church as an institution.

Many contemporary theologians feel that the term "laity" has no theological content, for strictly speaking, all Christians are laity—we are all part of the *laos* or people of God.

Landmarkism   A theological movement originating in Tennessee in the mid-nineteenth century, holding that only Baptist churches are true churches, that *baptism is only valid when administered by a Baptist congregation, and that *Communion is to be restricted to the members of a particular congregation, for there is no such thing as a universal church. Landmarkism also holds that there is an uninterrupted line of succession of true Baptists, linking the present-day congregations with Jesus and the apostles. In order to show this, Landmarkist historians seek to reinstate many in the past whom the church at large considered heretics, and whose views are now reinterpreted in order to bring them in line with Baptist teaching.

Lapsed, Restoration of the   The restoration of the fallen into the full communion of the church—particularly allowing them once more to partake in the *Eucharist. Ever since its inception, the Christian church had to deal with the undeniable fact that baptized Christians still sinned. In the middle of the second century, this issue weighed on the conscience of Hermas, who felt that he had sinned by lusting after a woman, and who worried about others in the church of Rome who had sinned. He came to the conclusion that there is one more chance for repentance and restoration after *baptism. This was to be done through a formal act of public confession, penance, and restoration. After that, the only hope for a believer who sinned again was to be chosen by God for martyrdom. Obviously, this referred to particularly grievous sins, for the common everyday sins of the believers were confessed regularly in the public act of worship, and there declared to be forgiven (*see* *Confession).

Of particular concern for early Christians was the question of the restoration of those who had fallen into one of the three sins of homicide, fornication, and apostasy. The subject of the forgiveness of fornication came to a head in the third century in the conflict between Calixtus (died 222), the bishop of Rome, and Hippolytus (ca.170–ca.235), one of the most distinguished theologians of his time. The latter was a moral rigorist, who was scandalized when he learned that Calixtus was readmitting into Communion some Christians who had committed adultery—a form of fornication—and who had gone through a process of repentance, confession, and penance. The two clashed, and after a long debate the position of Calixtus won the day: people guilty of fornication were not beyond the reach of grace and restoration.

The matter of the restoration of adulterers was hardly settled, when the restoration of those who had fallen into apostasy by denying their faith during a time of persecution came to the foreground. In Rome, there was now a debate in which Novatian took the rigorist side, and Bishop Cornelius (died 253) insisted that the church had to be ready to forgive sinners. In Carthage, a similar debate arose between Bishop Cyprian (ca.210–58) and some of the "confessors"—people who had confessed their faith and remained firm in spite of persecution, imprisonment, and torture. In this case, both agreed that the lapsed could be restored after proper repentance and penance; but Cyprian insisted that this should be done by proper ecclesiastical authority, and the confessors felt that they had earned the right to declare the restoration of the lapsed. While Cyprian eventually won the day, this did not put an end to controversies over the restoration of those who had fallen during times of persecution.

Finally, after the persecutions were over, the Council of Nicaea (325) sought to bring some order into the matter by establishing certain rules for the restoration of the lapsed.

Still, the debates on the restoration of the lapsed, and the final agreement to establish guidelines for such restoration, may be seen as a significant step in the development of the penitential system of the medieval church (*Penance), for the matter of what to do with sins committed after baptism has always been a difficult theological and pastoral issue.

Latin American Theology Although there have been Latin American theologians in the past, the term "Latin American theology" usually refers to a particular theological stance that developed in conjunction with the Medellín Conference of the Latin American Bishops' Council (CELAM) in 1968, and whose main exponent and leader has been Peruvian theologian Gustavo Gutiérrez (1928–). Other theologians of the same school are Juan Luis Segundo (1925–96), Leonardo Boff (1938–), Jon Sobrino (1938–) and, among Protestants, José Míguez Bonino (1924–).

Latin American theology is a particular form of *contextual and *liberation theology, seeking to interpret the gospel within a setting of poverty and oppression. It seeks to reflect theologically both on the causes of the evils that beset the entire region and on Christian responses to such evils.

As a hermeneutical tool to understand the situation of Latin America, Latin American theologians often use *Marxist and neo-Marxist analysis. Poverty is not just the result of ignorance or of lack of effort. Poverty has structural causes. Furthermore, the structures that produce poverty and oppression are justified by an entire apparatus of ideas and perspectives, by an ideology—and in this context "ideology" does not mean simply a set of ideas or of ideals, but rather the attempt to justify a sociopolitical agenda by making it appear logical, just, and unavoidable. Marxist analysis serves to unmask those ideologies, which often include theology. This does not mean, however, that Latin American theologians are Marxist in the sense of being communists, and for that reason some prefer to speak of themselves as "Marxians," rather than as "Marxists."

A common emphasis of Latin American theology is the insistence of the role of *praxis and its connection with reflection. If we run the risk of being blinded by ideology, one of the ways to avoid that risk is to be engaged in acts of liberation, seeking to overcome oppression, poverty, and their root causes, which is a clear mandate of the gospel. Thus, praxis is not just any action; it is liberating action. Such liberating action—and its failures and frustrations—then lead to further reflection. Thus, there is a circular process of action-reflection-action that constantly sharpens and focuses both the action and the reflection.

Another way of saying this is by referring to a "*hermeneutical circle." In the case of biblical hermeneutics, we have been told what a text says. We go out and work for liberation. This allows us to see a new meaning in the text. We then go and act according to that new meaning. And thus the circle continues—although it is more a spiral than a circle, for each full circle leads us to new discoveries and new actions.

Latin American theologians also tend to agree on their analysis of violence. While deploring violence, they insist that there are "states of violence" as well as "acts of violence." Quite often, the established order sees only the acts of violence—for instance, when someone takes a gun and robs a bank—while ignoring the states of violence—for instance, the social order that makes this particular man's children about to starve, and to which he responds by robbing a bank. Rather than joining the existing order by focusing only or primarily on acts of violence, Christians must focus on the states of violence that quite often stand at the root of acts of violence.

In its inception, Latin American theology had a markedly optimistic tone. It was hoped that a series of revolutions would lead to a drastic change, so that poverty and oppression would be reduced. In biblical hermeneutics, many theologians focused on the story of the exodus, and seemed to be almost expecting the Red Sea to open momentarily. In more recent decades, however, a more sober and somber spirit has prevailed, with the feeling that perhaps liberation is not as close as some expected. In biblical hermeneutics, there is much more emphasis on the exile, and on being faithful over the long haul. Some critics claim that this shows that Latin American theology was so tied to Marxist hopes that the demise of the Soviet Union will also mean the demise of Latin American theology. Others insist that Latin American theology is still as active and creative as it once was, although now responding to a context that has become even more oppressive than before—and that precisely because of that oppression this type of theology continues being particularly relevant.

Latino/a Theology   The *contextual theology developed by persons of Hispanic or Latino culture in the United States. It tends to differ from *Latin American theology in that its context includes being a *cultural—and in many ways disenfranchised—minority. In this sense it is sometimes parallel to those elements in Latin American theology that stress the situation of the Native peoples and cultures in predominantly Spanish or Portuguese-speaking Latin America.

One of the common themes in Latino theology is "*mestizaje*"—a term that has played an important role in discussions of Mexican identity, and which Mexican American theologian Virgilio Elizondo (1935–) has related to the condition of Mexican Americans in the United States and of Galileans in ancient Judaism. A *mestizo*—strictly speaking, a "mixed breed"—is a person who stands between cultures, considered alien by both, and yet creating a new culture that may well be the vanguard for both dominant cultures. Latino and Latina theologians have developed this theme as a paradigm for understanding their situation, in which they no longer belong to the culture of their homelands, and yet they do not fully belong to the culture of the United States.

Other themes of interest to Hispanic theologians in the United States are the paradigm of exile, the relationship between intergenerational and intercultural conflicts and tensions, their relation to Latin America, the relationship between language, culture, and identity, and the reading of Scripture—as well as theology and history—from their own cultural and social context.

A number of Latinas, feeling that Latino theology does not sufficiently take into account the experiences and contributions of Latinas, and that the term "feminism" does not quite express their concerns, have developed, within the context of Latino/a theology and as one of its expressions, *mujerista theology.

Law   In biblical studies, sometimes used as a synonym for the Torah—that portion of the Hebrew canon called the

"Law," as contrasted to the "Prophets" and the "Writings." In the Hebrew Bible, the law is God's good gift, and a sign of God's love. The law is also eternal, for it reflects God's very nature. There is, however, a hope expressed in the prophets, of the time when the written law will no longer be necessary, for the covenant will be written in human hearts.

In the New Testament, the term "Law" usually refers to the Pentateuch or to the Mosaic code. Jesus often speaks of "the Law and the Prophets" to refer to Scripture. He also declares that he has not come to undo the law, but to fulfill it. Thus, there is in the teachings of Jesus a positive valuation of the law. And yet, in the Sermon on the Mount we see him going beyond the law of Moses in the series of sayings: "You have heard that it was said. . . . But I say to you . . ."

In the Pauline epistles—particularly Romans and Galatians—there is a much more negative valuation of the law. While not rejecting the law, and affirming that it was given by God, Paul often speaks of it as manifesting the depth of sin, and as insufficient for justification. This has led many Christian theologians to establish a contrast between the law and the gospel, or at least to debate their relationship. (*See* *Law and Gospel; *Antinomianism.)

Traditionally, the law has been seen as having three basic functions. It serves to convince and convict us of sin; it provides guidance for the organization of society and the state, limiting the consequences of sin; and it provides guidance for Christians as they seek to serve God (*see* *Law, Third Use of).

At a civil level, the "law" is also the set of rules by which a society governs itself. Christians have long debated the degree to which they must obey such laws, and whether or not—and how— such laws should be reflective of the law of God. From a very early date, there has been a consensus that unjust laws should not be obeyed—hence the refusal of the early martyrs to worship the emperor, the insistence of pacifists on not accepting the military draft, or the civil rights movement. There has also been a consensus, however, that the good order of society is also a value (*see* *State), and that therefore Christians must not take their faith as an excuse to disobey the law at pleasure. Still, between these two principles there is much room for debate—as may be seen in the twenty-first century as Christians disagree on issues such as abortion rights, the death penalty, and many others.

Law and Gospel The Pauline contrast between law and gospel (*see* *Law) has led theologians to debate the relationship between the two. In general, all are agreed that both the law and the gospel come from God, and most patristic and medieval theology tended to see the two as continuous.

It was the Reformation, with its emphasis on *justification by faith, and not by "*works of the law," that brought the matter of the relationship between law and gospel to the foreground. In general, Luther and the *Lutheran tradition saw the law as the means whereby sin and human insufficiency are revealed and the way is opened for the gospel. In this context, however, it is important to understand that Luther did not believe that the law appears only in the Old Testament, and the gospel in the New. The law is God's demand on us, be it in the Decalogue or in the teachings of Jesus. The gospel is God's promise, even in spite of our failure to obey the law. God's Word always comes as law and gospel, as no and yes, crushing and uplifting, leading to despair in our own abilities and to hope in God's promises.

The result of these views is that Luther has little to say regarding the value of the law per se as guidance for the believer (*see* *Law, Third Use of). He is afraid that an emphasis on this function of the law—a function that he does not reject, but does not stress—will lead to justification by works, and thus to a denial of the gospel.

For this reason, the ever-present danger in the Lutheran tradition has not been too much reliance on the law, but its opposite, *antinomianism.

While Calvin agreed with Luther on justification by faith, he insisted that such justification must lead to a process of *sanctification, whereby believers seek to conform to God's will. Even though in its contrast to the gospel the law condemns and crushes the sinner, once the gospel has been heard the same law is a source of guidance for believers in the process of sanctification. This emphasis has marked the *Reformed tradition, and therefore, while the ever-present danger for extreme Lutheranism is antinomianism, its counterpart in the Reformed tradition is legalism, rigorism, and even lapsing into salvation by *works.

In the twentieth century, Reformed theologian Karl Barth (1886–1968) brought a traditional Reformed view into the discussion by insisting that the very order, "law and gospel," is wrong. One does not come to the gospel through the law, but vice versa, for the enormity of sin is not recognized until one experiences the even greater love of God. What gives the law its power to crush a sinner is that the gospel has revealed the love and the grace against which the sinner has rebelled.

Law, Natural   The law implanted in human hearts, allowing them to know what is good even apart from *revelation. The notion of such a law has its roots in Greek philosophy, and passed from *Stoicism into Christianity as the basis for a morality that is not necessarily grounded on revelation, but still follows the will of God. The principle of natural law was explored in some detail by Thomas Aquinas (1225–74), who used it as the foundation for ethical principles that should be common to all humankind. Thus, for instance, the natural law that leads parents to know and care for their offspring should serve as a call for monogamy even among peoples that do not know Scripture or Christian ethics. Over time, societies discover that there are certain practices that are disruptive of social life, and others that support it, and this is an expression of natural law at work.

Natural law has allowed theologians —particularly Roman Catholic theologians—to set guides of conduct that theoretically should be accepted by all human beings, not on the basis of revelation or authority, but on the basis of the law inscribed in their own nature. Expanding its influence beyond the field of theology, the principle of natural law gave rise to modern international law, which supposedly should be recognized as good by all humans, no matter what their culture or their religious convictions.

Protestant theologians have had more doubts about natural law. While most accept the notion and seek to relate it to their ethical stances, some argue that the corruption of humanity (see *Depravity, Total) is such that so-called natural law is twisted to our sinful inclinations, and cannot be trusted. Karl Barth (1886–1968), in particular, rejected any use of natural law in Christian ethics.

Law, Third Use of   The function of the law of God as guidance for believers. Although such listings vary, in general the other two "uses" of the law are as guidance to society, which is to order its laws and practices according to the law of God, and as proof of sinners' inability to serve God. Luther stressed this latter use of the law, which to him was closely related to his fundamental tenet of *justification by faith. The law crushes, condemns, even kills, and is thus a sort of negative preparation for the gospel. Although Luther did believe that the law of God could serve as guidance for believers, he never stressed this point, for fear that it might lead to justification by *works. Calvin, in contrast, while agreeing with Luther on the basic issue of justification by faith, felt that justification must lead to *sanctification, and that in this process the law serves as guidance for believers. Thus, an emphasis on the "third use of the law" has become one of the characteristics of the *Reformed tradition. (*See* *Law and Gospel.)

Lectionary   A list of scriptural readings for Christian worship, usually following the Christian *Year. Also, a book containing such readings. While there are also lectionaries for daily readings, and for the monastic hours of prayer, in contemporary usage most lectionaries focus on Sunday worship (usually the *Eucharist). Sometimes the readings from the Gospels and those from the Epistles are printed separately, in which case the books are called "evangelistaries" and "epistolaries."

Liberalism   A term with many different meanings according to its context.

In economic and political theory, the term "liberalism" is employed in the United States in a sense that is diametrically opposed to its meaning in the rest of the world. In the United States, a "liberal" politician or economist is one who believes that the state should intervene in economic matters in order to bring about a more just order. Elsewhere, a "liberal" is someone who believes that the market should be given free rein to determine itself. Thus, when *Latin American theologians, for instance, condemn the consequences of what they call "liberal capitalism," they are referring to something very different from what people in the United States generally understand by "liberalism."

In the history of Roman Catholic theology, "liberalism" refers to the call, early in the nineteenth century, for the church to accept the liberal political ideals of the French Revolution, and of the other similar movements that flourished at the time. The main leader of this movement was Félicité-Robert de Lamennais (1782–1854), an ardent supporter of the papacy, who urged the pope to take the torch of political freedom away from secular rulers, and thus to lead the way into the future. The papacy, however, was too much invested in the traditional order to listen to Lamennais, whose views were condemned by Gregory XVI in the encyclical *Mirari vos* (1832). The liberal movement, however, continued growing within Roman Catholicism, and this finally led to the condemnation in 1864 of eighty liberal tenets, listed by Pius IX in a *Syllabus of Errors*. Thus, Roman Catholic "liberalism" had to do more with the relationship between the church and civil society than with doctrines. (For a movement within Roman Catholicism that was akin to Protestant liberalism, *see* *Modernism.)

In the history of Protestant theology, "liberalism" is a movement that flourished in the nineteenth and early twentieth centuries. While liberals differed widely, in general they agreed on the need to reconcile Christian faith and doctrine with *modernity. This included a much more positive valuation of human goodness and potential for good than had become traditional in Christian theology. Such a valuation of human potential was usually accompanied with the hope that human progress would naturally lead to a more just and rational ordering of society. Given the newly discovered rational order of the universe, theology must also be fully rational, and must find its way among the sciences by showing its own rationality (*see* *Reason and Faith). This in turn means that *miracles and all recourse to the "supernatural" are to be eschewed. The Bible ought to be studied and critiqued with the same analytical and historical tools that scholars apply to other pieces of literature and supposedly historical records. While Jesus is certainly an exceptional figure, he probably was very different from what Christian tradition—including the Gospels—have made of him, and therefore theologians must seek to discover the *historical Jesus. Religion in general, and Christianity in particular, are valid mostly because they serve as guides for the moral life.

Protestant liberalism in this classical sense began to wane as the First World War, and many of the tragic events that followed in the twentieth century, produced increased doubts regarding such notions as the inevitability of progress, the essential goodness of humankind, and the objective rationality of modernity. The most influential Protestant theologian calling for an alternative to classical liberalism was Karl Barth, whose *Commentary on Romans*, published in 1919, set the stage for postliberal, *neoorthodox theology.

In the common mind, "liberalism" is now seen as the opposite of *fundamentalism, and is a term that fundamentalists themselves often apply to any who do not agree with their tenets.

Liberation, Theologies of

A general title joining a wide variety of *contextual theologies, each focusing on the issues of oppression and discrimination in its particular context. Thus, some liberation theologies center their attention on international economic oppression, while others are particularly concerned with classism, racism, ageism, homophobia, and other foci. Besides acknowledging and claiming their contextuality, these various theologies also share a view of salvation as including, not only life after death and a personal relationship with God, but also liberation from the various expressions of sin in the present order. While recognizing that the final order of justice, love, and peace promised in Scripture is *eschatological in nature, and cannot be achieved by human efforts, the various liberation theologies insist on the need to promote and practice justice and love, not only at the personal level, but also in societal practices and structures.

Since the term "theology of liberation" was coined by Peruvian theologian Gustavo Gutiérrez (1928–), sometimes people refer to *Latin American theology as "the theology of liberation." Yet, the characteristics listed above are true of a variety of theologies in diverse circumstances. (*See also* *Black Theology; *Feminist Theology; *Latino/a Theology; *Minjung Theology; *Mujerista Theology; *Womanist Theology.)

Limbo

In traditional Roman Catholic theology, the place for the souls of those who, while not fully redeemed and therefore not capable of entering the blessedness of *heaven, do not really merit punishment. Traditionally, limbo included both the *limbus patrum*—limbo of the fathers, where the patriarchs and other saints of the Old Testament awaited their redemption by Jesus, and the *limbus infantium*—limbo of infants, where the souls of unbaptized children dwell eternally. Whether the latter is a place of joy or of punishment is a matter of different opinions, St. Thomas Aquinas (1225–74) holding that there is a degree of joy—but not the supernatural joy of the redeemed—in limbo, and St. Augustine (354–430), particularly in his heated writings against *Pelagianism, claiming that it is a place of punishment and damnation.

Liturgical Renewal

The name generally given to a movement for the reformation of the *liturgy that began in the nineteenth century, but flourished in the twentieth. The French Benedictines took the lead, late in the nineteenth century, in calling for a reformation of the liturgy. What was originally meant by this was a return to what was then seen as the high point of Christian civilization, in the Middle Ages. By the twentieth century, however, renewed patristic studies shifted the focus to the study and restoration of earlier Christian worship, particularly by promoting the participation of the *laity and by employing the liturgy as a means for instruction and edification. As a result of these patristic studies, greater emphasis was placed on the significance of *baptism, on the regular renewal of baptismal vows, and particularly on the celebratory—rather than what by then had become the traditional funereal—character of the *Eucharist, and the Easter (or Paschal) Vigil, culminating with Easter itself, as the high point of the Christian *Year. The greatest success of this movement in the Roman Catholic Church was the promulgation of the constitution *De sacra liturgia* by the Second Vatican Council in 1963. This included, among many significant changes, the use of the vernacular in the Eucharist.

Meanwhile, a parallel and related movement was taking place within Protestantism. In general, this was accompanied by a general dissatisfaction regarding the forms and practices of worship that had become customary during the nineteenth and twentieth centuries—a dissatisfaction that also revealed itself in the creation of "contemporary" worship services, by which was meant worship that abandoned the traditional patterns and practices, often seeking to respond to the "felt needs" of worshipers, and with little theological content or critique. There was also much discussion in the "younger churches" as to the relation between liturgy and *culture, and how to relate their culture to the liturgy while retaining the essence of both. The patristic, historical, and theological studies that led to a renewal of the liturgy within Roman Catholicism had a similar effect among Protestants. The result was that many Protestant bodies, both in the traditional centers of Protestantism and in what had earlier been considered the "mission field," produced new liturgical books, hymnals, and other materials reflecting a new emphasis on such concerns as the Eucharist, the active participation of all believers, and the significance of rites for Christian formation and development.

Liturgy   A word derived from the Greek *leitourgia*, which literally means "the work of the people." In the Hellenistic world, it often referred to the days of labor that the residents of a state owed to the government—a sort of tax paid, not with money, but with labor in public works. In the Septuagint, it often refers to the service that the people owe God, centered on the Temple. It has thus come to mean the service or worship of God, and particularly the order that is followed in that service. Since the center of Christian worship has usually been the *Eucharist, in some cases "the liturgy" simply means the Eucharistic service. (*See also* *Liturgical Renewal.)

Loci theologici   Literally, "theological places." This was the title of an important work by Melanchthon (1497–1560), by which he meant "theological topics." The same title was later employed by a number of *Lutheran theologians, particularly during the time of Protestant *scholasticism. Among Roman Catholic theologians, the phrase is most commonly used to refer, not to themes or topics of theology, but rather to the "places" where theology finds its sources, such as Scripture, tradition, experience.

Logos   A Greek term of wide meanings, usually having to do with speech or reason. In various contexts it may be translated as word, treatise, study, discourse, speech, reason, or order. It has played an important role in Christian theology by making it possible to claim that the Second Person of the Trinity—the Logos or *Word of God—is the source of the rationality permeating all creation.

Since long before the advent of Christianity, Greek and Hellenistic philosophers had puzzled over the connection between the order of the world and the order of the mind. My mind tells me that two and two make four. If I then look at the world, I discover that indeed two rocks and two more rocks are four rocks. How can this be explained? Obviously, there must be a principle of order or of rationality that is present both in the world and in my mind. This principle the philosophers called "logos." While all agreed that without such logos knowledge would be impossible, exactly how this principle functions was open to debate.

The Fourth Gospel refers to a preexistent Word or Logos of God who was incarnate in Jesus. Most likely, this passage is drawing from Hebrew traditions regarding *Wisdom, and using the Greek term *logos* to refer to Wisdom, rather than actually drawing on the Hellenistic philosophical tradition. But for early Christians, trying to communicate their faith to a sophisticated Hellenistic audience, the possibility of connecting these two strands of thought would have been obvious. Thus they would say that the One who has become incarnate in Jesus is the same Logos who is the foundation of all reason and all knowledge—in Johannine terms, the "light which enlightens everyone."

This allowed Christians to claim, not only that their faith made sense, but also that any truth known to anyone anywhere is the result of the action of the same Logos who was incarnate in Jesus. Thus, by the middle of the second century *apologists such as Justin Martyr were claiming that whatever truth the philosophers of old knew, they had received from the Logos, and that therefore the sages of old, inasmuch as they spoke the truth, were Christians!

While most later theologians have not made such extravagant claims about ancient philosophers, there is a long tradition of employing the doctrine of the Logos as a means to recognize, explain, and accept any truth found beyond the confines of the Christian church and its doctrines. According to this tradition, all who possess any truth have received it from the Word of God, the Second Person of the *Trinity.

The doctrine of the Logos has played a less felicitous role in the development of the doctrine of the Trinity. Once Christian theologians had begun to think about *God and the divine *attributes along the lines of the Greek philosophical tradition, they found themselves heirs to a problem that had plagued that philosophical tradition before, namely, How can an immutable being relate to a mutable world? (In philosophical studies, this was often called the problem of "the one and the many.") An immutable being cannot communicate, and much less interact, with a mutable world. Yet in the biblical tradition it is quite clear that God relates and interacts with creation. How is this to be explained?

Some early theologians—particularly Justin Martyr, already mentioned above—suggested solving this problem by means of the Logos, now seen as an intermediate being, as a sort of bridge, between the immutable God and the mutable world. Justin went so far as to call the Logos "a second God"—an expression that was not acceptable to Christian *monotheism. At any rate, this does not really solve the problem of the relationship between the immutable God and the mutable world, for if the Logos is mutable it cannot communicate with God; and if it is immutable, it cannot communicate with the world.

Still, many theologians followed Justin's lead on this point, suggesting that the Logos must be understood as a secondary sort of divinity, and as *subordinate to the Father, while others insisted that the One incarnate in Jesus must be God truly and fully, or the incarnation is meaningless. In the fourth century, the subordinationist view was expressed and defended by Arius and his followers, and thus came to be called *Arianism—a doctrine rejected by the Council of Nicaea in 325, and again by the Council of Constantinople in 381. Since that time, Christian theologians have generally held that the Second Person of the Trinity, called "Son" or "Word" (Logos), is just as divine and just as eternal as the First Person, and therefore that it is not correct to claim that the Logos is an intermediate being between God and creation—more than creation, and less than God.

Love   The third and highest of the "theological *virtues." As such, it is to be the supreme rule of action for Christians, who are to imitate a God who "is love." Augustine (354–430) expressed this principle by declaring: "Love God, and do as you please." Others have insisted that love is more than a feeling, for it implies action—and sometimes even action when the feeling is absent. It is for this reason that Christians are commanded to love. As a feeling, love cannot be commanded; but as an action it can be. Thus, to "love the neighbor" does not mean primarily to harbor positive feelings toward your neighbor, but rather to act lovingly even when the feeling is absent, in the hope and prayer that the feeling will develop.

For some theologians, love is the prime attribute of God, who "is love." In discussions on the *Trinity, theologians have repeatedly asserted that the Trinity itself is the expression of God's love within Godself. Augustine declared that the Holy *Spirit is the bond of love between the Father and the Son—a view that has become traditional in Western theology.

One of the most influential theological treatises of the twentieth century was Anders Nygren's (1890–1978) *Agape and Eros*, which explores the various words for "love" and their different meanings. (*See* *Agape.)

Lundensian Theology   A theological school within *Lutheranism that flourished during the twentieth century, named after its center, the University of Lund in Sweden. Its great figures are Gustaf Aulén (1879–1977), Anders Nygren (1890–1978), and Gustaf Wingren (1910–2000). One of its characteristics was its renewed interest in Luther and his connection with patristic theology, particularly that of Irenaeus. Its methodology is the "investigation of motifs"— *Motifvorschung*. By a "motif" is meant a central idea or characteristic that lies behind various formulations. Thus, Aulén's book on the doctrine of redemption, published in English under the title of *Christus Victor*, explores various understandings of the work of Christ, seeking to rediscover and reinstate what he calls the "dramatic" view of Ire-

naeus—a view that sees Christ, not as a victim, but as a conqueror of the powers of evil (*Atonement). For his part, Nygren explored the various understandings of *love in his epoch-making book *Agape and Eros*, establishing a sharp contrast between these two as a means to recover Luther's understanding of *grace. (*See* *Agape.)

Lutheranism   One of the main traditions resulting from the Reformation of the sixteenth century (jointly with *Tridentine Roman Catholicism, the *Reformed tradition, *Anglicanism, and *Anabaptism). The name "Lutheran" was originally employed by its enemies to imply that it was a heretical innovation created by Luther. In this sense, it was applied by Roman Catholics to all Protestants. At first, "Lutheran" churches called themselves "churches of the Confession of Augsburg," after the document that their leaders presented before the Diet of Augsburg in 1530. Eventually, however, they took the name of "Lutheran," by which most are known.

The differences between Lutheranism and other branches of Protestantism —particularly the Reformed tradition— are subtle, but important. Most of Luther's teachings were adopted by these other Protestants, although with different emphases. Thus, the three main tenets of Lutheranism are common to Protestantism in general: *sola scriptura, sola gratia, sola fide*—Scripture alone, grace alone, faith alone. These are affirmations of the primacy of Scripture, as well as of *justification by faith through the *grace of God.

On the subject of the authority of Scripture, Luther and Lutheranism have generally insisted on its priority over tradition, but have not felt it necessary to reject those elements within tradition that do not contradict Scripture— vestments, crucifixes, rituals, and so on. In this, Lutheranism and Anglicanism contrast with the Reformed tradition— particularly in its Zwinglian wing—and with the Anabaptists, who have sought to restore biblical Christianity by divesting it of any accretions of tradition.

On the matter of justification by faith through the grace of God, all Protestants are agreed. Luther, however, feared that to speak too much of a process of *sanctification to follow justification risked returning to justification by works. Justification does not make the sinner just, but is, rather, the act of God's grace acquitting a sinner who is still a sinner. Calvin and the Reformed tradition, while agreeing with Luther on justification by faith, lay more emphasis on the work of God sanctifying the sinner—and therefore also on the value of the law of God as guidance for believers (*see* *Law, Third Use of).

Finally, Luther disagreed both with Roman Catholicism and with Zwingli and Calvin in affirming that in the *Eucharist, while the bread remains bread and the wine remains wine, the body of Christ is physically present, and believers partake of it.

After Luther's death, there was a long series of controversies within Lutheranism. In these controversies, the "strict Lutherans" opposed the more moderate views of Melanchthon and his followers. Eventually, these controversies led to the *Formula of Concord* (1577), which became one of the fundamental documents of Lutheranism.

In the seventeenth century Lutheranism—as well as the Reformed tradition—went through a period of detailed systematization often called Protestant *orthodoxy (or Protestant *scholasticism). This period produced some of the greatest works of systematic theology within the Lutheran tradition, but was also characterized by narrow dogmatism. As a reaction, much of eighteenth-century Lutheranism turned toward *Pietism, which emphasized personal faith, prayer, small groups of devotion and support, and works of charity. While at first most Lutheran theologians rejected Pietism, eventually the movement gave shape to modern Lutheranism, which emphasizes both orthodoxy and personal piety.

Macedonians   Named after Macedonius of Constantinople, this was the group that agreed with the *Nicene decision that the Son is of the same substance as the Father (*Homoousios), but were not ready to say the same of the Spirit. For this reason they were also called "Pneumatomachians"—enemies of the Spirit. Their position was rejected by a synod gathered in Antioch in 362, and finally by the Second Ecumenical Council (Constantinople, 381).

Magnificat   The song of Mary in Luke 1:46–55. Its name derives from the first word of the Latin translation, *Magnificat anima mea*—"My soul magnifies." Although it has traditionally been part of evening prayers, and often repeated in the Mass, its words of vindication for the poor and the humble have received particular attention with the rise of *liberation theologies.

Majoristic Controversy   A debate among *Lutherans precipitated by Georg Major (1502–74), who claimed that good *works are necessary for salvation. In reaction, some claimed that good works lead to self-assurance, and are therefore detrimental to salvation. Eventually the *Formula of Concord* (1577) condemned both extremes, declaring that good works are neither necessary nor detrimental to salvation.

Manichaeism   The doctrine of Manes (ca.216–276) and his followers. By extension, any extremely *dualistic view. In the latter sense, the notion that there are "good nations" and "bad nations," for instance, may be called "Manichaean."

In the strict sense, Manichaeism developed originally in the Persian Empire, and from there spread into India, China, and the Roman Empire. Manes himself had been influenced by *Gnosticism and other *ascetic tendencies, and therefore Manichaeism has much in common with Gnosticism. It holds that there are two eternal and indestructible principles, good and evil, the first purely spiritual, and the latter material. The human predicament consists of our being part of the divine substance, the substance of good, and yet existing here on earth in a mixture with the principle of evil, trapped in a physical body. Salvation therefore consists in returning to our divine origin. And the final consummation of all things is simply the final separation between the principle of good and the principle of evil—which will then continue existing, although separately from each other.

According to Manes, he knew this —as well as other secrets leading to salvation—through divine revelation. This revelation had come before him to others, such as Buddha, Zoroaster, and Jesus; yet Manes claimed to be greater than all these prophets, for he also had received the "true knowledge" that explains the origin and mysteries of the world.

Augustine (354–430) was a follower of Manichaeism for some time. After he became disenchanted with the Manichaeans' claim to wisdom, he wrote several treaties against them—particularly defending the *freedom of the will, which the Manichaeans denied.

Marcionism   The doctrine of Marcion (ca.100–ca.160). The son of a Christian bishop in Pontus, Marcion traveled to Asia Minor and then to Rome, where he was expelled from the church (ca.144). He then founded his own ecclesiastical community, which grew to such an extent that it became a major rival to the orthodox church—which in turn led a number of theologians to refute his views.

Although Marcion was a *dualist, he differed from the prevailing *gnostic views in that he did not believe in long sequences of spiritual or intellectual beings whose existence and eventual error led to the creation of the world. Nor did he believe that salvation was attained through a secret knowledge. According to Marcion, the world is the creation of the god of the Old Testament,

Yahweh. In this sense, the Hebrew Scriptures are true. Yet Yahweh is not the same as the Father of Jesus Christ, the Christian God. Yahweh is an inferior and vindictive god, who created this world either out of spite or out of ignorance, and caused human souls to be trapped in it. Yahweh judges and punishes. Thus, there is a radical contrast between the religion of Israel and Christianity, between Yahweh and God, between justice and love.

For our salvation, the Supreme God has sent his Son, Jesus, to lead us back to truth and freedom. Since matter is part of the domain of Yahweh, and is opposed to spiritual reality, Jesus did not really take human flesh. He was not even born, but simply appeared on earth during the reign of Tiberius. He was a celestial being with the appearance of a human body (*see* *Docetism), whose function was mostly to let us know of the love of God, and to invite us to receive divine forgiveness.

According to Marcion, this message of love and forgiveness was misunderstood by early Christians, who insisted on interpreting Jesus as the fulfillment of promises made in the Hebrew Scriptures. Only Paul understood it. This is why he had such a struggle with those other Christians who insisted on the need to obey the law of the Old Testament.

Having rejected the Hebrew Scriptures as the word of a lesser God, Marcion found it necessary to put something else in their place. This was his own version of what we now call the New Testament. Its core was the corpus of Paul's epistles, joined to the Gospel of Luke, whom Marcion held in high regard because he had been Paul's companion. Both the epistles and Luke, however, were edited in order to erase from them all positive references to the Hebrew Scriptures or to the material world.

The challenge of Marcion and his followers led the church at large to develop its own list of books of the New Testament—a list to be placed, not in contrast to, but alongside the Hebrew Scriptures (*see* *Canon). It also led the church in Rome to develop a baptismal creed built around the basic Trinitarian formula for baptism. This creed, which affirmed that the God who created and rules all things is the Father of Jesus, that Jesus was born, that he truly suffered, died, and was raised, that he will return to judge, and that the bodies of the dead will rise again—all these points in sharp contrast to Marcion's views—eventually developed into what is now called the Apostles' *Creed.

Marks of the Church   Also called "notes" of the church. Those characteristics by which the true church may be described and known. Although there are references to such "marks" in earlier times, the subject of the marks of the church came to the foreground at the time of the Reformation, when they were originally used in anti-Protestant polemics. The classical exposition of the marks of the church as showing the falsehood of Protestant churches is that of Cardinal Robert Bellarmine (1542–1621), who listed fifteen characteristics of the true church that he claimed the Protestants lacked. In spite of such an extensive list, the discussion on the marks of the church eventually focused on the four listed in the *Nicene *Creed: one, holy, catholic, and apostolic. In general, Protestants who accept the Nicene Creed agree that these four marks of the church are essential, but interpret them differently from Roman Catholics (*see* *Unity of the Church; *Holiness; *Catholicity; *Apostolicity). On the other hand, partly as a response to Roman Catholic polemics, some of the Reformers declared that the two essential marks of the church are the preaching of the Word of God and the proper administration of the *sacraments.

Marxism   The philosophy of Karl Marx (1818–83). The son of Jewish parents pressured into accepting Christianity, Marx became an atheist in his late teens or early twenties. Marxism is a

*materialistic version of *Hegelian *dialectics. Instead of interpreting history as the unfolding thought of the Mind or Spirit, as did Hegel, Marx interpreted it as the dialectical working out of systems of production and clashing class interests. At a time when psychology was beginning to explore the subconscious recesses of the mind, Marx proposed that much of what we consider purely rational truth in fact reflects hidden class interests—hidden even from ourselves. These result in "ideologies" claiming to be an actual depiction of truth, but being in fact a justification for an existing—or a desired—economic and social order.

Marxism sees this historical process as leading to and culminating in a just economic and social order in which all will receive according to their needs, and all will contribute according to their abilities. This utopian order—which may be interpreted as a secularized and atheistic version of Judeo-Christian *eschatology —is the communistic state, and will be the result of a revolt by the proletariat.

During most of the twentieth century, Marxism was the official ideology of a number of nations, often calling themselves "socialist"—the Soviet Union, the People's Republic of China, several Soviet satellites in Europe, Cuba, and elsewhere. During the cold war between these nations and the capitalistic West, in the minds of many Marxism became synonymous with communism, and communism with the oppressive systems of the socialist bloc. For that reason, the demise of the Soviet Union, and the movement away from socialism of most socialist countries, has created the impression that Marxism is no longer relevant.

This may be true of Marxism as an organized political movement; but at a deeper level the impact of Marx is felt everywhere. In theology, it is openly acknowledged by many *liberation theologians, particularly in *Latin America, who often call themselves "Marxian" in order to indicate that, while not being orthodox Marxists, and being neither communists nor atheists, they find Marx's analysis of social and economic reality useful to their enterprise. Furthermore, in the twenty-first century the impact of Marx's understanding of the relationship between class interests and ideologies is visible in a wide variety of manifestations—from *postcolonial and *postmodern theories to the manner in which politicians plan their campaigns and capitalist corporations plan their marketing.

Mary The name of several women in Scripture—and the New Testament form of the Old Testament "Miriam"—but most commonly the mother of Jesus, sometimes referred to as "the B.V.M."—the Blessed Virgin Mary, or the *Beata Virgo Maria*.

The virginity of Mary at the time of the conception of Jesus goes back to very early Christian tradition (*see* *Virgin Birth). Although the New Testament refers repeatedly to the brothers of Jesus, at a later point, but certainly by the fourth century, it was commonly affirmed that she remained a virgin throughout her life, never cohabiting with Joseph, and that the "brothers of Jesus" were either other close relatives of his, or Joseph's sons from an earlier marriage. By the ninth century, some were claiming that Jesus could not have been born through the birth canal, for this would have destroyed his mother's virginity. Ratramnus of Corbie (died 868) wrote against such notions, which he considered *docetic, and insisted that Jesus was born "by the natural door," although without violating Mary's physical virginity. Although others attacked Ratramnus's arguments, there seems to have been general agreement that Mary's "perpetual virginity" involved, not only that she never had intercourse, but even that the birth of Jesus preserved her physical virginity.

Long before that, in the fifth century, there had been another controversy regarding the title *theotokos—bearer or mother of God—as applied to Mary. Although the issues debated then had to do mostly with matters of Christology (*see* *Communicatio idiomatum; *Nestorianism), at a more popular level what was at stake was also the respect due to the Savior's mother. Thus the title "Mother of God," sanctioned by the Council of Ephesus (Third Ecumenical Council, 431), became the typical orthodox way of referring to Mary.

Mary was considered the "Queen of Heaven," and the first among the saints in heaven. For this reason, when the *iconoclastic controversy led to the distinction between the *latreia* due only to God and the *douleia* or veneration of the saints and their images, it was also declared that Mary was worthy of a higher form of veneration, or *hyperdouleia*.

The contrast between the old creation, whose head is Adam, and the new creation, whose head is Jesus, led to many connections and comparisons between Mary and Eve, claiming that, as it was Eve who brought Adam to the tree, it was Mary who brought Jesus into the world, and eventually to the tree on Calvary. Although such connections were already made late in the second century by Irenaeus, in later times they evolved into the claim by some that Mary's role in redemption is unique, and that she has a mediating role that goes beyond that of any believer or any saint in heaven, and thus she was sometimes given the title of "Mediatrix of All Graces," or even of "Co-Redemptrix."

Mary's close connection with the birth and saving work of Jesus eventually developed into the theory that she herself must have been preserved from *original sin at the time of her conception. This *immaculate conception of Mary was much debated during the high point of the Middle Ages. Thomas Aquinas (1225–74) rejected it, while Duns Scotus (ca.1266–1308) and other Franciscans defended and promoted it. It was finally declared to be *dogma of the Roman Catholic Church by Pius IX in his bull *Ineffabilis Deus* (1854).

Another recently defined Catholic dogma regarding Mary is her bodily *assumption, long held by popular piety, but proclaimed as dogma of the church by Pius XII in 1950.

Popular piety, often sanctioned by hierarchical authority, also holds that the Virgin Mary has appeared in various places and forms, such as Our Lady of Lourdes and Our Lady of Guadalupe.

Materialism   The belief that reality consists exclusively of physical matter, and that spiritual, nonmaterial realities are either nonexistent or irrelevant. Some among the ancient philosophers were materialists, and many early Christian theologians—from Tertullian to the young Augustine—had difficulty conceiving of realities that are not material. In general, however, most Christian theologians have rejected materialism as too simplistic an explanation for the mysteries of life, and have insisted that God is not material. Since during the time of *modernity many understood the universe as a closed system of material causes and effects, modern materialism has normally inclined toward *predeterminism. (*See also* *Marxism.)

In a different sense, "materialism" is the name give to the attitude of those who constantly seek their gain, particularly financial gain.

Matter   Usually, the "stuff" of which things are made. In *Aristotelian philosophy, and therefore in much late medieval theology, matter is individuated by receiving *form. At various points in the course of Christian history, but particularly during the thirteenth century, there have been debates as to whether matter is eternal or is created by God (*see* *Averroism). The doctrine of *creation *ex nihilo* was developed and stressed precisely against the notion that matter is eternal, and therefore not created.

Mennonites   The followers of Menno Simons (1496–1561), and the largest of present-day traditions emerging from the *Anabaptists of the sixteenth century. Menno himself was a pacifist, and therefore *pacifism has been one of the enduring characteristics of all Mennonite communities. Mennonites have repeatedly gone into exile rather than take up arms, thus spreading into Russia, North America, and the interior of South America. Their absolute refusal to take up arms was a major factor in the development of the category of "conscientious objector" to *war in a number of Western countries. While some Mennonites— notably the Amish—have sought to retain the simplicity of life in the sixteenth century by refusing to adapt to modern conveniences, and as a result have tended to be isolated from the rest of society, by far the majority of Mennonites are very much engaged in actions of social and humanitarian services.

Merit   The value of good human actions as deserving divine reward. While most theologians are agreed that God punishes evil and rewards good, the Protestant Reformers of the sixteenth century, and their followers thereafter, rejected the notion that such rewards could include God's *grace or *salvation—which are gifts freely given by God, and not earned by humans.

*Scholastic theology, while affirming the doctrine of merit, sought to establish some distinctions that would make it possible to affirm also the primacy of grace. The most important of these distinctions is that between merit *de condigno* and merit *de congruo*. The first refers to actions that in themselves merit a reward. The latter refers to actions for which a reward is befitting, although not truly earned or deserved. In the strictest sense, there can be no human merit *de condigno* in regard to God, for all that we are we owe to God. Yet God has determined and vowed that certain actions, performed with the support and help of divine grace, will gain certain rewards, and therefore there is a secondary sense in which believers acting in grace may earn merit *de condigno*, and thus attain to salvation. In contrast, merit *de congruo* is not the result of a state of grace, and is not true merit—not even in the limited sense in which actions resulting from grace are meritorious.

Even though strictly speaking merit is always the work of grace, the saints may perform more works than is required of them (*see* *Supererogation), which are then part of the *treasury of merits. Medieval theology extended the doctrine of merits to their transferability, so that the merits of Jesus and the saints are available to believers in the treasury of merits. This stands at the heart of the medieval understanding of *penance, by which such merits may be applied to the penitent sinner, and of the practice of selling *indulgences.

Metaphor   In contemporary theological language, particularly after the work of Paul Ricoeur (1913–) and Sallie McFague (1934–), a metaphor is not simply a figurative way of speaking about something that is like it. The power of metaphor is not only in its stating that one reality is like another, but also and most importantly in stating that the two are different. The power is not only in consonance, but also in dissonance. Therefore, once a metaphor has become a literal description, such as in the "leg" of a table, it is no longer a living, powerful metaphor. In this view, the parables of Jesus, for instance, are powerful metaphors because they not only say what the kingdom of God is like, but also declare the uniqueness of the kingdom —what Ricoeur has called "a logic of superabundance."

Thus, while all language about God is metaphorical, this is not to be seen as a hindrance or as a shortcoming, but rather as an indication of the uniqueness of God —a uniqueness that can only be approached through a variety of metaphors.

Metaphysics   The name given by the original compilers of the works of Aristotle to the section immediately after the Physics—hence the title *meta*, after,

physics. Since what was discussed there was the nature of being as such, the term came to mean any inquiry into the nature of being, and eventually almost any philosophical inquiry. After the work of Hume, Kant, and others, metaphysics has often been rejected as the investigation of matters beyond the realm of human experience or knowledge. However, much Roman Catholic theology continued employing metaphysics as a proper foundation for theological discourse. With the decline of *empiricism, a number of Protestant theologians and philosophers have done likewise—some employing the metaphysics of Whitehead (1861–1947) to develop *process theology, and others, such as Paul Tillich (1886–1965), returning to the "ontological" foundations of theology.

Methodism   The name commonly given to the movement and churches derived from the *Wesleyan revival, generally excluding those Wesleyans who are part of the *holiness movement or of *Pentecostalism. Following John Wesley (1703–91), Methodists generally stress personal piety, individual and social holiness, and the proclamation of the gospel to those outside the church. Following Wesley's lead, most Methodists are *Arminian, although there are also *Calvinistic Methodists derived mostly from the work of George Whitefield (1714–70) in Wales.

Millennialism   The expectation of a reign of Christ on earth, either before or after his *parousia. The millennium has been the subject of much debate, particularly among *fundamentalist Christians in the twentieth and twenty-first centuries, who do not agree on the interpretation of Revelation 20:2–7—Revelation being the only book in the New Testament where a reign of a thousand years is explicitly mentioned. In the second century, Christian theologians such as Papias and Irenaeus did believe in a reign of God on earth—a reign of peace, justice, and physical abundance—and they sometimes spoke of it as lasting a thousand years (*see* *Chiliasm). Others, such as Augustine (354–430), felt that such expectations were too materialistic, and preferred to understand the millennium as well as any scriptural reference to an eschatological abundance as *allegorical language referring to a purely spiritual reign or *kingdom of God (*Amillennialism). During the Middle Ages, due to the influence of Augustine and other theologians of *Neoplatonic tendencies, the millennium was generally understood as a figurative way of speaking of *heaven, or if not, as the present life of the church, in which evil is supposed to be bound. Many combined the saying in 2 Peter, that a thousand years is like a day in the eyes of God, with notions of a history of the world that would last seven thousand years, and thus developed schemes in which there would be a thousand years between the first and the second advents of Christ.

It was in the seventeenth century that *eschatological speculation and literalistic interpretations of Revelation 20 led to a renewed interest in the millennium, and particularly to the development of a series of schemes or programs for the events surrounding its coming. While the terms "premillennialist" and "postmillennialist" seem to stress the difference between these two views regarding the order of events, the difference between these two positions has to do, not just with an ordering of the final events, but with their entire view of history and Christian responsibility within it.

In general, premillennialists stress the millennium as the result of divine intervention, preceded by events such as the "great apostasy," the coming of the *antichrist, and the "great tribulation." In the nineteenth century, and then in the twentieth, these views gained many followers through the *dispensationalist teachings of J. N. Darby (1800–82) and Cyrus Scofield (1843–1921). The latter's "annotated Bible" provided many fun-damentalist readers with a scheme explaining the order and connection of the various eschatological events, and thus attained great success. Since in the various premillennialist schemes the millennium will be preceded by great evil, those who hold such views often see little need to improve society, to challenge injustice in the social order, or even to work for peace.

In contrast, postmillennialists hold that the preaching of the gospel and the reformation of society through the impact of Christian witness—and sometimes also of progress—will bring about the reign of peace and justice that is often called the "millennium." Thus, while premillenialism tends to be more prevalent among *fundamentalists, postmillennialism was most common among the classical *liberals of the nineteenth and early twentieth centuries.

It is important to note, however, that the subject itself of the millennium is of greater importance for premillennialists than for amillennialists or postmillennialists, many of whom do not even use the term "millennium." Indeed, the latter two categories are most often names imposed on them by premillennialists.

Minjung Theology   A form of *liberation theology originating in Korea in the second half of the twentieth century, as Christians reflected on the long struggles of the Korean people for social justice and human rights. The term "minjung" is a combination of *min*, "people," and *jung*, "masses." By combining these two, minjung theology refers to all the oppressed, excluded, ignored, and exploited; but not just as an amorphous mass of people. The minjung are these people as they determine themselves, not as they are determined or classified by others. One of the crucial points at which minjung theologians challenge traditional Christian understandings refers to the human predicament. For minjung theologians, the notion of "*sin," as traditionally understood by Western and imperialistic theology, has been a tool of oppression, often blaming the victim by failing to distinguish between sin, the sinner, and the sinned against. They then propose the traditional Korean notion of *han*, which is both the outrage and feeling of helplessness of the oppressed, and the conviction that this breach of justice will be overcome, thus leading to genuine hope. It is the notion of *han* that has sustained the Korean people over centuries of foreign invasion or exploitation. And it is *han* that leads the *minjung* to hope and to liberation in Jesus. According to leading minjung theologian Nam Dong Suh (1918–84), a true understanding of Jesus leads, not to *christological speculations and definitions, but to a true understanding of the minjung.

Minjung theologians have been involved in many of the most recent struggles of the Korean people, and also in an entire rereading, not only of Scripture and theology, but also of Korean history, which has often been told from the perspective of the powerful.

Miracles The term "miracle" comes from the same root as "to admire," and thus what stands at the heart of the notion of miracle is the dimension of wonder, amazement, and awe. In societies and cultures in which all events are seen as mysterious manifestations of unseen powers, all events are mysterious and awe-inspiring, and therefore particular events are seldom singled out as "miracles." It is in societies and cultures that take for granted that there is an established order in the world, that things may be expected to act and evolve in a certain way, that the notion of miracle as an unexpected event becomes significant. This is the background on which the New Testament sees the actions of Jesus as "signs" or "wonders." For his contemporaries, and for the church throughout most of its history, the miracles of Jesus were not unexplainable events. They were explained as signs of the power of Jesus himself— just as any other event was a manifesta-

tion of the power behind it. Thus, while miracles were seen as exceptional, overpowering, or amazing, they were not considered problematic.

It was *modernity that turned miracles into a problem. Modernity sees the universe as a closed system of causes and effects. No event takes place without being caused by another event, in a closed sequence that either we can explain or are convinced that we could explain if we only knew more. Thus, to claim that an event is the result of an intervention from beyond the system itself is to deny the very foundations of modern science and historiography. For this reason, *liberal theologians tended to reject any notion of miracle or of divine intervention in history or in human life—and, in response, those who believed that God does intervene felt that liberal theology had conceded too much to modern science.

The more recent critiques of the foundational paradigms of modernity, and the rise of *postmodernity, have once again opened the field for discussion on the ordering of the universe, on the possibility of *hope beyond the limits of the apparently possible, and on the need to construct new models for understanding the world and history. The notion of miracle, and its concomitant of hope for the hopeless, will be part of this discussion, which has not yet come to fruition.

Missio Dei Literally, the "mission of God." The term has been used traditionally in Trinitarian theology as one of the ways to refer to the inner relationships within the *Trinity—the Father sending the Son, and the two sending the Spirit. On the basis of John 20:21, it has been used to speak of the Christian mission as an extension or reflection of the mission of Jesus on earth—"as the Father has sent me, so I send you." It has become common in Protestant *missiology after the World Missionary Conference of Willingen in 1952. Its use has two major implications for mission: first, that the mission of the church is based on the inner sending within the Trinity, as well as on the sending of the Son in the *incarnation, second, that the mission is God's, and that therefore all that the church is to do is to join God in the mission that is already taking place for the redemption of creation.

Missiology   The discipline that studies missions. During the patristic and medieval periods, there were a number of treatises on the proclamation of the gospel to those who had not heard or had not received it. As a result of the Spanish conquests in the Western Hemisphere, Jesuit José de Acosta (1539–1600,) wrote what may be considered the first modern missiological treatise, *On Seeking the Salvation of the Indians*. However, missiology as such did not begin to gain a foothold in the theological curriculum, and in works on systematic theology, until the nineteenth century.

During its early stages, missiology was above all a "practical" discipline, concerned mostly with methods for the advancement of the missionary enterprise—language and intercultural studies, methods of communication and support, the training of indigenous leadership, how to *accommodate the gospel in a different *culture, and the like. Even then, while the emphasis in Protestant missiology lay on the conversion of individuals, the emphasis in Roman Catholic missiology lay on the planting of the church in a new land—*plantatio ecclesiae*.

Two significant developments in missiology during the second half of the twentieth century gave the discipline an entirely new focus. The first was the actual growth of a worldwide church, coupled with the growing secularization of society in the former centers of missionary work, so that it was no longer possible to speak of "Christendom," or of "Christian" and "heathen" lands. This led to a global perspective in which mission is to be carried out by people from every land, and must address people in every land—"mission in six continents."

The second development has been that missiology has moved away from its former preoccupation with methods and means, and has become more of a theological discipline, grounding its work on the *missio Dei* and advocating for an approach to the entire life and thought of the church that is grounded on that *missio*. Significantly, in many theological curricula missiology has been transferred from the "practical" area of studies to the "theological."

Modalism   *See* *Sabellianism.

Modernism   A term often applied in Protestant circles—particularly in conservative circles—to the general stance of a number of leading theologians early in the twentieth century who sought to reconcile Christianity with *modernity. In this endeavor, they tended to exclude the miraculous, to consider Christianity one religion among many, and to focus on the moral teachings of Jesus rather than on his person as Savior. While such views were widespread among intellectuals during the first half of the twentieth century, and while many considered the University of Chicago its fountainhead, Protestant modernism never became an organized movement.

The meaning of the term is more clearly defined in the case of Roman Catholicism, where it refers to the position of a number of theologians led by French theologian Alfred Loisy (1857–1940) and by British Jesuit George Tyrrell (1861–1909). They accepted and adopted the results of the critical methods for the study of Scripture and tradition developed by Protestants, and sought to have Catholic scholars and theologians follow similar paths. They then sought to produce an interpretation of Christianity and of its doctrines that could be reconciled with the views and discoveries of modern science.

While Protestant modernism reflected the views of many leaders in Protestant churches, who were convinced that the church and its doctrines should conform to the dictates of modernity, Catholic modernism was staunchly opposed by Rome and by much of the hierarchy, whose experience with the French Revolution and with other events of the times convinced them that Christianity and modernity were irreconcilable. With a brief and overly optimistic respite during the early years of Leo XIII's pontificate, the modernists found themselves opposed and eventually banned by the church—officially, by the decree *Lamentabili*, in 1907.

Modernity

The name often given to the worldview of the modern age—often by those who claim that the age of modernity is passing, and that we are now moving into "postmodernity." The main characteristics of this worldview are its claim to rational objectivity and therefore also to universality. Typical of this approach to reality is French philosopher René Descartes (1596–1650), whose famous "method" seeks to discover truths that cannot possibly be denied by any rational being, and which are therefore fully objective and universal. This objectivity of modernity is closely linked to a view of *reason as the very essence of humanity—to the point that one can affirm that one exists because one thinks. Its model is the objective truth of mathematics. Its goal is a series of universally accepted truths, for objective knowledge is so compelling that all will eventually come to accept it. Much impressed by the success of the physical sciences, modernity sees the universe as a closed machine, as an unbreakable and purely rational chain of causes and effects (*see* *Causality*), and therefore the modern universe has no room for mystery, and even beauty can be objectified into a series of ratios and proportions.

In theology, modernity has found its expressions in both *modernism and *fundamentalism, for each of these in its own way seeks the sort of objective universality that is the hallmark of modernity.

In recent times, as disciplines such as the sociology of knowledge and depth psychology, as well as *contextual theologies, develop, the very notions of objectivity and universality that stand at the basis of modernity are being questioned, and therefore—although the supposed "demise of modernity" has been greatly exaggerated—there is much discussion of new and different ways of looking at reality (*see* *Postmodernity*).

Molinism

The doctrine of Jesuit theologian Luis de Molina (1535–1600), particularly regarding *grace and the *freedom of the will. Molina insisted that freedom is not only "freedom from coercion," but also "freedom from necessity." A stone that falls is free from coercion, but is not really free, for it falls of necessity. The doctrine of irresistible *grace may preserve freedom from coercion; but it does away with freedom from necessity. Even after the *fall, God grants all humans a general grace or general help, and this is sufficient for a person to take the first step toward believing. This is then followed by the "*habit of faith," which is a supernatural gift of God to those who desire to believe, and to this God adds other gifts of the Spirit.

How, then, is it possible to affirm God's *omniscience and human freedom at the same time? By claiming that there are three different sorts of knowledge in God: God's "natural" knowledge includes all things, even those that do not exist. God's "free" knowledge includes those things that God has willed to exist. God's "intermediate knowledge"—*scientia media*—is that knowledge by which God knows those things that will exist or will happen, although not willed by God. These "future contingents" are willed by those creatures whom God has endowed with freedom. Therefore, future contingent events—including a sinner's conversion—do not depend on God's foreknowledge.

Molinism was staunchly defended by the Jesuits, and repeatedly attacked by the Dominicans, and became one of the main theological points of contention between these two orders.

Monarchianism The insistence on the unity of God to the point of denying the *Trinity. The term is employed of widely diverging positions. Thus, scholars speak of a "dynamic monarchianism," which holds that only the Father is God, and that what dwelt in Jesus was just the "power"—*dynamis*—of God. In sharp contrast with this, "Modalistic Monarchianism" claimed that Jesus was indeed God, and so is the Spirit, for Father, Son, and Holy Spirit are simply three "modes" in which God relates to the world at various times. (*See also* *Patripassianism; *Sabellianism.)

Monasticism A movement that has taken various shapes throughout Christian history, yet whose common thread has been the desire to serve God with greater dedication than seems possible in daily life "in the world." The term "monk" originally meant "solitary," for the first monks were hermits who withdrew to a life of solitude in remote areas—particularly the sparsely inhabited "deserts" of Egypt and Syria. However, quite soon monks began living in communities—"cenobitic" monasticism. The monastic life has always been open to both men and women, although the feminine branches of most monastic orders have remained more secluded than some of their masculine counterparts. In the West, most cenobitic monasticism bears the imprint of the Rule of St. Benedict (ca.480–547), which sets the pattern for monastic life and prayer.

Monasticism gained momentum after the conversion of Constantine, as a movement of protest against the organized church and its participation in the affairs and pomp of the world. But eventually it became a powerful arm of the church. Its theological justification was found in the distinction between the commandments of God—which all must obey—and the "*counsels of perfection," consisting primarily of chastity, poverty,

and obedience, which are the marks of monastic life.

Monasticism has evolved greatly through the ages, undergoing repeated movements of reform as the ancient ideals were abandoned, or as new challenges arose. At times, particularly in the West, monasteries have served as centers of learning, as pharmacies and hospitals, as schools, as centers where Bibles and other ancient books were copied and preserved, and as hostels for travelers. They became centers for missions, as in the cases of Iona and Lindisfarne. In connection with the Crusades and with the Spanish Reconquista, monastic military orders emerged. In the thirteenth century, with the rise of the Franciscans and Dominicans, monks became preachers, professors, and eventually Inquisitors. In the sixteenth century, the Jesuits and other orders became the right hand of the Spanish and Portuguese crowns in their efforts to evangelize the New World, and of the papacy in its struggle against Protestantism.

Luther and most Protestant Reformers rejected monasticism on the basis that it was a way to seek salvation through *works. Yet it is important to remember that the very Bible that the Reformers so cherished was copied and preserved mostly through the work of monastics, and that for quite a few centuries monastic houses had been the centers of learning throughout Christian Europe—until the rise of universities in the thirteenth century provided an alternative. Thus, most medieval theology—and much of later Roman Catholic theology—is in fact monastic theology.

Monergism (also monenergism) The view that, while there are in Christ two persons—as defined by the Council of Chalcedon (451)—there is only one principle of activity, one *energeia*, hence the name "monergism." This was proposed by Patriarch Sergius of Constantinople (died 638) as a means to gain the adherence of the more moderate *monophysites. The attempt failed, creating more divisions than reconciliations, and therefore in 634 Sergius himself prohibited all discussion as to whether Christ had one or two "energeias."

In an entirely different context, having to do with *soteriology, "monergism" is sometimes used as the opposite of *synergism.

Monism The view that all reality is ultimately one. Such is the case, for instance, of the *Neoplatonist theory of the world as a series of emanations from the ineffable One, and of all *pantheistic systems. The Christian doctrine of *creation, while insisting that all things come from God, also affirms that they are different from God, and not of the substance of God.

Monophysism (also monophysitism) The claim that there is in Christ only "one nature," the divine. This was first set forth by the monk Eutyches (ca.378–ca.450), who then gained the support of Patriarch Dioscorus of Alexandria, and eventually condemned by the Fourth Ecumenical Council, held at Chalcedon in 451. Although the thought of Eutyches is not altogether clear—some even claiming that he had declared that the body of Christ was made of a different, heavenly substance—the concern of most monophysites was that the doctrine of the "two natures" in Christ—one divine and one human—seemed to divide him into two, and came dangerously close to *Nestorianism. For that reason, some monophysites were willing to say that Christ was *of* two natures, but not *in* two natures—that is to say, that the humanity of Christ, although present after the incarnation, was so absorbed by the divine as to become one nature. Thus, the monophysite controversy was the continuation of the long-standing difference between *Antiochene and *Alexandrine *Christologies, monophysism being the outcome of the traditionally unitive Christology of Alexandria.

Although condemned by the Council of Chalcedon, monophysism did not disappear. There was great resentment against the Byzantine Empire in Syria, Egypt, and Armenia, and in all these areas monophysite churches developed that continue existing to this day. Since the Church of Ethiopia was closely related to Egypt, it too became monophysite.

It is important to point out, however, that scholars often speak of many of these churches and their theologians as "verbal monophysites" or as "Severians"—after Severus of Antioch (ca.465–538), the best-known early defender of this sort of monophysism. While rejecting the formula of Chalcedon, these "verbal monophysites" affirm that Jesus is both divine and human.

Monotheism The belief that there is only one God. A belief held in common, among other religions, by Judaism, Christianity, and Islam—although there are indications that at certain stages the faith of Israel was *henotheistic rather than clearly monotheistic. By its very nature, monotheism leads to the notion that, since there is only one God, there is also a single master or ruler of all events—in contrast with religions where there are different gods for different functions or realms of life. Thus monotheism is ultimately opposed, not only to polytheism, but also to *dualism.

In contrast to both Judaism and Islam, however, Christianity holds that the One God is also the Triune God (*Trinity), and therefore has frequently been criticized on this score by Jews as well as by Muslims. Within the church itself, there have been long and heated controversies as to how the One God can also be Triune. This has led, on the one hand, to views approaching tritheism, and thus endangering the fundamental monotheistic nature of the Christian faith; and, on the other hand, to views in which there seems to be no real distinction between the three divine persons (*Sabellianism). The response of most orthodox theologians is that the doctrine itself of the Trinity presupposes and requires an understanding of "One," not in the mathematical sense of a solitary being, but rather as an organic unity that is best understood as absolute and primal love.

Monotheletism   A second attempt on the part of Patriarch Sergius of Constantinople (died 638) to make the doctrine of the "two natures" in Christ more palatable to moderate *monophysites. After proposing *monergism and then withdrawing it, Sergius proposed that, although there are in Christ two natures, there is only one will—*thelema*—hence the name "monotheletism." Exactly what this meant is not altogether clear. At any rate, Sergius's proposal was never accepted by most monophysites, and was soundly rejected by the more traditional defenders of the Definition of Chalcedon—led by Maximus the Confessor (ca.580–662). Finally, the Sixth Ecumenical Council (Constantinople, 681) rejected monotheletism.

Montanism   The doctrine and sect of Montanus, a former pagan priest converted to Christianity around the year 155. Claiming possession by the Holy *Spirit, he and two women, Priscilla and Maximilla, declared that with them a new dispensation was dawning. This was a dispensation of greater moral rigor, for just as the *law of Moses had been superseded by the "law of the gospel," now the latter was giving way to the "law of the Spirit." The Montanists expected the end of the world to come soon, and gathered in a town in Phrygia where they expected the New Jerusalem to be established. They also organized themselves into a church that for a time rivaled the rest of the church.

Moral Theology   The name traditionally given in Roman Catholic theology to Christian *ethics. Although today the distinction is mostly a matter of nomenclature, the two different names do point to different approaches in the early stages of development of the discipline. While Protestant ethics were more inclined toward philosophical ethics, and during the nineteenth century tended to focus on Kant's quest for ethical autonomy, Roman Catholic moral theology was devoted mostly to the resolution of moral cases on the basis of *Thomistic psychological and moral presuppositions, *canon law, *Scripture, and *reason. Hence the name of "*casuistry" by which it was also known—a name that has acquired the negative connotation of seeking excuses and exceptions in order to avoid moral action, although such practices have been rare in true casuistry, except in some Jesuit circles in the seventeenth century (*see* *Probabilism).

Moral theology thus includes matters of ethics both individual and social, both private and public. It includes the proper ordering of society and of the state as well as personal sexual and economic practices, and also the matter of the degree to which, and the means by which, Christians and the church as an institution are to seek legislation governing the moral practices of a society.

Mortal Sin   In Roman Catholic theology, a sin so grave that it separates the sinner from God to such a degree that a person who dies with such sins unforgiven—a "state of mortal sin"—is condemned to *hell. In contrast, "venial sins" are either minor sins, or have been committed out of ignorance. A sinner who dies in a state of venial sin will go to *purgatory before finally being admitted into *heaven.

Protestants have generally rejected any such classifications of sin, for every sin separates the sinner from God, and every sin—no matter how small or how great—requires God's *grace in order to be forgiven.

Mujerista Theology   A term coined by Ada María Isasi-Díaz (1943–) to refer to the theology of Latinas in the United States. While agreeing with much of *feminist theology, mujerista theology insists that such theology has been so concerned about issues and perspectives in the dominant culture that it is unable to express the experience, the oppression, and the hopes of minority women—particularly Hispanic women. Also, while agreeing with much of *Latino theology, mujerista theology points out that Latino theology is so concerned over issues of culture, class, and race that it often does not pay sufficient attention to gender issues. Hence the need for a distinguishing name: "mujerista"—from the Spanish *mujer*, woman. The methodology of mujerista theology thus stresses the need to listen to the actual words and experiences of Latinas, and then interpreting these expressions in theological terms, rather than imposing traditional theological categories on the experienced life of Latinas.

Mystery Religions   A wide variety of religions that flourished in the Greco-Roman world early in the Christian era—the cult of Isis and Osiris, the Dionysian mysteries, Attis and Cybele, the Great Mother, and so on. They seem to have their roots in earlier fertility cults, whereby worshipers sought to explain and to enhance the fertility of the soil, herds, and people. Since such fertility is often cyclical, following the seasons of the year or the floods of the Nile, a common trait of mystery religions is their focus on the cycle of birth, life, and death, not only in nature, but also in the life of individuals. Just as nature dies and comes to life again, so do the gods of mystery religions follow a process or a basic *myth of death and rebirth, and their followers are likewise promised new life after death. Thus, what had originally been religions of fertility eventually became religions of *salvation. Such salvation was to be attained by joining with the gods in their death and resurrection, usually through rites called "mysteries"—hence the name commonly given to these religions.

The relationship between Christianity and mystery religions has long been debated. There are a number of points of contact or similarities. What is not clear—since there are few detailed sources for the practice of the mysteries before the advent of Christianity—is to what degree Christianity impacted the mysteries, and to what degree the opposite was true. At any rate, the mysteries were one of the chief rivals of Christianity in its expansion throughout the Mediterranean world, and most likely left their impact on a number of Christian practices.

Mysticism   A widely defined term, and therefore one whose meaning is not always clear, nor always the same. Strictly speaking, mysticism is the experience of an immediate and sustained or repeated connection with the divine, this connection being the ordering principle of all of life. Thus, while sudden experiences of conversion, charismatic events, and visions may be said to have a mystical dimension, and sometimes are an element in mystical experience, they are not the essence of mysticism. Nor is religious zeal tantamount to mysticism.

Mysticism exists in all major religions. In Christianity, it has taken several distinct forms. One is profoundly influenced by the *Neoplatonic tradition, and its goal is for the soul to be so united with the divine as to lose the sense of self—much like a drop of water dissolving into the ocean. Another centers on bridal imagery, speaking of a spiritual marriage between the soul and Christ. Some Christian mystics have had experiences of union with God as the source of all being. Others have centered their contemplation on Christ, and particularly on his sufferings. Some Christian mystics have been drawn into a life of solitude and contemplation, while others have been propelled into activities such as service to the needy or the reform of the church. Some have felt that their communion with God was such that they could practically dispense with the services of the church, while others have been drawn into more intensive participation in the communal life of the church.

Given this variety of experiences, it is not surprising that many theologians have looked askance at mysticism or rejected it altogether as being excessively subjective, individualistic, or *quietistic, or as attempting to achieve salvation by works.

While there is wide variety in the shapes and experiences of mysticism within the Christian tradition, mystical theology—reflection on, and guidance for, the mystical experience—tends to agree that the mystical life is a process involving several stages. Although there are several such outlines or schemes, most commonly these stages are three: purgation, illumination, and union. Thus, the mystical life is often accompanied by a discipline of reflection and contemplation, and is not just a single moment of *ecstasy. The "purgative way" is the cleansing of the soul from its sin. The "illuminative way" enlightens the disciple to see more clearly the path to perfection and to practice love and purity more fully. The "unitive way" seeks union with God as the final goal of all discipleship. While these are usually called "ways," they are most often depicted as stages, so that the mystical life begins with a stage of cleansing (purgative), advances through illumination and the practice of the virtues that illumination entails, and ends in union with the divine. On this final union, Eastern mysticism tends to emphasize the loss of the individual into the divine, while Western mysticism tends to insist on the permanent consciousness of difference.

Myth   A very confusing term, whose meaning has to be determined by its context and by the intentions of the author. In common usage a "myth" is something that is not true—as when one speaks of "the myth of the self-made man." In its classical usage, a myth is a story about the gods or about celestial or primal beings, whose purpose is to explain certain phenomena or to promote a certain form of conduct. Thus, the myth of Isis and Osiris explains the cyclical flooding and the fertility produced by the Nile, and the myth of Pandora warns about the dangers of unbounded curiosity. As modern historiography began to develop, historians sometimes distinguished between "myth" and "fact," meaning by the first a story that was not factual, and had been developed in order to promote a certain view or interpretation of events. In the middle of the twentieth century, Rudolf Bultmann (1884–1976) argued that, since *modernity has left behind the mythological worldview of antiquity, it is now necessary to *demythologize the message of the New Testament. More recently, a number of scholars have argued that since a myth is a narrative that interprets reality, and that since reality itself is meaningless without interpretation, myth is an integral part of knowledge and of life.

Natural Theology   A theology that claims to be based on the natural gifts of the human mind, and on the "general revelation" granted to all (*see* *Revelation), rather than on a "special revelation" in Scripture or in Jesus Christ. The early apologists (*see* *Apologetics) argued that items such as the existence of one Supreme Being and life after death had already been discovered by the ancient philosophers, and therefore they could be said to have promoted a sort of natural theology. For them, as for most of the *scholastic tradition, this did not suffice, for the special revelation of God in Scripture and in Jesus Christ added much that reason alone could never discover. Thus, Thomas Aquinas (1225–74) claimed that there are certain truths that are attainable by the powers of *reason properly applied, and others that are beyond the reach of reason, and are known only through revelation. These two overlap, for God has revealed those matters—such as God's own existence—that, while accessible to reason, are necessary for salvation, thus making salvation possible for those who cannot follow the philosophical arguments proving them.

In general, the Reformers were less enthusiastic about natural theology, in part because they rejected much of the scholastic tradition, in part because it tended to render special revelation, and particularly Scripture, less necessary, and in part because it granted fallen human beings powers of correct reasoning that the Reformers themselves saw as corrupted by sin. For some of them, natural theology sufficed only to show human sin and need, but was unable to provide an answer to such need.

It was the *Deists who brought natural theology to its apex, arguing that it was possible, by the mere exercise of reason and common sense, to arrive at a "natural religion" that did not depend on a special revelation on the part of God, and on which therefore all reasonable human beings could agree. They believed true Christianity to be nothing else than this natural religion, and held that claims to special revelation were in fact lapses into unreasonable superstition.

In the twentieth century, Karl Barth (1886–1968) led a spirited attack on natural theology. It was this attack that led to the final break between him and another leading *neo-orthodox theologian, Emil Brunner (1889–1966). Although later he moderated his stance, Barth rejected any attempt to construct theology—even part of it—on human reason or on the gifts of nature, insisting that there is a chasm between nature and grace, and therefore between philosophy and theology, and between reason and faith. This was important for Barth because he saw natural theology as an ally of the attempt on the part of the "German Christians" to show that Christianity had reached its climax in German civilization, and thus to justify the politics of Nazism. Another German theologian of the same generation, Paul Tillich (1886–1965) saw natural theology as asking the question and posing the

existential predicaments that only the gospel could answer.

Neo-orthodoxy Also called "dialectical theology" and "crisis theology," because it stressed the dialectical tension—in Greek, *krisis*—between the divine and the human. Neo-orthodoxy was a reaction against the *liberal theology of the nineteenth century, whose optimism regarding human capabilities was sorely tried by the First World War. Karl Barth's (1886–1968) *Commentary on Romans*, published in 1919, is usually regarded as the beginning of this theological school. Early collaborators of Barth in this enterprise were his lifelong colleague Eduard Thurneysen (1888–1974), as well as Emil Brunner (1889–1966) and Friedrich Gogarten (1887–1968). Neo-orthodoxy criticized liberal theology for having minimized the distinction and the distance between God and humans, thus losing sight of divine *transcendence and leaving itself open to the suggestion that God is nothing but a projection of human need and aspirations. In so doing, the neo-orthodox claimed, liberalism had underestimated the power and prevalence of sin, which twists all human knowledge, and had rendered the church incapable of responding with a prophetic word to the dreams of human progress that had led to the First World War—and would eventually lead to fascism and other forms of totalitarianism and to the Second World War. By stressing the need for *revelation and the authority of Scripture, and also by drawing more consistently on the tradition of the Reformation and the early church, this theology merited the name of "neo-orthodoxy." Several neo-orthodox theologians were among the principal proponents of the Barmen Declaration against Nazism as idolatry.

Neoplatonism The form that *Platonism most commonly took after the work of Plotinus (205–270), a pagan philosopher who lived in Alexandria and then in Rome. It differs from Platonism in its more religious and mystical tendencies, and in that it reflects the impact of *Stoicism, many of whose views it assimilated. According to Plotinus, all reality derives from the Ineffable One as a series of emanations. In these emanations, the One moves toward multiplicity. Evil as such does not exist, but is rather the deprivation of the good, so that something is said to be "bad" or "corrupted" as it moves toward multiplicity and away from the One. True knowledge is attained through the contemplation of higher realities, and specifically of the One, and its goal is to culminate in *ecstasy, where the soul contemplates the One directly and loses itself into the One.

While the early Neoplatonists rejected Christianity, and saw it as a rival to true philosophy, eventually many of their teachings were absorbed into Christianity. Augustine (354–430) found Neoplatonism helpful in dealing with some of the difficulties he had with Christian doctrines such as the incorporeity of God and the *soul, and in dealing with the problem of how evil can exist in a world created by a good God (see *Theodicy). He thus became one of the main channels through which Neoplatonism impacted Western Christian theology. Slightly later, around the year 500, an anonymous author who claimed to be Dionysius the Areopagite, but who in fact was very much a Neoplatonist, wrote a series of treatises on *mystical theology that became very influential during the Middle Ages.

Thus, a form of Neoplatonism divested of its earlier anti-Christian elements was dominant in Western Christian philosophy and theology until the reintroduction of Aristotle (see *Aristotelianism; *Thomism) in the thirteenth century. And, even after that time, much Christian mystical theology bears the imprint of Neoplatonism.

Nestorianism   The doctrine of Nestorius, patriarch of Constantinople, declared heretical by the Third Ecumenical Council (Ephesus, 431). Nesto-

rius's *Christology was of the *Antiochene type, and he therefore sought to preserve the full humanity of Jesus by making a clear distinction between it and his divinity. The debate broke out in 428, when Nestorius defended the attacks of his chaplain on the title of *Theotokos—mother or bearer of God—as applied to *Mary. Although quite naturally devotion to Mary played a role in the controversy, in fact the debate was on the character of the union of divinity and humanity in Christ. Nestorius's opponents, led by Patriarch Cyril of Alexandria (died 444), insisted that the union in Christ is such as to allow for the *communicatio idiomatum—the transferral of properties or predicates from one nature to the other. It was this principle that made it possible to say that God spoke in Jesus, that God walked in Galilee, or that God was born of the Virgin Mary. Without such communicatio, Cyril argued, there is no true incarnation.

Against Cyril and his party, Nestorius and his defenders argued that only "incomplete natures" can come together fully. The body and the soul are both incomplete, and when they come together they form a complete nature, a human being. In Jesus, however, both the divinity and the humanity are complete natures, and therefore they cannot come together as the soul and the body come together to form a complete nature. This means that the union is not "natural" or "*hypostatic," but "moral." In Christ there are two complete natures in two persons, united by their common will or purpose.

Twenty years after his condemnation by the Council of Ephesus, Nestorius learned of the decisions of the Fourth Ecumenical Council (Chalcedon, 451), and felt that those decisions vindicated him. The book that he then wrote in defense of his Christology, and trying to show that it agreed with the Chalcedonian Definition of Faith, was discovered late in the nineteenth century, and has raised many questions as to the exact nature of Nestorius's Christology, which until then was known mostly through the writings of his adversaries.

Many of the followers of Nestorius, as well as others of the Antiochene school of theology who felt threatened by the decisions taken at Ephesus, went into exile beyond the borders of the Roman Empire, where they made of the city of Nisibis the center of a flourishing school of theology. The result was that the church in the Persian Empire became Nestorian. To this day there are remnants of this Nestorian church, not only within the borders of the former Persian Empire, but also in the Western Hemisphere, where Nestorians found refuge from persecution in their original lands.

Nicene As a noun, an abbreviated title for the Nicene *Creed—which is not in truth the creed originally promulgated at the First Ecumenical Council (Nicaea, 325), but that creed with a number of later additions. (*See *Filioque.*)

As an adjective, "Nicene" means pertaining to or agreeing with the decisions taken at Nicaea. In this sense, it is often used to refer to the party that, under the leadership first of Athanasius and later of the Cappadocians, defended the *homoousios.

Nominalism In the debate regarding the nature of *universals, the position holding that they do not really exist, but are only names—*nomina*—given to things. Extreme nominalism was rare, for even if universals are mere names it is clear that they are not entirely capricious. (There is something common to all horses that allows us to group them together, and to say that a table does not belong in the same category.) Yet nominalism, even in its more moderate forms, made it more difficult to explain *original sin, or to hold to a strictly *hierarchical notion of the church. If humanity is not as real as are individual human beings, how can one claim that in the sin of one all have sinned? And, if the reality of Christianity is not in the church as an eternal entity (*see *Ecclesiology), but rather in believers themselves, does this not mean that authority should reside in the faithful, rather than in the hierarchy claiming to represent the eternal church?

In the late Middle Ages there was a resurgence of criticism to *realism as a way to understand universals, and this resurgence was often called *nominalism—even though its position regarding universals was more moderate than earlier, extreme nominalism. This was closely connected with efforts to reform the church through *conciliarism, and with a sharp critique of the manner in which traditional *scholasticism had understood the relationship between faith and *reason. (*See also *Potentia Dei absoluta.*)

Notes of the Church See *Marks of the Church.

Novatianism A rigorist movement named after Novatian, who in the third century clashed with ecclesiastical authorities in Rome over the issue of the restoration of the *lapsed during persecution. The result was a schism that lasted several generations after the death of Novatian himself. Novatian also wrote a treatise *On the Trinity*, in which he opposed *modalism, and which became an important step in the process toward the definition of the doctrine of the *Trinity.

Nunc Dimittis The first two words of Simeon's song in the Latin translation of Luke 2:29–32, and hence the traditional name for that song.

Occasionalism The theory of French cardinal Nicolas de Malebranche (1638–1715), by which he sought to resolve the question left open by *Cartesianism regarding the "communication of the substances." If, as Descartes had suggested, a human being is composed of a thinking reality—*res cogitans*—and an extensive or physical reality—*res extensa*, how do these interact with each other? How does the mind perceive what happens to the body, and how does it communicate its decisions to the body? Malebranche's response was that these two realities—as well as any other substances—do not actually affect each other. It is God who intervenes to make a body do what a mind decides, or to make a billiard ball move when another hits it. Thus, what we commonly call "causes" are not really such, but are "occasions" of God's activity. Hence the name of "occasionalism" for his theory.

Omnipotence   One of the traditional *attributes of God, meaning that *God possesses all power to its maximum degree. While this is a fairly common statement, its exact meaning is not altogether clear, simply because finite minds cannot really conceive or understand the full meaning of the "all" expressed here by the root *omni*. This limitation of human understanding has often been pointed out by posing questions such as, "Can God make two plus two be five?" or, "Can God make a stone so big that even God cannot move it?" The first question raises the issue of the relationship between divine omnipotence and logical order. Does divine omnipotence mean that even logic is subject to God's decision? Or is God's omnipotence limited by logic, so that God is not truly omnipotent? The second question points to the logical conundrum implicit in the very notion of omnipotence.

Through the ages, philosophical theologians have debated these issues—although usually with more sophisticated examples. Some have argued that omnipotence means that God can do whatever is possible, and others have countered that true omnipotence requires that nothing is impossible for God. Some have argued that God can only do that which is good, and others have responded that whatever God does is good, for it is God who determines the good and the bad (see *Potentia Dei absoluta*).

On the other hand, there is a different way of understanding omnipotence, not as a philosophical notion derived from the nature of the Supreme Being, but rather as an expression of believers' experience of and faith in the power of God. The term that the Apostles' *Creed translates as "almighty" does not literally mean "all-powerful" or "omnipotent," but rather "all-governing." What the creed affirms is not that God has limitless power, but that all things are under divine rule. Thus, omnipotence may be understood and explained, not in terms of some ideal, logical, infinitude of power, but rather in terms of God's rule over all things, and God's final victory over all evil.

Omnipresence   One of the traditional *attributes of God, meaning that *God is fully present everywhere. In this definition the word "fully" is crucial, for God's presence is not like that of the air, which may be present in a number of places, but only partially present in any one place. This is what is often meant by the "*immensity" of God. In Scripture, the divine omnipresence is seen both as a gift and as a fearful reality. It means both that God is readily available everywhere and that it is impossible to flee or to hide from the divine presence. This particular attribute of God has caused much less debate than its traditional companions *omnipotence and *omniscience.

Omniscience   One of the traditional *attributes of God, meaning that *God knows all things. As in the case of *omnipotence, this apparently simple notion gives rise to many difficulties and debates. One may debate, for instance, whether in God willing and knowing are the same, in which case everything that God knows God does, and therefore all that God knows comes into being. However, if that is the case, then God does not know the impossible, and all events as well as all existing beings are necessary, for nothing is contingent (see *Contingency). Or one may debate whether God's knowledge affects divine *impassibility, since in knowledge the object that is known impacts the knower. Finally, the very notion of omniscience has led to many debates regarding *pre-determinism, *predestination, and *free-dom. If God knows the future, how can the future not be already determined by such knowledge? If God knows our future decisions, how can we still be free to make such decisions?

Such difficulties have led many theologians—particularly those in the *neo-orthodox tradition—to declare that attributes such as omniscience and omnipotence must not be understood as the result of philosophical speculation, or as derived from the notion of God as the Supreme Being. From this perspective, omniscience and omnipresence are best understood in terms of divine *judgment and *grace. They are not attributes we know by considering the necessary characteristics of a Supreme Being, but affirmations of our conviction, grounded on *revelation, that God loves and judges us and creation, that we cannot hide from God, and that God will not remain forever hidden from us.

Ontological Argument An argument seeking to prove the existence of God, taking as its starting point, not the existence of the world (*Cosmological Argument), but rather the notion itself of God. Its classical expression dates from the *Proslogion* of Anselm of Canterbury (ca.1033–1109), who inquired why Psalm 53 declares that to deny the existence of God is folly. According to Anselm, God is "that-than-which-no-greater-can-be-thought," or the perfect being. On the basis of that definition, to think that such a being does not exist is to fall into contradiction, for any existent being would be greater and more perfect than this nonexistent God. In other words, the very notion of fullness and perfection requires existence, and therefore the perfect being must exist.

Even though Anselm's argument can be expressed in these few words, it has been much debated through the ages. Almost immediately after its publica-

tion, a monk named Gaunilo wrote a treatise *In Defense of the Fool*, in which he argues that, while he can conceive of a perfect island, this does not imply that such an island must exist, for in that case it would be less perfect than any existing island. Anselm responded by insisting that his argument is valid only for a being with the supreme order of perfection in itself, in which case existence is the necessary corollary of its essence.

It is precisely at this point that Anselm's argument has found most critics. Most notably, Kant (1724–1804) argued that existence is never a corollary or a necessary predicate of an essence, and that Anselm's fallacy is in making it such. Later, other theologians and philosophers have proposed modifications of the ontological argument, in which they sought to overcome Kant's critique. Most notable among these is Charles Hartshorne (1897–2000), a *process philosopher who believed that, within the parameters of process philosophy, Kant's objections are not valid.

In any case, there are also numerous theologians who feel that, no matter whether the ontological argument in any of its various forms is valid or not, all that it may prove is the existence of a Supreme Being, but this is not necessarily the same as the God of Scripture and of Christian faith.

Ontologism A development in the nineteenth century within Roman Catholic theology, in reaction to Kant's criticism of ontological speculation, and to the ensuing metaphysical skepticism of many philosophers. The ontologists, led by Italian theologian Vincenzo Gioberti (1801–52), held that all knowledge is in a sense knowledge of God, and that therefore every truth implies an immediate and intuitive perception of the divine truth. These views, which seemed to lead to *pantheism, were rejected by the Inquisition in 1861.

Ordo salutis Latin for the "order of salvation." The term is traditionally employed to refer to the various elements in the process whereby the sinner is saved and brought to final redemption. While the term has fallen into general disuse, many earlier controversies in theology revolved around the *ordo salutis*. This could be said about the controversy of Augustine (354–430) with the Pelagians and later with the Semipelagians, where the issue at stake was the primacy of grace in salvation, and whether the *initium fidei* is in grace or in human freedom. Medieval theology developed a fairly structured *ordo salutis*, including not only *repentance, *regeneration, *penance, *sanctification, and the *beatific vision, but also *purgatory and *limbo. Luther's struggles during his monastic years may be seen as the quest for an *ordo salutis* that responded to his profound sense of sin and inadequacy. The debates first between Lutherans and Calvinists, and then between Calvinists and Wesley regarding sanctification also revolved around the *ordo salutis*.

While these debates are important, it must be pointed out that the great variety of Christian experience would seem to indicate that any description or definition of the *ordo salutis* must remain tentative and flexible, and also that the traditional debates regarding this *ordo* tend to consider *salvation as an individual matter, and to neglect the more cosmic dimensions of God's plan of *redemption.

Original Righteousness   In traditional theology, the state of the human creature before the *fall. In most traditional theology, it is taken for granted that, had Adam and Eve not fallen, they and all humankind would have remained in their original state of righteousness. Irenaeus (second century) and many other theologians, however, have held that God always intended for the human creature to grow in righteousness, and that therefore the state of *redemption is higher than the original state of innocence. In that case, redemption is not merely the restoration of orig-

inal righteousness, but a process whereby greater righteousness and communion with God is attained.

Original Sin   The classical way of referring to the fact that sin pervades all human life from birth, and is therefore, more than mere acts we commit, a state in which we live. It is customary to contrast original sin with "actual" sins, which are those individuals commit on their own. Although the most common view of original sin in Western theology has been as an inheritance from Adam and Eve, in the early church there were alternative understandings. In the second century, Irenaeus believed that, since Adam was the head of all humankind, in him all humanity literally sinned. At about the same time, Clement of Alexandria held that original sin, rather than an inheritance, is a symbol expressing the fact that all humans sin. Thus, for him original sin was simply an expression of the inevitability of actual sin. Writing just a few years after Irenaeus and Clement, Tertullian was the first to understand original sin as something we all inherit from our first parents. Two hundred years later, it was Augustine who first developed the theory of original sin as an inheritance, and who connected it with the *concupiscence that he held was inevitably involved in the act of conception. In contemporary theology, original sin tends to be understood as a description of the condition into which all humans are born, which makes sin inevitable even before we are aware of it, and is often connected with the view of sin, not as an act, but rather as a state in which all humans are born and live. (*See* *Sin.)

Orthodoxy   Strictly speaking, "orthodoxy" means "correct doctrine," and therefore all churches consider themselves orthodox. The term is sometimes used with somewhat pejorative overtones, to describe a sort of theology that seeks to define every possible point of doctrine or belief, claiming that those who do not agree are heretics. It is in this sense that historians often refer to the seventeenth century as the period of "Protestant orthodoxy." In a third sense, the term is used to refer to those essential points of Christian doctrine on which the church—or most of it—has long agreed, and therefore many traditional Protestant churches define "orthodoxy" as agreement with the doctrinal decisions of the first four—or in some cases seven—ecumenical councils.

Finally, "Orthodoxy," when capitalized, usually refers to the Eastern churches that have evolved out of the ancient Greek-speaking church and its missions, such as the Greek Orthodox Church, the Russian Orthodox Church, the Bulgarian Orthodox Church, and others. These churches agree on the validity of the decisions of the first seven ecumenical councils and hold intercommunion with each other, even though they are "autocephalous"—the church in each nation having its own hierarchy and its own head—and therefore structurally independent, granting the Ecumenical Patriarch of Constantinople only a precedence of honor, but not of jurisdiction. (A number of churches not in communion with the rest of Orthodoxy, because they do not accept some of the decrees of the early councils, call themselves orthodox, and are sometimes considered part of Eastern Orthodoxy, because they hold many practices and traditions in common with it. Such is the case of the Coptic Church and the Church of Ethiopia.)

Orthopraxis A term often employed, particularly by *liberation theologians, to indicate that proper *praxis* is just as important as proper doctrine—or rather, that a doctrine, no matter how correct, that does not lead to and derive from the praxis of love is flawed.

Ousia See *Hypostasis.

Oxford Movement A movement that developed in the Church of England during the nineteenth century, seeking to counteract the influence of both *liberalism and *evangelicalism, and to return to some of the more "catholic" elements in Christianity. Its views were expressed in a series of *Tracts for the Times*—which led the movement to be known also as "Tractarianism." The first of these was published in 1833 by Oxford theologian John Henry Newman (1801–90), who eventually joined the Roman Catholic Church and became a cardinal. Most of the members of the movement, however, remained loyal Anglicans, where they developed and promoted a form of piety that found profound value in the doctrinal, ritual, and devotional traditions of the church, while remaining Protestant in their fundamental theological outlook.

Pacifism The position of Christians who hold that violence, and war in particular, are contrary to the teachings of Jesus and to the will of God, and that therefore Christians should abstain from all forms of violence. There is no doubt that the early church was pacifist, teaching that Christians could not be soldiers. By the end of the second century, there were some Christians in the Roman army, and several theologians—most notably Tertullian (ca.155–ca.220)—wrote against such practices. Pagan philosopher Celsus criticized Christianity by arguing that if all Romans were to become Christians there would be nobody to defend the Empire—to which Origen (ca.185–ca.254) replied that in that case the enemies of the Empire would also be Christian, and there would be no need for military defense. By the time the Empire began supporting Christianity, early in the fourth century, there were already a number of Christians in the army; and by the middle of the fifth century, under Theodosius II, only Christians could join the army. Thus, a total about-face had taken place in the church's attitude toward war and military service, which now justified military activity in terms of the principles of a "just war" (*see* *War).

During the Middle Ages, it was mostly heretics and other dissenters—*Albigensians, *Waldensians, and some *Hussites—who revived pacifist ideas and practices. In the case of the Albigensians, a crusade against them led many of their number to renounce their earlier pacifism.

At the time of the Reformation, some *Anabaptists took a pacifist position, while others resorted to violence to promote and to defend their views. Pacifism was from the beginning the position of Menno Simons (1496–1561) and his followers, now known as *Mennonites. The wars of religion of the seventeenth century led many to adopt pacifist positions—*Quakers, the Brethren, and others. Pacifism was also adopted by Martin Luther King Jr. (1929–68) in the struggle for civil rights, and by Mohandas Gandhi—who declared that Jesus had influenced him on this point—in the struggle for Indian independence.

While some pacifist groups have eschewed all participation in civil society at large, fearing that such participation would inevitably involve them in violent activity, others have advocated and practiced nonviolent resistance as an active tool for social change. Those who practice and advocate such resistance feel that, by drawing violence against themselves, they unmask and thus begin undoing the evil and hidden dimensions of violence.

Panentheism A term derived from Greek words meaning "God in everything," and coined by philosopher K. C. F. Krause (1781–1832) to differentiate his position from *pantheism. While according to the latter the universe is God, according to panentheism, while all things share in the divine nature, the divine is not limited to them. Thus, God is immanent to the universe, which itself is divine; but God is also transcendent, existing beyond the totality of the universe. The term has also been employed to describe the positions of *process philosophers Alfred N. Whitehead (1861–1947) and Charles Hartshorne (1897–2000). The latter employed the relationship between a person and the person's body as an example of the relationship between God and the universe: just as the body is part of the person, but is not the whole person, so does the universe relate to God.

Panpsychism The notion that all things in the universe have a certain degree of consciousness. Elements of such views were common in the ancient world, where many held that the planets and other heavenly bodies had souls, and where some natural phenomena—for instance, a rock falling—were sometimes explained in terms of the consciousness of the things involved—in this case, the rock. Such views have also appeared repeatedly in the history of Western thought, and Thomas Aquinas (1225–74) explicitly rejected and refuted them. They were resurrected in the nineteenth century, and in the twentieth some saw similar tendencies in Teilhard de Chardin's (1881–1955) claim that all things move toward a higher degree of consciousness.

Pantheism The claim that the universe in its totality is God. It differs from *panentheism in that the latter does not believe that the universe exhausts the being of God, who does transcend the universe. There have been pantheistic tendencies in a number of Christian theologians and mystics. The *Neoplatonic doctrine of the whole of reality as a series of emanations of the One has led a number of theologians of Neoplatonic inclinations, such as John Scotus Erigena (ca.810–ca.877), to espouse pantheism. Many mystics, such as Meister Eckhart (ca.1260–?1327), have been accused of pantheism while they in fact tended more toward panentheism. In modern philosophy, the classical pantheistic system is that of Baruch Spinoza (1632–77), who claimed that all reality is a single substance, and that thought and matter are only attributes of the divine substance—a substance that may have many other attributes that we are incapable of perceiving.

Paraclete *See* *Spirit, Holy.

Paradise A term, apparently of Persian origin, that made its way both into the literature of Israel and into the Greek of the Septuagint and of the New Testament. In its original Persian usage, it referred to an enclosed garden of pleasures, and it is in this sense that the Septuagint employs this term to refer to the Garden of Eden. Out of that usage, first rabbinic and then Christian literature began referring to the place of blessedness reserved for the faithful as "Paradise." Medieval theologians believed that Paradise, or Eden, was a place on earth, and therefore many ancient maps include its supposed geographic location. On the other hand, the frequent identification of Paradise with *heaven, and the manner in which such heaven was then seen, implied that the final Paradise was higher than the original Eden, and not identical with it.

Paradox A term whose Greek roots mean "against common opinion," and which is used in literature to refer to statements whose seeming contradiction point to a deeper reality—such as "sweet bitterness," or "saving one's life by losing it." In ancient philosophy, it referred to points at which logic seems to contradict fact—as in Zeno's famous paradox, that since space is infinitely divisible, movement is logically impossible. In theology, it was employed by Søren Kierkegaard (1813–55), and later by *neo-orthodoxy, to insist that all language about God is but an approximation, and never fully describes God's nature or God's activity. According to this view, at the heart of the Christian faith stands the paradox that Kierkegaard calls "the scandal of particularity," whereby the act of God's becoming incarnate in a particular man, at a particular time and place, has universal significance for all humankind, at all times and places.

Parousia A term of Greek origin, meaning "arrival" or "presence," and commonly used in Christian theology to refer to the "second coming" of Christ (*see* *Eschatology). While the early church expected the imminent return of Jesus, as that return was delayed several different positions emerged. Some have sought to explain this delay by declaring that conditions for the Parousia have not been fulfilled. Thus, for instance, some have felt that Christ will not return until the gospel has been preached in every land, and therefore have devoted themselves to translating the New Testament into every possible language, thus hoping to hasten the Parousia. Along similar lines, others believe that Jesus will not return until Israel is restored to its biblical boundaries, and therefore support extreme Zionism, not because they particularly respect Judaism, but rather because they believe that in so doing they hasten the return of Jesus—when, according to their expectations, all Jews will see the error of their ways! The delay of the Parousia has led others to try to determine the date for such return, thus developing dozens of schemes that have obviously proved faulty. Still others have reacted by declaring that the Parousia is just a symbol for the coming of the *kingdom, which is being established by Christian activity on earth. Finally, the majority of Christians through the ages have held that, while the return of Jesus in glory is part of Christian hope, it is not for us to try to discover when this will take place, and much less are we given the task of hastening the time; what we are to do, rather, is to live now as those who truly believe that their Lord will reign, and that God's kingdom of peace and justice will come.

Patripassianism (or Patripassionism) A name often given by their opponents to *modalism and *Sabellianism, on the basis that if there is no real distinction between the Father and the Son, one is led to the conclusion that the Father suffered in Christ—hence the word "patripassionism."

Patristics   The discipline that studies the writings, lives, and theology of the "fathers of the church"—a term that includes a number of "mothers." Their theology as a whole is sometimes called "patristic theology." There is no consensus as to the date on which the "patristic age" ends. Some extend it through the twelfth century, claiming that it ends with the advent of *scholasticism. Others limit it to the first eight centuries of Christian history. Most of the writings studied by this discipline are in Greek or in Latin, although significant numbers exist also in Syriac, Coptic, Armenian, and other ancient languages. Books dating, reviewing, and analyzing the writings of these ancient authors are usually called "patrologies."

Patronato Real   A Spanish term denoting the series of privileges and responsibilities that the popes gave the Spanish crown in relation to the emerging church in the "Indies." The Portuguese *Padroado* refers to similar arrangements vis-à-vis the Portuguese crown and its colonies. At the time of the "discovery" of the Western Hemisphere, the popes were too engrossed in European politics, and in the ideals of the Renaissance, to be burdened with the enormous missionary task that was opening before their eyes. Therefore, in a series of papal bulls—particularly under Alexander VI, who reigned from 1492 to 1503—they placed the responsibility for such missionary work on the colonial powers, whose sovereigns were given "royal patronage" over the emerging church in their colonies. Under these arrangements, all such missionary work was the responsibility of the crown, which would also collect tithes and offerings, and be responsible for all expenses of the church. (At the time when these bulls were issued, Europe did not yet know of the gold of Mexico and Peru.) The colonial powers had the right and the duty to establish dioceses and parishes, to found convents and monasteries, to determine who could enter their colonies as missionaries, and even to "present" to the pope those candidates whom the pope would then name as bishops for the churches in the colonies.

The net result of all this was that the newly founded churches in the colonies were arms of colonial policy, and were run from the colonial centers rather than from Rome.

At the time of Latin American independence, in the nineteenth century, this arrangement created serious difficulties for the Roman Catholic Church, for the newly established nations claimed for themselves all the ancient rights and privileges of the crown, and Rome was not ready to allow them to name their own bishops. The result was that dioceses remained vacant for decades.

Pelagianism   The doctrine of Pelagius, a learned and saintly British monk who went to Rome late in the fourth century and there raised objections to Augustine's doctrine of *grace (*see* *Augustinianism), which he felt undercut Christian obedience to God's *law, making *salvation totally dependent on God's *predestination and free gift of grace. While little remains of the writings of Pelagius, and therefore it is necessary to reconstruct his doctrines depending mostly on the testimony of his opponents, it would seem that Pelagius rejected the notion of *original sin, claiming that all children are born in a state of innocence similar to that of Adam before the *fall. Also, sin has not corrupted human nature to such a degree that a sinner no longer has the ability to refrain from sin, as Augustine held. On the contrary, sinners still retain the *freedom of the will necessary to accept God's grace, and therefore the *initium fidei*—the beginning of faith—is in the human will, and not in God's grace.

Pelagianism was repeatedly rejected, first by theologians such as Augustine and Jerome, and then by the Council of Ephesus (Third Ecumenical Council, 431), and by the Synod of Orange in 529. This did not mean, however, that Augustine's views on grace and predestination were accepted without further discussion, for *Semipelagianism still raised objections, and even after this too was rejected many ways were found to mollify Augustine's teachings on the matter.

For this reason, the accusation of "Pelagianism" has been leveled against their opponents by many who have sought to restore the Augustinian doctrine of grace and predestination. Thus, Luther felt that practically all the *scholastics were Pelagian, the orthodox *Calvinists gathered at Dort accused the *Arminians of Pelagianism, and the *Jansenists said the same about their opponents.

Penance   One of the traditional seven *sacraments of the Roman Catholic Church, commonly called "*confession"—although it involves much more than the act of confession of sins—and, after Vatican II, "the *reconciliation of the penitent." Traditionally, the sacrament of penance includes repentance for sin (see *Contrition; *Attrition), an act of acknowledging or confessing sin, and works of repentance that serve as a punishment or payment (*Satisfaction) for the sin committed and confessed. Since "penance" literally means "punishment," sometimes the term "penance" refers, not to the sacramental practice as a whole, but only to this last element.

It is clear that in the early church it was customary to confess sins publicly within the congregation. This was sometimes done in detail, confessing specific sins, and sometimes in more general terms. Grievous sins, such as idolatry, fornication, and homicide, led to the *excommunication of the sinner, who joined the official ranks of the "penitent" until such a time as proper satisfaction had been accomplished. At that point the penitent was officially declared forgiven, and was readmitted to Communion.

Apparently in the early church such repentance was allowed only once, and the process of satisfaction was so stringent that it often lasted a lifetime. However, as time went by the practice of penance evolved, with the confession of sins becoming more detailed, including all sorts of sin and taking place in secret, between the sinner and a priest. Beginning in the fifth century, and originally in the Celtic church, "penitential books" were produced to serve as guidance for priests hearing confessions. These included questions to be asked of the sinner, as well as the penance to be prescribed for each sin. A parallel development altered the original—and logical —order of the elements in the rite, so that it became customary for the priest to declare the *absolution of the sinner at the time of confession—such absolution being contingent on the sinner's fulfillment of the prescribed penance.

As the Middle Ages advanced, it became common to substitute one form of penance for another. Someone who was unable to go on a prescribed pilgrimage could perform special works of charity at home, or could provide the resources to make it possible for another person to go on pilgrimage. Such commutations were eventually called "*indulgences." At the time of the First Crusade, Pope Urban II proclaimed a "plenary indulgence" in connection with it. Then it became customary to grant special indulgences to pilgrims to Rome in specific "holy years." Eventually, the sale of indulgences became an important source of income for the church—and the precipitating factor in Luther's protest.

Pentecostalism   The name commonly given to a widespread movement derived from the *holiness movement and, through it, from the *Wesleyan, or *Methodist, revival. Like these predecessors, most Pentecostals espouse *Arminianism and the *freedom of the will.

While most accept traditional *Trinitarian theology, there is a branch of the movement that rejects such theology, partly on the ground that the doctrine of the Trinity is not found in Scripture, and insist on baptizing only "in the name of Jesus."

The theological trait characterizing the movement is the belief in a further experience after conversion similar to the "second blessing" of the holiness movement, but consisting in the outpouring or baptism of the *Holy Spirit on the believer—sometimes, particularly in the early stages of the movement, called a "third blessing" beyond conversion and sanctification. Such outpouring is manifested in outward signs, of which the most common is speaking in tongues—*glossolalia. This speech may be in actual languages unknown to the believer who speaks, or in "mystical" or "angelic" tongues whose meaning remains mysterious.

Other extraordinary gifts of the Spirit include healing and prophecy. For this reason, it is common in Pentecostal worship to set aside a time of prayer for the ill, often joined with the imposition of hands and anointing with oil. And it is also common in a Pentecostal service to allow anyone to speak who claims to have received a "word from the Lord" for the congregation—or to give testimonials as to what God has done in one's life.

Pentecostals are often considered fundamentalists. However, while Pentecostals do tend to be literalistic in their interpretation of Scripture, it would not be quite exact to call all of them "fundamentalists." *Fundamentalism is a conscious reaction against *liberal interpretations of Scripture. In contrast to this, most Pentecostals do not know of any such liberal interpretations, and therefore are not reacting against them, but simply practicing what could be termed a "naive" or "immediate" reading and interpretation of the text.

It is also common to think that the main trait of Pentecostalism is its emotional worship. There is no doubt that Pentecostal worship allows for freer expression of the emotions than does most traditional Christian worship. However, what makes Pentecostalism such is not so much its worship as its theology, insisting on the baptism of the Holy Spirit as an experience beyond that of conversion.

The movement itself began in the United States early in the twentieth century. While other events of glossolalia preceded it, the 1906 revival in Apostolic Faith Gospel Mission on Azusa Street in Los Angeles is usually credited with the birth of the movement. In a few years, it had spread throughout the United States and abroad, to the point that by the end of the century Pentecostalism was the fastest-growing form of Christianity throughout the world, and in several countries its membership had far exceeded that of more traditional churches.

Perfection   While in most traditional philosophy that which is "perfect" is incapable of change or improvement, this has not always been the view of Christian theologians. Thus, Irenaeus and other early Greek-speaking theologians taught that Adam and Eve were created perfect, but also that they were "like children": they had to grow and to develop in righteousness. In this view, perfection is more dynamic than in its more traditional understanding, allowing for growth and development.

The place of "perfection" in Christian life has been much debated, particularly since John Wesley (1703–91) and early *Methodism insisted on the need to preach perfection or "entire *sanctification" as the goal of the Christian life—not as something that one attains, but as a gift from God, just as salvation is a gift from God. Wesley himself did not believe that such entire sanctification was a common occurrence, and there were only two or three names that he mentioned when asked to give instances of entire sanctification. But he insisted that if such perfection is not preached as the goal of the Christian life, there is the danger that people will cease striving in the path of sanctification.

Wesley also made it clear that Christian perfection did not mean absolute freedom from sin and error, but only from sin committed willfully against the known will of God. And it consisted primarily in "perfection in love," rather than in obeying a set of rules or prohibitions. Furthermore, even those who have received this unparalleled gift must continue moving on to perfection—in which one may perceive an echo of the views of early Greek theologians, with whom Wesley was acquainted.

As *Wesleyanism developed after the death of Wesley, there were those who felt that the Methodist tradition was abandoning Wesley's emphasis on sanctification, and particularly on entire sanctification. This unease with the direction that Methodism was taking led to the rise of the *holiness movement.

Perichōrēsis   See *Circumincession.

Perseverance

In a theological context, usually the "perseverance of the saints." This doctrine, first taught by Augustine (354–430), holds that those who have been predestined for salvation will persevere to the end, in spite of every temptation and shortcoming. This is both a corollary of the doctrine of *predestination and a pastoral issue, for the doctrine of perseverance gives believers *assurance of their salvation and frees them from a constant preoccupation with it. Both Luther and Calvin agreed with Augustine on this point, as did the Synod of Dort (1618–19), which defined the perseverance of the saints as one of the essential characteristics of orthodox *Calvinism. It was rejected by the *Arminians, both because it was based on a view of predestination which they rejected, and because they feared that such a doctrine would invite believers to complacency. On this point Wesley and the tradition flowing from him (see *Methodists; *Holiness Movement; *Pen-

tecostalism) rejected orthodox Calvinism, insisting on the possibility of what is popularly known as "backsliding."

Person

A word whose meaning has changed drastically in modern times, and which therefore often hampers our understanding of earlier theological formulations. In contemporary usage, a "person" is a conscious individual. Thus, when modern writers speak of a "personal" God they mean that God relates with us as one person to another, that God is capable of love, mercy, and so on. And for the same reason, when we read of "God in three persons" (*Trinity) we tend to think in terms of three individual centers of consciousness, and therefore of three gods.

In earlier theology, however, the term "persona" had a different meaning. Introduced into Trinitarian and *christological language by Tertullian, it would seem that he understood it in a manner similar to that in which lawyers today speak of a "legal person." Several individuals constituting a corporation become a single legal person; and an individual variously incorporated becomes more than one legal person. When the term was translated into Greek, there were two options: *prosōpon and *hypostasis. The former was the name of a mask worn by an actor in the theater, and thus would have been similar to our word "role." In the course of a play, an actor could play several roles, and thus have several prosōpa. The other possible translation was hypostasis, a philosophical term meaning subsistence, or that which makes a thing exist. Significantly, by and large the majority of the Greek-speaking church rejected the term prosōpon in favor of hypostasis. Thus, in Trinitarian and christological contexts, a "person" is not an individual center of consciousness, as it is in modern usage, but is rather an eternal principle of subsistence within the Godhead.

Personalism

A name given in philosophy to any system that focuses on

the value of persons as the touchstone for understanding and interpreting reality. In theology, personalism is the name of a theological tendency that became prevalent in Boston University late in the nineteenth century under the leadership of *Methodist theologian Borden Parker Bowne (1847–1910), and later continued by Edgar S. Brightman (1884–1953). It became quite widespread in North American theological circles during the first half of the twentieth century, and could be said to have been the typical North American form of *liberalism. Like other theologies of liberal tendencies, personalism stressed human creativity and potential for good, and tended to underplay the power of *sin as a state of corruption of human nature.

Phenomenology The philosophical school founded by Edmund Husserl (1859–1938), who sought to develop a method of inquiry that would be totally objective and free from the influence of the researcher's own views or prejudices. In order to do this, the researcher must concentrate on the phenomena—that is, on events as they come to us, completely devoid of interpretation. As a result of this method, Husserl believed, one is able to attain to the essence of the matter, untainted by prejudices or judgments of value. This phenomenological method was very influential in the *philosophy of religion of the early and mid-twentieth century, when students of religious systems and beliefs sought to study them as phenomena that appear in human society, without seeking to evaluate or decide on the truth or falsehood of a particular doctrine, view, or practice. In more recent times, with the *postmodern critique on claims of objectivity and universality, Husserl's method has been criticized as being itself based on the very sort of prejudgment on the part of the researcher that the method sought to avoid.

Philosophy and Theology See *Reason and Faith.

Philosophy of Religion A discipline originating in the eighteenth century and seeking to apply philosophical methods to the study of religion. For this reason, there are practically as many philosophies of religion as there are philosophical systems. In general, however, philosophies of religion seek either to study the religious phenomena, experiences, and doctrines, or to propose an understanding of God and the world based on purely philosophical categories. In the first sense, during the early twentieth century the field was dominated by *phenomenology, and later by logical and linguistic analysis, often concentrating on the study of such categories as *myth and *metaphor. There have been a number of studies of *mysticism as it appears in various religious traditions, seeking to elucidate the common characteristics of mysticism, no matter its cultural, religious, and doctrinal context. In the second sense, philosophy of religion has sought to validate elements in religious worldviews that are traditionally based on *revelation. Thus, in the eighteenth and nineteenth centuries, the field was dominated by attempts to ground religion on Kant's ethical imperative, or on Hegel's dialectics, and in the twentieth century the focus shifted to analytical logic, *existentialism, and *process philosophy. (See also *Process Theology.)

Pietism A movement that first appeared in Germany under the leadership of Philipp Jacob Spener (1635–1705), mostly as a reaction to Protestant *scholasticism, seeking to awaken and nurture the personal faith of believers. The beginning of the movement is usually dated in 1675, when Spener published his influential book *Pia Desideria*. Here he expressed six "pious desires," which became the program for Pietism. The first of these was that Christians should organize into small groups to study Scripture in a spirit of devotion. Since Spener called these small groups *collegia pietatis*, this first point of the program, jointly with the title of the book itself, gave the movement the name of "Pietism." Second, Spener desired that the commonly held doctrine of the universal *priesthood of believers be made effective by entrusting *laity with the leadership of the small groups. Third, he hoped that believers would move beyond Christianity as a set of doctrines, and come to experience it as a living faith. As a consequence of this third point, the fourth would be that controversies among Christians would always take place within the framework of a spirit of love. Then, points five and six had to do with the pastoral leadership of the church: the fifth being that pastors be trained in the devotional tradition of Christianity and in the practice of leading a flock, and not only in theology and other academic matters; and the sixth, that the pulpit cease being a place for obscure and detailed theological disquisitions, and recover its role in inspiring, instructing, and feeding the disciples.

Although missions were not included among Spener's six points, very soon Pietism came to be known for its eagerness to share the faith with others, and thus was one of the fountainheads of the modern missionary movement among Protestants.

Platonism   Strictly speaking, the philosophy of Plato, who lived in Athens in the fourth century before the Christian era. More generally, however, the term is used for a long philosophical tradition that has had profound impact on Christian theology—in the *patristic age, particularly on the *Alexandrine school of theology, and eventually on most theological traditions (see *Neoplatonism). In the seventeenth century, a group known as the "Cambridge Platonists" sought to use Platonist philosophy as a tool to mediate between *Puritanism and the more traditional elements within the Church of England.

At the time of the advent of Christianity, Plato and his teacher Socrates were held in high regard by the Greco-Roman intelligentsia, and their philosophy pervaded much of popular culture in the Mediterranean basin. Thus, when Christians were criticized as uncultured people teaching strange and irrational doctrine, many responded by seeking to build bridges between Christianity and Platonism, and thus claiming that much of what Christianity taught was similar to what had been said earlier by Plato and other sages (see *Apologetics). While this did serve to present Christianity under a more favorable light, it also resulted in a Platonic interpretation of a number of Christian doctrines, particularly regarding God, the nature of Christian hope, and the manner in which knowledge is acquired.

Regarding the doctrine of *God, Christians found that much of what Plato had said about the Idea of the Good and the origin of the world could be used to promote both *monotheism and the doctrine of *creation. In the *Timaeus*, Plato had spoken of an absolutely impassible supreme Idea of the Good, and of a Demiurge who created the world under the inspiration of this supreme Idea. Using these themes, Christians began equating the Idea of the Good with God, and also speaking of creation much as Plato had done. This led to a view of God as impassible, impersonal, and distant, and of the one who created the world as a being who, while existing before and apart from the world, is lesser than the supreme Good. Such views stand behind the issues debated much later in the *Arian controversy.

Secondly, regarding Christian hope, Plato's notion that there is a higher world of eternal realities above the present world of shadows was soon joined with the Christian notion of *heaven or of the *kingdom of God, and Plato's doctrine of the *immortality of the soul came to take the place of—or to take a place next to—the Christian doctrine of the *resurrection of the body. Thus, what was essentially a hope for a triumph of God in the future was progressively transmuted into a hope of moving away from the present world into a higher one.

Finally, Plato's theory of knowledge (*see* *Epistemology), with its distrust of the data of the senses, dominated Christian theology from the fourth to the thirteenth centuries. Since Plato explained the possibility of knowledge on the basis of the *preexistence of the soul, and Christians soon rejected that option, the result was the *Augustinian theory of *illumination.

Pneumatology   Derived from the Greek *pneuma* (spirit, wind, breath) and *logos* (discourse, study), pneumatology is that heading in theology devoted to the doctrine of the Holy *Spirit. (Some confusion may arise on this matter, for sometimes in philosophical anthropology "pneumatology" has to do with the human spirit or soul.) It has been a much-neglected heading in traditional theology, and is receiving much closer attention in the twenty-first century, partly as a result of the enormous growth and impact of *Pentecostalism.

Pneumatomachians   *See* *Macedonians.

Polysemia   From the Greek *poly* (many) and *semeion* (sign or meaning), and thus referring to the variety of meanings that may be found in a text— particularly, in the field of theology, in scriptural texts. From a relatively early date theologians such as Origen (ca.185–ca.254) have claimed that biblical texts have a variety of meanings. In Origen's case, this was a hierarchy of meanings, so that the more one ascended in spiritual insight, the better one understood the text. Apart from such views, polysemia has traditionally been viewed as a flaw in the text, similar to ambiguity. Yet in more recent times, as scholars have become more aware of the impact of the reader and the reader's location and experience on the reading of a text (*Reader Response Criticism), and particularly under the impact of *postmod-

ern views, polysemia has come to be regarded, not only as inevitable, but also as the positive outcome of reading from a variety of perspectives, so that instead of speaking of a variety of mutually exclusive meanings there is a tendency to speak of the "aggregation" of meaning to a text thanks to polysemia.

Positive Theology   The name commonly given, toward the middle of the twentieth century, to theology based on *revelation and on the authoritative pronouncements of the church, rather than on *reason and common experience. It thus stands in contrast to *natural theology.

Positive Thinking   The doctrine of Norman Vincent Peale (1898–1993), a popular preacher and author who taught that one must not allow oneself to be overwhelmed by obstacles and difficulties, which can be overcome by "positive thinking" and with the help of God. Underplaying the power and prevalence of sin, both in its individual and in its social dimensions, Peale held that through his techniques of positive thinking, self-help, and emotional relaxation people could build their own happiness.

Positivism   A mode of thought promoted by Auguste Comte (1798–1857), who held that in the interpretation of the world humanity had progressed from a "theological" stage, in which explanations are based on the gods and their will, to a "metaphysical" stage, in which explanations are based on the supposed nature of things, to a final "positive" stage, on which conjectures are left aside in favor of strict empirical observation. By extension, "positivism" came to mean any system that, on the basis of a radical *empiricism, rejects *metaphysics, theology, or any other sort of thought that is not completely based on provable observation. For a time, "logical positivism" dominated much of the philosophical scene, claiming that a priori propositions such as those of mathematics and logics provide no information regarding the actual world, and that only a posteriori propositions, based on empirical observation and verification, provide such information. In consequence, the discourse of such disciplines as theology, ethics, and metaphysics was dismissed as not strictly false, but simply irrelevant and meaningless. Toward the end of the twentieth century, however, logical positivism was severely criticized for not applying to itself and its own basic principles the same skeptical criteria that it applied to other disciplines and philosophical systems.

Post-Vatican A term often applied, normally as an adjectival phrase, to the practices and theology of Roman Catholicism after the Second Vatican Council (1962–65). It is often contrasted with "*Tridentine" Roman Catholicism, which covers the period from the Council of Trent (1545–63) to the Second Vatican Council. Post-Vatican Catholicism tends to be much more open to the role of the *laity, making the *priesthood of all believers more effective, and seeing the church, not so much as a *hierarchy of prelates and priests, but rather as the pilgrim people of God (*see* *Ecclesiology). This is reflected in the *worship of the church, which is now in the vernacular, with greater lay participation, and with the priest facing the congregation in the act of consecration of the *Eucharist. Post-Vatican Roman Catholicism is also much more open to other Christian bodies (*see* *Ecumenism) as well as to other religions, providing more space for religious freedom, even in countries that are mostly Roman Catholic. Finally, its theology is much more missional, seeking to respond to the needs of the world, and no longer limiting itself to the more technical and *apologetic discourse that dominated earlier Catholic theology.

Postcolonial Criticism A type of cultural criticism, often analyzing literary texts produced in the colonial context both by the colonizers and by the colonized. In biblical studies, the term is used with a slightly different connotation, meaning the study of the manner in which colonial relationships have been reinforced and justified by certain readings of Scripture, as well as the manner in which Scripture may now be read from a postcolonial perspective. In some cases, this is paralleled with a discussion of the function of texts vis-à-vis the ancient empires in which they were produced and canonized.

Postmillennialism The view regarding the *millennium that sees it coming before the *Parousia, and preparing the way for it. In general, postmillennialists reject the notion that the millennium will come after great evil, and that therefore such evil is to be seen as God's preparation for the millennium.

While classical *liberalism was not overly concerned with the millennium, and seldom spoke of it, thus being generally "amillennialist," *premillennialists have often dubbed liberals "postmillennialists" on the basis that many liberals sought to improve society and the world as if they were seeking to bring about the millennium—and indeed, among classic liberals it was customary to speak of "building the *kingdom," or even of "bringing about the kingdom."

Postmodernity The new age that according to some has emerged or is emerging at the demise of *modernity. According to this view, as the world becomes more pluralistic, the foundational "metanarrative"—or basic *myth by which a worldview lives—of modernity is losing power. While modernity was characterized by an "epistemological optimism," believing that knowledge was an objective and ever-expanding reality leading toward the universal acceptance of its findings, postmodernity is quite skeptical of all metanarratives, of all claims to objectivity or universality, and particularly of all political, literary, or religious discourse that claims to represent the totality of reality, or to be free of perspectival bias.

In the field of theology, postmodernity has opened the way for a worldview that no longer sees the universe as a closed system of cause and effect, with no room for divine activity, as is the case with the modern metanarrative. On the other hand, by denying the value of any metanarrative, postmodernity may undercut attempts at correcting injustice or at promoting equality—for justice, equality, and the like are powerful notions only insofar as they are accepted by others as part of their metanarrative.

Potency   *See* *Act.

Potentia Dei absoluta   Part of a distinction, originating in the eleventh century but coming to the theological and philosophical foreground in the late Middle Ages, between two manners or levels of God's power: the *potentia Dei absoluta*, and the *potentia Dei ordinata*—God's absolute and God's ordered power. This was a way of escaping some of the difficulties caused by the notion of divine *omnipotence. If God is omnipotent, can God act contrary to logic? Can God change the principles of logic? According to God's absolute power, God certainly can. But God has determined that the divine omnipotence will function within certain parameters, and therefore within those parameters—God's ordered power—God cannot change the principles of logic. John Duns Scotus (ca.1266–1308), for instance, declared that, under the *potentia Dei absoluta*, God did not have to accept the *merits of Christ as infinite, nor to apply them to sinful humanity; but, within the parameters of the *potentia Dei ordinata*, God has indeed freely determined to accept the merits of Christ as infinite payment for all human sin. Other later medieval theologians carried this distinction much farther, claiming that arguments for the rationality of God's incarnation in a human being, while valid under the *potentia ordinata*, were

not absolutely true, for God could also have decided to become incarnate in a beast or in a rock.

Poverty   The theme of poverty and the poor came to the foreground of Christian theology during the second half of the twentieth century, when various theologies of *liberation, as well as the development of some extreme forms of free-market capitalism, brought attention to the growing inequality in standards of living throughout the world. Christian tradition has consistently held that poverty—in the literal sense of lacking the resources necessary to sustain life, in terms of food, shelter, clothing, and the like—is not the result of God's will, but of sin—even though not necessarily nor exclusively the sin of the poor. In *patristic literature, poverty is usually seen as the result of extreme wealth and the selfish use of power, and Christians are repeatedly called to share their goods with the needy. During the Middle Ages, such calls were not as radical as they had been in earlier times, and usually invited the rich to give alms to the poor. After the Reformation, as capitalism began to develop, the notion began to develop that the poor were such as a result of their own decisions, their sloth, and their lack of creativity, and that the rich were such thanks to their good qualities. The ancient view that extreme wealth and extreme poverty are two sides of the same coin was abandoned in favor of a different interpretation, namely, that the poor were simply "left behind" as the rich forged ahead toward progress and its benefits. The inequality among nations was expressed in a similar way, by calling some nations "developed" and others "underdeveloped." It was as a reaction against such views, and against the growing inequality in the world, that liberation theologies as well as *postcolonial criticism developed, both making poverty and dependent inequity significant subjects of theological discussion.

While throughout most of its history Christianity has deplored and sought to ameliorate poverty in this sense, there is another sense in which poverty has been praised and even sought. This is what is often called the "voluntary poverty" of *monasticism. Such "voluntary poverty" is one of the *counsels of perfection, not having the binding character of the commandments, but still pointing the way for those who seek a higher degree of discipleship. One of the traits of monasticism that has remained fairly constant through the many variations of monasticism itself has been the centrality of voluntary poverty. Voluntary poverty has often been inspired by the sense that it is easier for Christians to devote their lives to God if they are not overly burdened by possessions. Many monastics have seen possessions as an obstacle to contemplation, and have chosen extreme simplicity of life as conducive to contemplation. Then, a second reason for voluntary poverty has been what many reformers have called "the freedom of the church": if the church and its leaders have few possessions, and care little for them, this will make it more difficult for secular rulers to impose their will on the church. The history of monasticism is marked by an unending series of attempts to reform the institution by returning to a stricter rule of poverty after its own success and prestige had rendered it wealthy.

One of the most radical calls for voluntary poverty came in the early thirteenth century, as the monetary economy was being reestablished in Western Europe after long centuries of a barter economy. This was led by Francis of Assisi (ca.1182–1226) and the founders of other mendicant orders. Francis himself insisted that neither the friars as individuals nor the order as such should own anything. When this rule was mitigated by papal decree, the result was a sharp division between the more moderate and the more radical Franciscans.

The mendicant movement led to strong theological debates, particularly in the University of Paris, where teachers who did not have vows of poverty felt threatened by the newly arrived Franciscans and Dominicans. As a result of those debates, it was eventually decided that the imitation of "the poverty of Christ," while commendable, was not to be expected of all Christians, nor even of all clergy and other church leadership. This has been the stance of the Roman Catholic Church since that time. Protestants, on the other hand, by rejecting the distinction between commandments and counsels of perfection, have frequently forgotten the ancient calls to voluntary poverty, with the result that sometimes wealth is seen as an unambiguous sign of divine favor.

Pragmatism   A philosophical school appearing in the United States late in the nineteenth century and early in the twentieth, under the leadership, first, of Charles Sanders Peirce (1839–1914), and later of William James (1842–1910) and John Dewey (1859–1952). Reacting against the idealism of much earlier philosophy, pragmatism claimed that the value of a doctrine depended not so much on its truth as on its usefulness for life. Although this was not the purpose of its founding philosophers, in some circles pragmatism eventually developed into the theory that whatever works, producing the results intended, is acceptable, and that whatever does not produce tangible results is irrelevant. It is in this latter, less technical sense, that the term is generally used today.

Praxis   From a Greek word meaning action, activity, deed, endeavor. In contemporary theology it is commonly used by *liberation theologians who insist that it is not enough to speak or to believe the truth, for Christian truth is always truth in action, truth in deed. Thus, praxis is involvement in liberative action. However, praxis must not be confused with activism, for not all action is liberative, and praxis can take the form of resistance or of liberative reflection. (*See also* *Orthopraxis.)

Predestination   The view that God has determined beforehand who is destined for eternal life—in other words, who are the "elect" (*Election). While many theologians defending the doctrine of predestination avoid taking a stand on the matter, others affirm that the logical counterpart is also true: that God has also determined who will be eternally damned—in other words, who is a "reprobate." This latter position is usually called "double predestination," some being predestined to eternal life, and others to eternal damnation.

There is no doubt that the term "predestination" and its many derivative forms appear repeatedly in the Bible, particularly in Pauline literature. However, it was with Augustine (354–430), in his controversies with Pelagius and his followers, that the first fully developed Christian doctrine of predestination appeared (*see* *Augustinianism; *Pelagianism; *Semipelagianism). Augustine was convinced through his own experience that his conversion was not due to his own free initiative (*see* *Freedom of the Will), but rather to God's *grace working in him. He felt that the consequences of *sin are so great that sinners cannot do anything on their own that is not sin. They are free, but all their options are sinful. It requires a divine intervention to make it possible for a sinner to accept God's offer of salvation and new life. This intervention cannot be due to anything the sinner does or desires, but simply and solely to divine initiative. Without God's grace, humankind is nothing but "a mass of damnation." Were it up to us, in our sinful state we would simply reject God's grace. But God's grace is irresistible, working within the sinner to produce the act of conversion. As Augustine would say, before we believe God's grace "operates" in us so that we may believe, and after we believe God's grace "cooperates" with us so that we may produce fruits worthy of God. If grace is irresistible, and not all believe, this is because God grants this grace to some,

and not to others. God does this according to God's own hidden counsel, for no particular reason on the part of the sinner or the sinner's actions. Hence the doctrine of predestination. As to the number of the predestined, Augustine speculates that this must be the same number as the angels that fell, and that the purpose of predestining some sinners for salvation is to fill the number of the angelic host, decimated by sin.

Leaving aside this latter speculation, it is clear that Augustine's doctrine of predestination is not simply the logical corollary of God's *omniscience and *omnipotence, nor of speculations as to the nature of God. It is rather the result of Augustine's eager desire to attribute salvation only to God and to God's grace, and to make sure that believers cannot claim that they have believed because they were in any sense better or wiser than those who did not believe.

While in theory Augustine's doctrine was generally accepted, it was usually sufficiently mitigated or underplayed so as not to create much difficulty or reaction. It did become the subject of a bitter controversy in Carolingian times, when the monk Gottschalk revived its most extreme form, insisting on double predestination. The opposition was such that Gottschalk was imprisoned for the rest of his life. Later, most of the *scholastics—including Thomas Aquinas (1225–74)—affirmed the doctrine of predestination, but often mitigated it, or moved it to the background so it did not really affect people's views of the *ordo salutis.

Most of the Reformers, particularly Luther and Calvin, reaffirmed the essential points of Augustine's doctrine of predestination. For both Luther and Calvin, as earlier for Augustine, this doctrine is not the result of speculation on the nature and power of God, but rather an expression of the experience of salvation by God's grace, and grace alone. This was one of the main points of conflict between Luther and Erasmus, who argued that predestination destroys freedom and responsibility. However, in the course of time the *Lutheran tradition, while still holding to predestination, did not emphasize it as much as the *Reformed tradition. In the seventeenth century, Calvinist orthodoxy so insisted on predestination and its related doctrines of irresistible grace, the *perseverance of saints, and limited *atonement (particularly in its controversy with *Arminianism) that these became the hallmark of *Calvinism.

Finally, in the twentieth century Reformed theologian Karl Barth (1886–1968) disagreed with both Augustine and Calvin on this point, while still holding to a version of predestination. According to Barth, the great flaw in the traditional doctrines of predestination is that they focus on the individual's salvation, and not on Jesus Christ, who is the center of theology and the Elect One. The doctrine of predestination means that Jesus Christ is both the Elect One of God and God's Reprobate One, in that he carries the sins of all, and in him all are elected. While Barth's doctrine on this point is not altogether clear, it has been accused of leaning toward *universalism.

Predeterminism The doctrine that all events are predetermined. This is to be clearly distinguished from *predestination, which has to do only with the final destiny of persons, and not with other events. Predeterminism has a long history, for it was held by many *Stoics, and in more recent times there have been those who claim that, since the universe is like a vast machine, in which everything is caused by what existed before, all its movements and events are predetermined. Obviously, such predeterminism denies human *freedom as well as responsibility.

Although there is an important difference between predeterminism and predestination, in the heat of debate some have sought to defend predestination with arguments that are in fact predeterministic. Thus, the argument claiming that since God is *omniscient the future

is already set tends to prove, not only predestination, but also predeterminism. Most theologians who have defended the doctrine of predestination have taken pains not to lapse into predeterminism.

Preexistence of Christ Orthodox *Christology has long held that the One who was incarnate in Jesus existed before his physical, earthly birth. Those who oppose such teaching are usually called "adoptionists," meaning that they hold that Jesus was a human being like any other who was adopted into sonship by God. (Technically, however, the term "*adoptionism" is often reserved for the position of certain Spanish theologians in the eighth century who did believe in the preexistence of the Second Person of the Trinity, who was then incarnate in Jesus.)

In the great debates of the fourth century between *Arians and *Nicenes, what was at stake was not the preexistence of Christ, on which both parties agreed, but his *eternal* preexistence, and therefore his full divinity, which the Arians did not accept.

Preexistence of Souls The view that souls exist before being born in their present earthly body. Such theories are common in many religions and are often connected with the *transmigration of souls—the notion that souls undergo a cycle of various incarnations. In his dialogues, Plato presents Socrates as explaining knowledge (*Epistemology) as the result of the soul's having learned from the contemplation of ideas in the purely intelligible world. Among Christians, Origen (ca.185–ca.254) suggested that all souls were originally created as pure intellects, and that the physical world was created as a temporary abode for fallen souls. Those that fell farther have become demons, and eventually all souls will be restored to their primal nature as pure intellects. Augustine toyed with the idea of the preexistence of souls, but eventually rejected it—as has most Christian tradition since that time.

Premillennialism The position that sees the *millennium as coming after the *Parousia, usually after a time of great corruption known as "the great tribulation." Although premillennialism has medieval antecedents, contemporary premillennial views began developing early in the seventeenth century, and began increasing in popularity, first in England and then in the United States, in the nineteenth century. Their sense that the millennium will come after the great tribulation often leads premillennialists to ignore social and political structures of evil, or at least not to resist them, on the ground that such evil is inevitable as preparation for the coming of the Lord. In the late twentieth century, there were political leaders in the United States who argued that, since the return of Christ would set things aright, Christians should not be too concerned about the degradation of the environment, and should feel free to exploit it for their benefit.

Presbyterianism The name given to those branches of the *Reformed tradition that are characterized by a "Presbyterian" polity, that is, a form of government in which the "elders" or "presbyters," joined in a body often called "presbytery," perform the functions of a corporate *bishop. Presbyterianism originated in Scotland, and from there expanded to North America, Australia, New Zealand, and other lands colonized by the British.

Priesthood A priest is a person who intercedes before God on behalf of the people, often offering sacrifices. In the New Testament, and in early *patristic literature, those who led the worship of the church were never called "priests" in this sense; but by the middle of the third century some Christians were referring to such a person as a *sacerdos*, or priest.

The English term "priest" is a contraction of "presbyter," from the Greek *presbyteros*, elder. Although in English the adjective "sacerdotal" is commonly employed, there is no corresponding

noun. Since in the Middle Ages the presbyter also performed sacerdotal functions, a single word was retained in English, thus resulting in the term "priest" having come to mean both an elder or presbyter and one who carries sacerdotal functions. In most Christian tradition, ministerial orders have three major ranks: deacon, presbyter, and bishop. As a result, in English the term "priest" is the equivalent of "elder" or "presbyter" in those traditions that affirm the sacerdotal function of the person presiding at the *Eucharist, and is not employed in traditions such as *Presbyterianism, *Methodism, and other Protestant traditions that prefer to speak of the presiding officer as an "elder" or a "presbyter."

Priesthood of All Believers The principle that all Christian believers are priests by virtue of their *baptism. This has its historical background in the Old Testament view of the people of God as "a kingdom of priests," and in its continuation in the New Testament. Historically, however, this universal priesthood was eclipsed by the place of the ordained priesthood in the *hierarchy of the church. It was Luther, and the Protestant Reformation with him, that made this once again a fundamental point of Christian doctrine—although Luther himself, and most of the Reformers, were unable to find ways to make such universal priesthood an experienced reality in the life of the church. *Post-Vatican Roman Catholicism also recognizes the priesthood of all believers, although still insisting that the difference between this priesthood and that of the ordained clergy is more than a mere matter of degree.

Probabilism A view proposed by Bartolomé de Medina (ca.1528–80) while commenting on the *Summa theologiae* of Thomas Aquinas at the University of Salamanca. Medina extended to moral action a principle that had long been held in theological matters: just as it is lawful to hold a probable opinion, even though it has not been proved, so is it lawful to follow a probably correct course of action. The "probable" is not mandatory, since it has not been proved; but the very fact that it is probable means that it is somewhat reasonable, and therefore acceptable.

Later moralists extended Medina's argument by claiming that as long as it is not certain that an action is sinful it is lawful, and therefore "probabilism" became synonymous with moral permissiveness.

Process Theology A twentieth-century school of theology built on the foundations of the process philosophy developed by Alfred North Whitehead (1861–1947). Two of its leading figures are, in the first generation, Charles Hartshorne (1897–2000) and in the next generation, John Cobb (1925–). Process philosophy sees reality, not as a series of given objects, but rather as a continuum of events. Reality is constantly becoming—hence the name of "process." The fundamental building blocks of reality are events or, in more technical terms, "actual occasions." These actual occasions are guided by the highest principle of all reality, creativity.

Building on these philosophical foundations, Hartshorne, Cobb, and others have developed a theology that sees God, not as a static being, but rather as the actual occasion that includes all others. This means first of all that God too is becoming. God is not finished. God is part of the process. And it means also that all other actual occasions are part of God. However, since God transcends the totality of the universe, this system is *panentheistic rather than *pantheistic.

Thus, process theology sees God as both part of the universe and beyond it, but always in process. This means that the future is unknown and unpredictable, even for God, who is also being shaped by that future as it unfolds. This is one of the reasons why many traditional theologians have criticized process theology. On the other hand, this theology has gained supporters among believers, particularly because it means that God can actually respond to events, that God is free, and that it is possible to speak of God using the metaphor of a person who responds to other persons.

Since God is revealed in all actual occasions, everything is a divine *revelation, and therefore process theology usually has difficulty with the notion of a special revelation. For the same reason, process theologians tend to speak of Jesus, not as God incarnate (*see* *Incarnation), but rather as the clearest of the multitudinous incarnations of God in actual occasions.

Procession Apart from its liturgical usage, in which it refers to a devotional —sometimes celebratory and sometimes penitential—march toward the altar or toward a place of pilgrimage, the term "procession" is used in theology to denote the special relationship of the Holy *Spirit with the other two persons of the *Trinity: according to the Nicene *Creed, while the Son is "begotten" by the Father in what is usually called "*filiation," the Spirit "proceeds" from the Father. It was the Cappadocians—Basil the Great, Gregory of Nazianzus, and Gregory of Nyssa—who first sought to establish this distinction, claiming that, while the Son is begotten directly by the Father, the Spirit proceeds "from the Father, through the Son," by *spiration. In the West, however, Augustine understood this procession in a different way. For him, the Spirit was the bond of love joining Father and Son. This difference lies at the root of the controversy surrounding the *Filioque, when the Western church altered the creed to declare that the Spirit proceeds "from the Father *and the Son.*"

Proofs for the Existence of God
See *God.

Prophecy A Greek term that appears in the New Testament, as well as in the ancient Greek translation of the Old Testament, the Septuagint. It usually refers to speaking in the name of God, under divine mandate and inspiration. In the Old Testament, the prophets speak words of judgment, direction, and consolation. In the early church, they spoke in the midst of the congregation, proclaiming the word that God had given to them—thus "prophesying" was parallel to what today we call "preaching."

While sometimes the content of a prophecy refers to the future, that is not always the case. Prophets may speak of the future in the sense of warning their audience of impending judgment if they do not mend their ways, or of promising restoration after a time of suffering and punishment. They also speak of the final hope for a time of perfect peace and justice, for a new heaven and a new earth. Thus, without discounting the future-oriented dimension of some prophecy, it is necessary to correct the commonly held notion that a prophecy in the biblical sense is a foretelling of the future, or a program for the end times (see *Eschatology).

The early church, faced with the need to interpret the Hebrew Scriptures in line with their experience of Jesus Christ, had recourse to *allegorical and *typological interpretation, but also to the reading of some texts as a prophetic announcement of the coming of Jesus. Thus, and also through the influence of an environment in which oracles and fortune-tellers were common, the notion of prophecy became increasingly tied to foretelling the future, to the point that there are Christians who believe that every word called a "prophecy"—from Isaiah in the Old Testament to the book of Revelation in the New—is a detailed foretelling of future events.

Propitiation A gift or sacrifice offered to the Deity to appease divine wrath, usually in expiation for sin. In Christian tradition, it is common to speak of Christ's death as a propitiation for the sins of humankind. In *Tridentine theology, the *Eucharist is a "propitiatory" sacrifice offered before God. The language of propitiation is also employed frequently in connection with *penance. In all these instances, however, it is important to remember that, even when the death of Christ is conceived in propitiatory terms, it is God who offers the sacrifice, and thus the wrath of God to be appeased is the counterpart of God's love.

Prosōpon A Greek word originally meaning a face, or even the mask that actors wore in the theater. Since the Latin *persona* could have a similar meaning, the use of *persona* in *Trinitarian theology made some Greek theologians suspect that the Latins held to *modalism, as if Father, Son, and Holy Spirit were only three masks, or faces, of God. Similar confusion resulted when some Greeks used the term *prosōpon* in a *christological context. Eventually, it was decided that the Latin *persona* was best translated into Greek by *hypostasis, and *prosōpon* fell into disuse.

Protestant Principle A phrase coined by Paul Tillich (1886–1965) by which he meant the Protestant resistance to granting final and absolute authority to any creature, be it church, hierarchy, rite, or even the Bible. The reason for this is that God and God's grace exceed the bounds of any such authority, and therefore faith is always *paradoxical, knowing that its own content is not its true object. According to Tillich, this "Protestant principle" is not limited to Protestantism, nor even to Christianity, but is fundamental to any authentic faith. Needless to say, in thus speaking Tillich was expressing his own view of Protestantism, and ignoring or discounting the strong tendency in many Protestant circles to grant Scripture precisely the sort of ultimate authority that the "Protestant principle" should disallow.

Providence Often understood in the sense that God provides, "providence" implies much more. The word derives from the Latin *providere*, which means to foresee. For that reason, in its classical usage it often referred simply to God's *foreknowledge (*Omniscience). In most theological systems, however, it implies that God foresees and therefore moves events toward the intended end of *creation. It is in this sense that Calvin stresses the importance of providence—a stress that has become characteristic of the entire *Reformed tradition.

In some cases, providence is understood in such a way that it implies that all things are predetermined, and so there is no freedom (*see* *Predeterminism). Yet this is not necessarily the case, for it is possible to understand divine providence as the way in which God brings about the intended ends, both in spite of and through the actions of sinners.

Purgatory In Roman Catholic and Eastern *Orthodox doctrine, a place where the souls of the dead go to be cleansed and thus prepared for their admission into *heaven. The notion is fairly common in *patristic literature that believers who die and are not ready for the divine presence must undergo a process of purification before being admitted to that presence. Origen (ca.185–ca.254) and others speak of the soul's being purified "as if by fire." Augustine suggests the possibility that there may be a place for those who die in a state of *grace, but not quite ready to go to heaven. Very soon what Augustine proposed as a possibility became the commonly held doctrine of the church and its leaders, who then proceeded to systematize the notion of purgatory and its precise place in the order of salvation (*see* *Ordo salutis). According to the doctrine proclaimed at the Councils of Lyons (1274) and Florence (1439), purgatory is a place of temporal—that is, not eternal—punishment and purification, so that all souls in purgatory will eventually be admitted into heaven. In the West—but not in the East—the official position was defined by the Council of Trent (1545–63), which followed Thomas Aquinas (1225–74) in distinguishing between the guilt (*culpa*) and the penalty (*poena*) for sin. Although the guilt is erased by the grace of God, the penalty remains, and it is this that is paid in purgatory.

The notion of purgatory is closely connected with masses and prayers for the dead, so that they may be released from purgatory and admitted into heaven. The *indulgences being sold at the time of the Reformation were said to be able to release a soul from purgatory.

The Reformers rejected the notion of purgatory, mostly on the ground that it was based on a view of *salvation as based on *works, and not on grace. This led them also to reject prayers for the dead, on the ground that those in heaven do not need such prayers, and those in *hell have no use for them—even though prayers for the dead are already attested in some of the earliest patristic writings.

Puritanism Although in common speech "puritanical" has the connotation of moral rigorism, strictly speaking Puritanism was a movement that developed in England in the second half of the sixteenth century and the first half of the seventeenth. Its purpose was to "purify" the church from all "popish" practices, particularly in worship and in church order, thus restoring the "pure" Christianity of the New Testament—hence the name, "Puritanism." The movement eventually led to armed revolution, to the reorganization of the Church of England following *Presbyterian polity, to the Westminster Assembly, and to the execution of King Charles I in 1649. After the restoration of the monarchy, the Act of Uniformity of 1662 resulted in the deposition of approximately two thousand Puritan ministers. Long before that, large numbers of Puritans fled the country, and many eventually settled in New England.

Although most Puritans favored a Presbyterian form of government, there were also among them Congregationalists, Baptists, and Independents, as well as the socially radical "Levelers," the more *mystical "Seekers," who sought the direct inspiration of the Holy *Spirit, and the wildly *eschatological "Fifth Monarchy Men."

Quakers The name commonly given to members of the "Society of Friends of Truth," founded in England by George Fox (1624–91). After a long spiritual quest, Fox discovered what he called "the inner light," which he equated with Christ living in the believer. He claimed that, once one has this inner light, the traditional exterior means of *grace, such as the church and the *sacraments, are no longer necessary. It is more important to eat and drink spiritually from Christ's flesh and blood than to partake of the physical *Eucharist, which may in fact be a hindrance to true communion with God. Church buildings he simply called "houses with steeples." After much persecution, including beatings and incarceration, Fox gained a measure of recognition and tolerance, and his movement spread throughout England and eventually to America, where one of its members, William Penn, founded a colony that was to be run on Quaker principles.

From its very beginnings, the Society of Friends has held fast to *pacifist and egalitarian ideals, refusing to participate in violence, and allowing all who are moved by the *Spirit —including women —to speak in its gatherings. Government is to be by consensus, rather than by majority vote, so that when there is disagreement the entire society must await the guidance of the Spirit producing consensus. Religious freedom must be granted to all, including those who strongly disagree with Quaker or even with Christian principles. Throughout their history, the Quakers have been active in social causes, practicing charity and promoting justice.

Quietism In a general sense, any doctrine or practice that suggests that the role of humans in their relationship with God is one of absolute passivity—a passivity that is reflected in a similar attitude vis-à-vis the life of society. Strictly speaking, however, the term "Quietism" usually refers to a movement begun by Spanish mystic Miguel de Molinos (1628–96), whose *Spiritual Guide* advocated total passivity before God. All that the soul is to do is to wait for God to act. Moral or even devotional actions do nothing to bring the soul closer to God. Even prayer must be an attitude of silence rather than of speech, of patient awaiting rather than of petition. Quietism—or "Molinism," as it was also called—spread throughout Italy, where Molinos had lived, and particularly into France, where Madame de Guyon (1648–1717), in her *Short and Easy Method of Prayer*, popularized Molinos's views. As part of their passive devotion, Quietists tended to bypass the *sacraments of the church, and for this and other reasons were severely criticized by the Jesuits and others. The movement was condemned as heretical by Pope Innocent XI in 1687.

Rapture A common theme in *premillennialist *eschatology. Derived from the Latin for being "caught up," the doctrine of the rapture is based on 1 Thess. 4:15–17, and claims that the church will be "caught up" into union with Christ at the time of the *Parousia. Among those concerned over the rapture and the order of the last events, there are three diverging opinions regarding the chronological relationship between the rapture and the "great tribulation." "Posttribulationists" hold that the church will be part of the great tribulation, and only then will be caught up into union with Christ. "Pretribulationists" believe that the rapture will come before the great tribulation, and that the church will thus be spared the trials and pains of the tribulation— hence the popular fiction series "Left Behind." Finally, "midtribulationists" believe that the rapture will come during the great tribulation, after the rise of the *antichrist, but before the more drastic trials and judgments.

Rationalism   A very ill-defined term whose exact meaning depends almost entirely on its context. In general, it refers to any system of thought or methodology of research that employs *reason as the final measure of truth. This, however, may be understood in a number of different ways. The medieval Roman Catholic *scholastics, and in the seventeenth century the Protestant scholastic theologians, developed highly systematic and rational systems, but such systems were ultimately based on the accepted doctrines of the church and on authoritative *revelation, and not exclusively on rational argumentation. *Deism is a different sort of rationalism, setting aside all claim to revealed authority and trying to develop an entirely rational and self-evident "natural religion." Kant's critique of reason, undercutting the arguments of deists as well as others, may be considered a form of rationalism, even though what Kant did was in large measure to demonstrate the limits of reason. Many *liberal theologians of the nineteenth century were also rationalists, in that they sought to develop an interpretation of Christianity that could be expressed and defended in rational terms.

Reader Response Criticism   An approach to the study of texts, proposed late in the twentieth century, that focuses on the reader as an active contributor to the meaning of the text. Such readers may be considered at different levels. At a very basic level, presumably every text was written with a certain reader or readers in mind—often called the "implied readers"—and those addressees have impacted the very process of composition of the text. But even more, every reader impacts the meaning of a text, for the very act of reading is a construction of meaning.

Real Presence   An affirmation of the presence of Christ in the *Eucharist. Such real presence may be physical, as in the case of *transubstantiation or of *consubstantiation, or it may be spiritual, as in Calvin's *virtualism. The term is most commonly used to exclude the view that the presence of Christ in the Eucharist is merely symbolic, that Christ is present simply because the eucharistic symbols bring him to mind. However, in some circles that affirm the physical presence of the body of Christ in the consecrated bread and wine, anything short of the affirmation of such physical presence is considered a denial of the "real presence."

Realism   Regarding the nature of *universals, the position that claims that they are real. This position in philosophy has theological consequences. For instance, if the reality of individual humans is in their common nature, the impact of *original sin on all humankind presents no difficulty, and it is easier to understand how the death and resurrection of the one man Jesus can avail for all. Likewise, realism tends to see the church as a celestial reality, represented on earth by a *hierarchy, while the contrary position, *nominalism, tends to see the church as the community of believers (*see* *Ecclesiology).

Extreme realism believes that the universal is more real than the particular, and that the more inclusive a universal, the more real it is. The inevitable conclusion is *monism and *pantheism.

Reason and Faith   The question of the role of reason in faith has been debated throughout Christian history. In the early *patristic period, we already encounter those who felt that Christian *revelation had nothing to do with reason—at least with philosophical reason—and those who claimed there was a connection or a continuity between the two.

Typical of the first of these tendencies was Tertullian (ca.155–ca.220), some of whose statements to that effect have become famous: "What does Athens have to do with Jerusalem? What does the Academy have to do with the church?" And, "It is to be believed, because it is absurd." (The latter phrase did not mean that irrationality was the reason for accepting something, but rather that some things that Christians know cannot be understood, thus leaving no other alternative than simply believing in them.) Even before Tertullian, Tatian had held similar views. They could even claim to ground their position on the apostle Paul's famous words to the effect that divine folly is greater than human wisdom. This attitude has persisted over the ages, taking different shapes. It often appears, for instance, in connection with *mysticism, which sometimes claims that its experiences and visions supersede reason and logic. In the nineteenth century, Søren Kierkegaard (1813–55) adopted this attitude against the prevailing and overwhelming influence of *Hegelian *rationalism.

The second tendency is illustrated by Justin Martyr (ca.100–ca.165), Clement of Alexandria (ca.150–ca.215), and Origen (ca.185–ca.254), who agreed that the *Word who was incarnate in Christ was the same Word that enlightens all who come into this world, and whose wisdom therefore the philosophers of old reflected (see *Alexandrine Theology; *Logos). For them, the rational structure of the universe and of the mind is part of God's creation, and is therefore a preparation for the gospel. Thus, there is an essential continuity between faith and reason, and between philosophy and theology.

Although the impact of the second of these tendencies was such that much of Christian doctrine came to be understood in philosophical terms (*Neoplatonism), particularly through the influence of Augustine (354–430) and the false Dionysius the Areopagite (ca.500), in general the early Middle Ages followed the tendency of Tertullian, granting primacy to faith and devoting little effort to rational and philosophical speculation—with the notable difference that, while Tertullian believed that there was a conflict between philosophy and theology, the early Middle Ages in general were quite unaware of such possible conflicts. The most notable exception was John Scotus Erigena (ca.810–ca.877), whose extremely Neoplatonic speculations led him to a *monistic *pantheism that most of his contemporaries rejected.

It was in the intellectual renaissance that took place in the twelfth century that the issue came to the foreground once again, as a number of scholars began to apply "*dialectics"—essentially, *Aristotelian logic—to issues of theology. A leading figure in this enterprise was Peter Abelard (1079–ca.1144), and the enmity of Bernard of Clairvaux (1090–1153) against him was mostly due to Abelard's use of reason to explore issues on which Bernard was convinced that faith sufficed.

As part of the same intellectual renaissance, and slightly before the conflicts between Bernard and Abelard, Anselm of Canterbury (ca.1033–1109) combined faith and reason in a way that would become typical of the high point of the Middle Ages. He applied reason to matters of faith, not because he felt that without reason he could not believe, but rather because thinking about what one loves is an expression of that love. As he put it in a prayer, "I do not seek, Lord, to penetrate your heights, with which I cannot compare my mind; but I do wish in some way to understand your truth, which my heart believes and loves." And then he concludes: "I do not seek to understand in order to believe. I believe in order to understand." Thus, Anselm's famous *ontological argument for the existence of God, and his discussion of the reason for the *incarnation and the rationality of Christ's *expiation are not really attempts to prove these doctrines, but rather attempts to understand them more rationally.

In the thirteenth century, these issues were further complicated by the introduction into Western Europe of a number of long-forgotten writings of Aristotle, which often were joined by the works of his Muslim commentators, particularly Averroës (1126–98) (*see* *Averroism). Soon their philosophical outlook was seen in some circles as the epitome of philosophy and reason. The old *epistemology, based on Platonic and Neoplatonic (*see* *Platonism; *Neoplatonism) presuppositions, was severely questioned. The new philosophy challenged many of the traditional Christian doctrines, such as *creation *ex nihilo*, making them appear irrational. Some argued for the primacy of philosophy and reason over theology and faith. Eventually some sought to avoid conflict with ecclesiastical authorities by claiming what they said was Averroës's doctrine of a "double truth," so that what is true in philosophy may not be true in theology. Others reacted by rejecting most of the new philosophy.

It was at this point that Thomas Aquinas (1225–74) produced his imposing synthesis, employing Aristotelian logics and metaphysics, and yet retaining the freedom of theology to ground its work, not on such metaphysics, but on revelation. According to Thomas, everything that is necessary for salvation, God has revealed. Such truths are equally available to the most learned and to the most ignorant through divine revelation. Otherwise, people would be saved through philosophical knowledge. Yet, some of these truths that God has revealed are also attainable through reason (for instance, the existence of God), while others, such as the *Trinity and the *incarnation, are known only through revelation and faith. These are not rational truths in the sense that reason can prove them. But they are not irrational. They do not contradict reason, even though misguided reason may contradict them. Such is the case, for instance, of some philosophers' denial of creation *ex nihilo*. Here, faith warns us that the

philosophers have erred, and thus calls the philosophers to look again at their arguments, seeking the flaws that have led them astray.

While for Thomas the truths that can be known only by faith were only a few, their number grew as the Middle Ages moved toward their end. Eventually, William of Ockham (ca.1285–ca.1349) declared that natural reason is quite incapable of knowing anything about God. On these matters, reason and philosophy can prove no more than a possibility or a probability.

Luther himself was trained by philosophers who agreed with Ockham on this point. Thus, it is no surprise that he spoke of "dirty reason" as the cause of many an error in theology, and insisted on the primacy of revelation over reason. On the other hand, Calvin, Melanchthon, and several other Reformers had been trained in the *humanism that had developed in part as an attempt to overcome some of the negative characteristics of the late Middle Ages, and therefore were more appreciative of reason, not as a source for religious truth, but certainly as an instrument for understanding, organizing, and applying revealed truth.

The scientific developments of the centuries after the Reformation, coupled with the Thirty Years War and other atrocities based on conflicting claims to revealed truth, led to increasing *rationalism among European intellectuals. René Descartes (1596–1650) was willing to doubt anything that he could not demonstrate by means of an indubitable proof, and thus constructed a system that claimed to be purely rational and not dependent on revelation or any exterior authority. In Great Britain, the *empiricist tradition followed a parallel path, although basing its conclusions, not on pure reason working on itself, as did Descartes, but rather on the observation of phenomena and experiences. The result was a series of systems claiming to deal with traditionally religious matters in purely rational terms (*see* *Rationalism*). The most pervasive of these systems was *Deism, which often presented itself as a defense of Christianity, but was ready to defend only those elements in Christianity that could be proved by reason, and which therefore could be reduced to a "natural religion" that would be acceptable to thinking people of any culture or faith tradition.

All of this was brought to a halt by Immanuel Kant (1724–1804) and his *Critique of Pure Reason*, where he showed that reason, rather than reflecting things as they are, is an active participant in knowledge, making things fit into its own molds and categories. This made it impossible to claim that "pure reason" could say anything meaningful about God and other traditionally theological subjects. Having dethroned reason as the basis for proving religion and its doctrines, there were in essence three options open.

The first of these options—which Kant himself took—was to ground religion on something other than reason. Kant argued in favor of certain religious principles, such as the existence of *God and the *immortality of the soul, not on the basis of "pure reason," but rather on the basis of "practical reason," which serves as the ethical foundation of life. Later, Schleiermacher (1768–1834) claimed that the seat of religion is not in knowledge (reason), nor in action (ethics), but in the "feeling of absolute dependence."

A second alternative after Kant's critique was to base religion on revelation, and lay aside every claim to justify or prove it on the basis of reason or philosophy. This was the path followed in the nineteenth century by Kierkegaard, and in the twentieth by Karl Barth (1886–1968).

The third alternative was to agree with Kant on the active role of the mind in knowledge, and arguing that such is the very nature of all things and events, which are no more than the unfolding of the cosmic mind or reason. This was the path followed by Hegel (1770–1831) and his followers (*see* *Hegelianism).

More recently, the work of Karl Marx (1818–83) and of Freud (1856–1939) has shown that the mind is not as objective as *modernity thought, for social and psychological factors, many of them unknown to the thinker, play a role in shaping reason and its processes. The result has been a growing tendency toward greater skepticism regarding the supposedly "universal" and "objective" claims of reason, eventually leading to the critique of modern reason in the name of *postmodernity.

Recapitulation Also *anakephalaiosis*. Literally, to place under a new head. In patristic theology it does not mean, as in common usage, to summarize or to repeat briefly. It refers rather to the work of Christ in becoming the Head of a new humanity. The term, which appears in Ephesians, is used extensively by Irenaeus (2nd cent.) and others. Within their theological framework, Adam is the head of the old humanity, and in his sin we have all sinned. To undo the work of Adam, Jesus is offered as the new Head. The notion of the *church as the "body of Christ" is to be taken quite literally. Because he has conquered sin, and because he lives, believers, as members of his body, will also conquer sin, and will also live.

Since recapitulation involves recreating humankind under a new Head, much of the work of *redemption is an undoing of the *fall of the first creation, and therefore Irenaeus and the entire tradition that stresses recapitulation see many parallels between the story of Adam and that of Jesus. Adam was tempted through the woman, who was still a virgin; Jesus was brought into earth by a virgin mother. Adam was defeated through a tree; Jesus won his victory through the tree of the cross. Recapitulation thus becomes also an undoing of the history of damnation through a new history of salvation.

Reconciliation   The setting aside of alienation and conflicts, restoring broken bonds of love. In this sense it is often used in common speech, as when we say that a couple has been reconciled. In Christian tradition, it refers most often to the restoration of the bonds of love and obedience between humankind and God. In this case, some have spoken of reconciliation as both an abating of the wrath of God and a human return to God. In more recent times, however, the stress has generally been placed on the latter, on the ground that God's love for us has never ceased, and that therefore it was we sinners, and not God, who were alienated and had to be reconciled.

The term is also used for the restoration of the bonds of love and respect that ought to exist among humans, which have been broken by sin. In this context, the point is repeatedly made that reconciliation with God implies and requires reconciliation among believers.

Redemption   A concept common to many religions, which appears also in Jewish and Christian Scriptures. In the Old Testament, there are frequent references to redeeming a prisoner by paying a ransom, or to redeeming a piece of land by paying a debt on it. It is from this sense that the common usage today, as in "redeeming a coupon," is derived. Normally, redemption implies a purchase price, a ransom for the redeemed. However, in the Old Testament, Yahweh repeatedly redeems Israel, and it is not always clear that a price is paid for such redemption. In the New Testament, the work of Christ on our behalf is also called redemption, and it is in this sense that the term is most commonly used in Christian theology, where "redemption" is usually a synonym for "*atonement."

In using this term, however, it is important to remember that, although it certainly has connotations of ransom and payment, what Christ has done for sinners—his atoning work—is more than paying for sin, and that therefore in this case redemption means more than buying back or paying a ransom.

Reformata semper reformanda   A traditional dictum of the *Reformed tradition, that the Reformed church must be always in the process of being reformed by the *Word of God. Reformation is not something that has been achieved, and then the church can move to other matters. Reformation is the continuous action of the Word within the church. The church, like each of its members, is always in a process of *sanctification—and, as in the case of the individual, this is not the work of the church itself, but of God within the church.

Reformed Tradition   One of the main theological traditions stemming from the Reformation of the sixteenth century, the others being *Tridentine Catholicism, *Lutheranism, *Anabaptism, and *Anglicanism. The Reformed tradition is derived mostly from the Swiss Reformation, and most particularly Huldrych Zwingli (1484–1531) and John Calvin (1509–64), although it soon expanded to include churches such as the Reformed churches in Holland, the *Presbyterian church in Scotland and those derived from it, the French Huguenots, the Hungarian Reformed Church, several regional churches in Germany, and many others.

The Reformed tradition agrees with the Lutheran on most of the points separating Lutheranism from Tridentine Catholicism—the authority of *Scripture, *justification by faith, the *priesthood of all believers, for example. With Lutheranism, Catholicism, and Anglicanism—and in contrast with some elements within Anabaptism—it acknowledges the authority of the ancient creeds and councils, particularly on such matters as the *Trinity, the *incarnation, and infant *baptism. It differs from Lutheranism on its understanding of the *real presence of Christ in the *Eucharist, as well as by the emphasis it places on matters such as the sovereignty and *providence of God, the process of *sanctification, the use of the *law among believers, the impact of *sin on all of humanity and creation, and the obligation of Christians to participate actively in the ordering of civil society. Although at a later date the Reformed tradition became known also for its emphasis on *predestination, on this point Calvin agreed with Luther, and it was only a series of controversies among the Reformed themselves that led to what has become the particular stress of *Calvinism on predestination and its corollaries.

During the sixteenth century, the main point of disagreement between Lutherans and Reformed was the manner of the presence of Christ in Communion. Luther believed that this presence was physical, so that the body of Christ was present in, around, and with the bread, which, however, also remained bread (see *Consubstantiation). This means that all who receive the sacrament receive Christ—even though some do so for their own condemnation. Zwingli was more inclined to think of the significance of Communion in terms of symbols pointing to Christ and to his death, and rejected any notion of a real presence in particular connection with the eucharistic service. While Calvin disagreed with Luther, he also disagreed with Zwingli, for he believed that Christ was really present in the Eucharist, but that this presence was spiritual, revealed to believers by faith. The body of Christ is in heaven, and it is by virtue of the Holy Spirit (see *Virtualism) that the believer is joined to that body—taken to heaven, as it were—and receives its benefits. Thus, there have always been within the Reformed tradition two conflicting views on the eucharistic presence of Christ, a situation that continues to this day.

The Reformed emphasis on the sovereignty and providence of God implies that within this tradition there is great confidence that God is working out the divine purposes even while sin seems to prevail, that evil shall be overcome, and that believers should trust God on this point.

The Reformed emphasis on sanctification comes largely from Calvin, who was convinced that Christianity is much more than a way to be saved. While he agreed with Luther that salvation is by an unmerited act of God's grace and does not require justice or works on the part of the sinner, he was also convinced that justification is only the beginning of a process whereby God is working to make people what they were intended to be. The final goal is not just to save the souls of sinners; it is also to make them more like God. For this reason, while the great danger of Lutheranism carried to an extreme is *antinomianism, the parallel danger within the Reformed tradition has always been legalism.

Closely connected with this latter emphasis is the Reformed stress on the positive value of the law for the life of the believer. Both Luther and Calvin, with Paul and many others, saw the law as a means to lay sin bare, to show human insufficiency, and thus to point to its counterpart, the gospel. Both believed that the law has a place in shaping civil society. But Calvin, much more than Luther, stressed the need for Christians to study the law of God as guidance in the process of sanctification (see also *Law, Third Use of).

Finally, on the matter of the pervasive impact of *sin Luther and Calvin tended to agree, but while much of the Lutheran tradition has laid little stress on this point, it has become one of the characteristic traits of the Reformed tradition, jointly with a similar stress on predestination. This was the result of a series of controversies that led in the Netherlands to the Synod of Dort (1618–19), and in England to the Westminster Assembly (1643). There it was established that orthodox *Calvinism must affirm, not only the doctrine of absolutely unconditional predestination, but also that *grace is irresistible, that humans are totally depraved (*Depravity, Total); that Christ died only for the elect (*Atonement, Limited); and that, since their faith is based on the divine decree of predestination, the saints will persevere and not fall away (*see* *Perseverance).

On the ordering of society, the Reformed tradition has historically been much more proactive than the Lutheran. Luther held that there are "two kingdoms," one civil and one religious, and that while Christians belong to both, that distinction must always be kept. For this and a number of other reasons, Lutheranism has tended to be politically more conservative than the Reformed tradition. In contrast, Zwingli died in the field of battle, and ever since the Reformed tradition has been involved in movements of rebellion in places such as Scotland, England, the Netherlands, and even the British colonies in North America. Quite often, these rebellious movements have set the goal of reforming society so as to bring it into greater agreement with the will of God—which may be seen as the sociopolitical side of the doctrine of sanctification.

Regeneration Literally, "new birth." Christians have always declared that it is necessary to be born anew, as Jesus told Nicodemus. However, the manner of such birth, and in particular its connection with *baptism, is a point of wide disagreement. It is clear that in early *patristic times baptism was closely joined with regeneration, as a dying to the old life and being born to the new. However, as the civil society became coextensive with the church, so that being born into the world was practically tantamount to being born into the church; as this was reflected in the practice of baptizing every infant shortly after birth; and as the efficacy of baptism came to be understood in almost mechanical terms, there was no need to emphasize regeneration, for this theoretically took place in every infant in the very act of being baptized. It was at the time of the Reformation that a wide variety of views emerged regarding regeneration. The *Tridentine Roman Catholic Church insisted on the efficacy of baptism as regeneration. At the other extreme, most *Anabaptists saw baptism as a sign following the new birth, and not effecting regeneration itself, which is an action of the Holy Spirit in the believer. Most in the *Anglican, *Lutheran, and *Reformed traditions, while also stressing the initiative of the Spirit in regeneration, retained infant baptism, usually interpreting it as an effective promise of regeneration. However, as time passed, these very traditions tended to speak less of the need for regeneration, thus prompting a series of movements in their midst that insisted on the need for new birth, and which were often regarded askance by the more established elements in each of those traditions. Some such movements, drawing attention to regeneration, are *Pietism, the Moravians, the *Methodist revivals, and the Great Awakenings in the United States. It is mostly as a result of these movements that the subject of a new birth or regeneration has been brought once again to the foreground.

Religionsgeschichtliche Schule Literally, the "school of the history of religion(s)." This was a movement that flourished late in the nineteenth century and early in the twentieth, whose purpose was to apply to the early history of Christianity the same historical criteria that are applied to the study of any ancient movement or event. Also, the growing contact with other religions, as a result of missionary work and of colonialism, led many to explore the parallelisms and differences among various religions. While many of the conclusions of its early proponents (Wilhelm Bousset, 1865–1920; Johannes Weiss, 1863–1914; Hermann Gunkel, 1862–1932; Ernst Troeltsch, 1865–1923) have been questioned by later scholars, their general methodological principles impacted historical scholarship well into the twentieth century.

Remonstrants   Another name by which the original Dutch *Arminians are called. The name is derived from the *Remonstrance*, a document they signed in 1610. While on many points their differences with the more traditional *Calvinists was subtle, they insisted on the point that Christ died for all (*Atonement, Limited), and that *grace is not irresistible. These became two of the crucial points at which their teachings were rejected by the Synod of Dort.

Repentance   The recognition, rejection, and abhorrence of one's sin. In the strict sense, repentance implies *contrition, although some theologians have argued for the value and even the sufficiency of *attrition. The Greek word in the New Testament that is usually translated as "repentance" in fact means also turning away from sin, and thus may also be translated as "conversion." Since the Vulgate translated it as *penitentia*, the ensuing sacrament of *penance laid particular stress on the penitential aspects of repentance, and on the penalty that follows sin and its *confession.

Reprobation   *See* *Predestination.

Resurrection   The notion that the dead will rise again does not appear in Jewish literature until fairly late—no earlier than the end of the third century BCE—and even then it was strongly contested by the more traditional elements within Judaism. During New Testament times, while the Pharisees believed in it, the Sadducees rejected it, and in this point Jesus and the early church sided with the Pharisees. From the very beginning, there was lack of clarity as to the relationship between the bodily resurrection of the dead and the continuing life of the soul after death (*see* *Immortality of the soul). Such ambiguity has continued throughout most of Christian history, with those who are most influenced by Hellenistic thought and philosophy stressing the continuing life of the soul, and others reminding them that in the New Testament Christian hope is expressed more often in terms of the resurrection of the dead than in terms of the continuing life—much less the immortality—of the soul.

For Christians, the resurrection of Jesus is much more than the "happy ending" of the story. It is the beginning of the final resurrection. In being raised from the dead, Jesus not only proved who he was, but also accomplished part of what he was sent to do. His resurrection is the dawning of the *kingdom of God in the midst of history. For this reason, Christians gathered on the first day of the week, the "day of the Lord" or the day of his resurrection, in order to join with him in a holy meal (*Eucharist). In that sense, every Sunday was Easter. When eventually the Christian or liturgical *year developed, one particular Sunday was set aside as the Great Easter, one of the two foci around which the liturgical year is built.

Revelation   God's self-disclosure. The principle that God can only be known through God's self-disclosure or revelation is common throughout the history of Christian theology. Yet, it is also clear that throughout the ages and in various cultural and historical contexts people who have never heard of the Judeo-Christian tradition have some notion of God or gods. This has led many Christian theologians to distinguish between "general" and "special" revelation, the first being that which is available to all human beings through their own experience, and the latter being that which is specifically available through Scripture and in the person of Jesus Christ.

That something may be known of God by contemplating the wonders of creation is a common theme in the Judeo-Christian tradition, clearly expressed in Psalm 19:1: "The heavens are telling the glory of God; and the firmament proclaims his handiwork." Likewise, Paul (Rom. 1:19–20) speaks of certain things about God being evident from the very beginning through the things that God has made; and, furthermore, that the Gentiles have a law written in their hearts (Rom. 2:15). Thus, it is possible to say that something may be known of God by looking both at nature and at the inner life and conscience.

On the other hand, it is also clear that when looking at nature one sees the law of tooth and fang, the survival of the fittest, the destruction of the weak, and other such things that could be interpreted as signs of a God very different from the loving creator of Scripture. And likewise, it is clear that human conscience can be twisted and manipulated in such a way as to justify whatever we wish (*Depravity, Total).

For these reasons, many Christian theologians affirm that such "general revelation" may be misleading, that the psalmist is speaking as a person of faith, part of a people who have received God's "special" revelation, and that in the best of cases any "natural" knowledge of God suffices only to condemn, and never to save. Luther, for instance, referred to such knowledge of God as knowing only "the left hand," the word of condemnation, and never revealing the word of love and salvation. Others have held that whatever good and truth people know apart from Scripture and the preaching of the gospel, they know because of the revelation in them of the *logos or *Word that was in Jesus Christ, and that therefore in this sense all revelation and even all knowledge is "special," and even christocentric.

For most Christians, the "special" revelation of God is that which we can only know because we have heard and accepted the gospel. Its center and essential content is Jesus Christ. It is attested in *Scripture. It is appropriated by the work of the Holy *Spirit.

Yet matters are not so simple. There is also the question of the degree to which in every revelation God is both revealed and hidden. It is clear that God is far above human understanding, and that "no one can see God and live." Therefore

God's self-disclosure is always given in hiddenness, for the revelation of the divine is *accommodated to human ability to see and to understand. The mystery is unveiled, and yet remains. Luther expressed this quite starkly by contrasting a "theology of glory," which errs in trying to see God as God is in glory and power, and a proper "theology of the cross," which sees God in suffering, in weakness, and in hiddenness.

Rule of Faith   Literally, the *canon of faith, the rule of faith was a summary of the main tenets of Christian belief that circulated in the early church, at least by the second century, and to which several Christian writers of the period attest. It seems to have been devised as a shorthand method to determine what doctrines were to be rejected, so that believers who did not have all of Scripture at hand, and who were not sophisticated in theological matters, could recognize and reject false teaching. It does not seem to have been a fixed text, but rather a list of items, with some flexibility allowed, for ancient writers quote it in a number of different ways. Some of these summaries of the rule of faith are so reminiscent of the Apostles' *Creed that it seems likely that the baptismal creed of the church of Rome—the Old Roman Symbol, from which the present Apostles' Creed evolved—was an expression or a condensation of the rule of faith.

Sabbath   The seventh day of the week, which the law of Israel commanded should be kept as a day of rest. Although it was also a day for worship and meditation, the emphasis lay on rest. For the same reason, the land was to be allowed to rest one out of seven years, in a "Sabbath year." While the New Testament repeatedly reports that the early Christians gathered on the first day of the week (Sunday), there is no indication that they rejected the practice of keeping the Sabbath. Apparently the Sabbath was still kept by Jewish Christians, as by all Jews; but they also gathered on Sunday—which they often called "the Lord's Day"—to celebrate the *resurrection of the Lord by breaking bread (*see* *Eucharist). As the church became increasingly Gentile, Sabbath-keeping was abandoned, and Sunday became both a day of worship and a day of rest. Much later, in their attempt to restore ancient biblical practices and to reject all that had evolved through tradition, *Puritans and others began applying the Old Testament laws regarding the Sabbath to the Christian day of worship, Sunday, thus making it a day when certain activities were forbidden. Finally, some among them, in an effort to carry the movement of biblical restoration even farther, began insisting that the day of Christian worship and rest should not be Sunday, but Saturday, the seventh day of the week. In this, they have been followed by several groups that insist on keeping the seventh day as the time set aside for worship, and are therefore called "Sabbatarians." The largest of these is the Seventh-Day Adventists.

Sabellianism The most common name given in antiquity to *Modalistic *Monarchianism. It is impossible to know exactly what Sabellius (second and third centuries) taught. He certainly believed that the Father, Son, and Holy Spirit are but three modes in which God is manifest. Perhaps all he did was include the Spirit in a discussion that until his time had dealt almost exclusively with the Father and the Son. Possibly he understood the *Trinity as three successive modes in which God is manifest.

Sacrament A term derived from the Latin *sacramentum*, meaning an oath of allegiance, and employed in the early Latin-speaking church to translate the Greek *mystērion*, which the Greek-speaking church used to refer particularly to the *Eucharist, but also to *baptism and to other rites. Augustine (354–430) defined a sacrament as "the

visible form of an invisible *grace," and most traditional definitions include words in the sense that a sacrament is "an outward and visible sign of an inward and spiritual grace."

For centuries, the term "sacrament" was used rather loosely. Augustine, for instance, spoke of the Lord's Prayer, the creed, and several other elements in Christian worship as sacraments. Hugh of St. Victor (1096–1141), in his treatise *On the Sacraments of the Christian Faith*, lists no less than thirty, including in his list anything that "by similitude represents, by institution signifies, and by sanctification contains, a certain invisible and spiritual grace." However, he paid special attention to seven: baptism, confirmation, Communion, penance, extreme unction, marriage, and ordination, thus showing that the process by which the official number of sacraments was fixed at seven was well advanced. Slightly later, Peter Lombard (died 1160) listed the same seven. Since his four books of *Sentences* became the most widely read textbook on theology, this number prevailed, and was officially fixed in 1439, by the Council of Florence. The Eastern Orthodox churches were represented there, and they too count the number of sacraments as seven. The Protestant Reformation tended to reserve the title of sacrament for the *Eucharist and *baptism, which could be shown to have been instituted by Christ, even though most of the others were retained as rites of the church—and the Church of England listed all seven, while also declaring that baptism and the Eucharist were the two "principal" sacraments. Some of the more radical elements within Protestantism rejected the term "sacrament," which they saw as "popish," and preferred to speak of the "ordinances of Christ." Others added footwashing as a sacrament instituted by Christ. Eventually, some groups, particularly the *Quakers, rejected the physical sacraments altogether.

As to the efficacy of the sacraments, standard Catholic doctrine declares that they work *ex opere operato, so that their efficacy does not depend on the virtue of the person administering them. As to the recipient of the sacrament, if there is no faith and repentance, the sacrament is still there, but is not efficacious—and may even work for the recipient's damnation. Medieval theology, beginning in the thirteenth century, also declared that a sacrament consists of matter and form. In the Eucharist, for instance, the matter is the bread and wine, and the form are the words of institution. In baptism, the matter is the water, and the form is the Trinitarian formula. Both of these have to be present in order for the sacrament to be truly such and to be valid. There were ambiguities, however, in determining what the "matter" was in sacraments such as marriage and *penance. Among Protestants, there are wide disagreements regarding the efficacy of the sacraments. Some see them as actually effecting what they represent—thus, for instance, baptism effects the new birth. Some see them as an effective sign of the promises of God, bringing the believer to those promises. Some see them as a mere symbol or representation.

Sacramental   Besides its obvious use as an adjective for things referring to the *sacraments—as in the phrase "the sacramental wine"—the word "sacramental" as a noun refers to rites, practices, and objects that aid or express the faith of the church, but are not considered sacraments. Such are the sign of the cross, the benediction, liturgical vestments, prayer vigils, the rosary, and many more. Some Protestants also apply the term to rites that Roman Catholics consider sacraments, but Protestants do not, such as matrimony and the anointing of the sick.

Salvation   *See* *Soteriology.

Sanctification   The process whereby a believer is brought closer to the will of God. In *Tridentine Roman Catholicism, sanctification is connected with *justification in such a way that the latter tends to be made dependent on the former. Sanctification is the process whereby God, through *grace cooperating with the believer, makes the sinner just and therefore able to abide in God's presence. This was the generally accepted medieval doctrine against which Luther protested, declaring that sinners are justified by the attribution to them of the *merits of Christ, and that therefore a justified sinner is still a sinner, no less than before justification (see *Simul justus et peccator; *Justice, Imputed). Although Luther believed that God works in the justified sinner to mold life and character, he feared that too much emphasis on sanctification would lead back to justification by *works, as if justification depended on one's holiness. Calvin, while agreeing with Luther on his understanding of justification, held that the event of justification, where the justice of Christ is imputed to the sinner, is to be followed by the process of sanctification, whereby the *Spirit conforms the believer to the will of God. Yet even then, any holiness that believers may achieve does not make them worthy of the *grace of God. In this process, Calvin did speak of the believer's moving toward perfection as the goal of the Christian life, even while also insisting that such perfection is unattainable in this life. In this regard, Wesley (1703–91) disagreed with Calvin. He too believed that justification is an event, and sanctification a process that builds on justification; but he insisted on the need to preach and teach Christian *perfection, or "full sanctification," lest the call to sanctification sound hollow and unattainable. He did not believe that many were actually "perfected on this life," and when pressed he could point to no more than three or four names; but he insisted on the need to present full sanctification as the goal of Christian life. It is out of this *Wesleyan emphasis that the *holiness movement emerged, part of it claiming that the "second blessing" of full sanctification is much more common than Wesley himself thought.

Satan The original meaning of the term in Hebrew is simply "adversary," and as such appears several times in the Old Testament, usually referring to people. However, in some of the more recent books of the Old Testament the "adversary" is represented as the enemy of God, or at least as one who questions and tests the faithfulness of believers. By the intertestamental period, particularly in *apocalyptic literature, the figure of Satan and his angels becomes more prominent, as it is also in the New Testament. While Scripture does not explicitly say that Satan is a fallen angel (the various texts that have been interpreted in that sense may well have other meanings), this notion is fairly common both in early Christian and in rabbinic writings.

In discussions of Satan and his power, Christian tradition has generally sought to avoid two extremes. On the one hand, it has made it very clear that the existence of Satan is not to be understood in *dualistic terms, as if there were two eternal principles, one of good and one of evil. Even Satan is God's creation, and in the end even Satan will be subjected to God's power. On the other hand, it has also made it clear that Satan's opposition to God is real, that evil is truly an opponent of God, and not a sham (see *Theodicy).

Satisfaction A payment made in order to expiate a fault. By the third century it was fairly common to speak of making satisfaction before God by means of fasting, caring for the needy, and other good works. Eventually this notion was applied to the atoning work of Christ (see *Atonement; *Expiation), and this view received its classic formulation in Anselm's (ca.1033–1109) treatise on Why God Became Human [Cur Deus homo?], thus resulting in the dominance throughout the Middle Ages, and even later, of the "substitutionary" or "juridical" theory of atonement.

The notion of satisfaction also plays a part in the theory and practice of *penance, for *repentance and *confession must be followed by satisfaction for the sins committed.

Schism A break in the unity of the church, usually manifested in the creation of competing organizations—rival bishops, denominational bodies, and the like. It does not necessarily imply a difference in doctrine, as does the term "*heresy." In the ancient church, and still in Eastern *Orthodoxy and Roman Catholicism, its most visible sign is the breaking of communion, so that the separated parties can no longer partake of the same *Eucharist. This break in communion is signified by deleting each other's names from the diptychs—the list of names for which prayer is made at the *Eucharist.

Scholasticism A theological method that developed in the medieval schools, particularly universities, beginning in the twelfth century, but reaching its apex in the thirteenth and fourteenth. The name itself, "Scholasticism," was given to it at a later date, by humanists who felt that this type of theology was purely theoretical and irrelevant, good only for the schools—just as they thought that the entire period between antiquity and themselves was irrelevant, and they therefore called it the "Middle Ages."

Scholasticism was born precisely at the time when cities began to grow, after long decline during the early Middle Ages. As a result, the old monastic schools were overshadowed by the cathedral schools, and eventually by the universities that developed from them. Thus, the two main forerunners of Scholasticism, Peter Abelard (1079–ca.1144) and Peter Lombard (ca.1095–1160), both taught in connection with the Cathedral of Paris, while Thomas Aquinas (ca.1225–74), commonly regarded as the high point of Scholasticism, taught in the University of Paris.

As most earlier theology, Scholasticism based its work on the authority of written texts, to which it then applied *reason—particularly, *Aristotelian logic. These written texts were essentially the Bible, the writings of the "fathers" of the church (*Patristics), and the philosophers—particularly, after his reintroduction into Western Europe, Aristotle. The basic textbook for scholastic theologians was the *Four Books of Sentences*, by Peter Lombard, which was essentially an ordered compilation of texts dealing with each heading of theology.

However, such texts did not always agree. Peter Abelard had clearly shown this in his book *Sic et non* [Yes and No], in which he posed 158 questions and then offered a series of quotes in which various authorities seemed to respond to those questions in a contradictory manner. Apparently his purpose was not to question the authority of such texts, but rather to point to the need to work more carefully with them. This was not well received, and was one of the many reasons for what Abelard called his "calamities."

The scholastics, however, did take up Abelard's challenge. Thus the method developed of posing a question, giving a series of arguments and quotations leading to one answer, and another series in the opposite direction, then offering a solution, and finally responding to the objections raised by the arguments that would seem to prove the opposite of the solution. This was often done in the form of *quaestiones disputatae*—debated questions—an exercise that took different forms, but in which essentially the teacher posed a question, the more advanced students offered arguments for both sides, and then the teacher offered his solution and his response to the objections raised. Quite often this was done following the *Sentences* of Peter Lombard, and therefore the works of most scholastic teachers include a *Commentary on the Sentences*. Or a teacher could develop his own overview of theology, also following the scholastic method, and resulting in the grand "*summas*" of the Middle Ages, of which

the most famous and influential is the *Summa theologiae* of Thomas Aquinas.

In the fourteenth century, and even more in the fifteenth, Scholasticism moved to the discussion of ever more subtle distinctions, becoming increasingly distanced from the life of the believers, and thus resulting in the scorn of the humanists who eventually gave it its name.

In the seventeenth century, there developed among Protestants a sort of theology that, by its attempts to classify all matters and to discuss them in absolutely logical order and in minute detail, by its connection with the universities, and by its use of philosophy, earned the name—usually pejorative—of "Protestant scholasticism." (*See* *Orthodoxy.)

Scripture   From the Latin *scriptura*, writing. Most major religions have sacred writings that help define them and preserve their continuity through the centuries. In some cases, the claim is made that these sacred writings were directly given or dictated from heaven, or by an angel. In others, the normative writings are simply the sayings and stories of the ancient sages of the faith.

Christian Scripture includes both the sacred writings of the Hebrews—which Christians call the Old Testament—and specifically Christian writings—the New Testament. While there has long been a general consensus among Christians as to which writings are to be considered "Scripture" in the authoritative sense, there have always been differences on some specific points.

Regarding the Old Testament, Christians generally accept the authority of the Jewish *canon, with its three main divisions of Law, Prophets, and Writings. However, since this canon was actually established in the year 90, after Christianity had come onto the scene, it does not include a number of books that some Jews had earlier considered authoritative, and which Christians had also used as authoritative. Hence the difference between the Protestant canon of the Old Testament, which coincides with the Jewish canon, and the Roman Catholic canon, which includes these "deuterocanonical" books, also known as the Old Testament *Apocrypha. The Eastern Church accepts some of these deuterocanonical books, but not others. The Roman Catholic Church defined its canon, which had long been in use, in 1546, at the Council of Trent (see *Tridentine). The Eastern churches generally follow the Synod of Jerusalem of 1672, which included in the Old Testament canon, besides the books in the Hebrew canon, four of the apocryphal books: Judith, Tobit, Wisdom, and Ecclesiasticus.

On the canon of the New Testament there is no difference among the main bodies of Christianity. From a very early date, the *Synoptics were read in church services, as well as the epistles of Paul, Acts, and—with some resistance at least well into the second century—the Gospel of John. The latter part of the canon remained fluid for some time, some excluding some of the universal epistles, others including writings such as the *Shepherd of Hermas*. While various groups had their own gospels, no other gospel was ever considered Scripture beyond the sect or group within which it originated. For some time, an important segment of the Syrian church used the *Diatessaron*, a compilation of the four canonical Gospels produced in the second century by Tatian.

At the time of the Reformation there was great debate on the authority of Scripture vis-à-vis *tradition. Protestants generally felt that the church and its doctrines had been corrupted by a false tradition that had developed over the centuries, and that it was necessary to return to Scripture as the pure source from which to draw proper doctrine and practice. While there was general agreement on this point among Protestants, there was great diversity of positions as to exactly how much of tradition was to be abandoned for the sake of Scripture— some being willing and even eager to retain all traditional practices that were not actually contradicted by Scripture, and some insisting that all that was not strictly biblical should be rejected. Over against all these positions, Roman Catholics generally claimed that, since it was the church that had determined the canon of Scripture, the church and its tradition had authority over Scripture, and that therefore any interpretation of Scripture that contradicted tradition and its authority as defined by the church was erroneous. With the passing of time, both extreme positions have been softened, with Roman Catholics acknowledging that centuries of tradition need to be cleansed and corrected by looking back at Scripture, and Protestants coming to recognize that Scripture itself has been preserved and transmitted through tradition.

As to the authority of Scripture and how it functions, there is a wide variety of opinions. Some hold that the true author of Scripture is the Holy *Spirit, who dictated or inspired in the writers what they were to write, and that therefore Scripture is *inerrant. Others hold that Scripture attests to a "progressive *revelation" of God, and that therefore the most ancient texts must be read under the correction of the more recent—and, in the view of some, of the continuing and progressing revelation of God even after the end of the writing of the New Testament. Still others hold that Scripture is a witness or record of the great acts of God in salvation, and that revelation is not in the words of Scripture, but in the events to which it attests. Still others point out that, according to Scripture itself, Jesus Christ is the *Word of God, and that therefore Scripture is the Word of God in a derivative sense, as pointing to the eternal Word, the Second Person of the Trinity.

Finally, it is important to remember that the very act of reading Scripture is also an act of interpretation. No text ever comes to us in its purity, as if we were passive receivers of whatever the text says. We read the text from where we stand, from our experiences. our traditions, and our perspectives. This makes the discipline of *hermeneutics particularly important, and for this reason much recent biblical scholarship has focused on hermeneutics, rather than on debates about the "authority" of Scripture on its own.

Second Coming of Christ   *See* *Parousia.

Semiotics   From the Greek *sēmeion,* sign, is the discipline, developed late in the twentieth century, that studies signs, their interrelationships, and the laws governing sign and meaning. In this context, a "sign" is anything capable of standing for another, or representing a meaning beyond itself. Thus, signs include words, symbols, gestures. While semiotics is the concern of many different fields, including literary criticism, linguistics, philosophy, education, anthropology, and even media and design, it is of particular interest to theologians as a tool for analyzing texts—particularly the texts of *Scripture. At a different level, it has also been used to discuss the significance of actions and events—particularly the *miracles of Jesus, which the Fourth Gospel often calls "signs." (*See also* *Polysemia.)

Semipelagianism   A doctrine that could also be appropriately named "semiaugustinianism," for what the Semipelagians sought to do was to reject *Pelagianism without following *Augustine to the extremes of his doctrines on *grace and *predestination. In order to avoid the ultimate consequences of Augustine's emphasis on the priority of grace, the Semipelagians held that the *initium fidei*—the very first act of believing—is in the hands of the sinner, and not of God. These views became particularly popular in the south of France, in and around Marseilles, where monastic teachers such as John Cassian (360–435) wrote treatises proposing an intermediate position between Pelagius and

Augustine. The latter wrote a number of treatises attempting to refute Semipelagianism. In the end, while declaring itself to be Augustinian, most of the medieval church was Semipelagian, for it refused to follow Augustine on such matters as irresistible grace and predestination.

Sempiternity   The quality of existing endlessly toward the future, but still having a beginning. According to this distinction, which was fairly common in the Middle Ages, only God is eternal, for only God has no beginning and no end. The life of the faithful in God's presence, although commonly called "eternal," is in fact "sempiternal." The same is true of *heaven and *hell. (*See also* *Eternity.)

Sexuality   A term that refers, not only to sexual activity, but to every way in which sexual drives, differences, and inclinations help determine human nature, goals, activities, and relationships. In Scripture, both sexuality and sexual activity are part of God's good *creation. Gender appears as a central characteristic of the human creature in both stories of creation in the first two chapters of Genesis. The relationship between Yahweh and Israel is often depicted as that between husband and wife; and the same is true of the relationship between Christ and the church.

On the other hand, since sexuality is such a central feature in human nature, and since it is so deeply ingrained in all human relationships, Scripture and all of Christian tradition have deemed it necessary to provide guidance as to its expression, particularly in sexual acts and practices. Adultery and various forms of fornication are repeatedly condemned in Scripture, not because sex in itself is evil, but rather because it is so powerful that wrongly used it can undermine and destroy all human and social relationships. For this reason, the only moral subject that the Bible discusses more often than sexuality is economic justice and the use and distribution of physical resources. While neither sex nor using economic resources is of itself evil, both sexuality and economic resources can easily be used in oppressive and destructive ways.

When Christianity first made its way into the Greco-Roman world, there were already there—as well as within Judaism itself—a number of religious and philosophical traditions that saw sex as evil, or at least as an obstacle in the way to wisdom. Some of these traditions felt that passion was contrary to reason, and that therefore the more one avoided passion—and therefore sexual desires and activity—the wiser one would be. Interestingly enough, while these traditions often decried sex, they affirmed a number of stereotypes supposedly based on sexuality, thus declaring women to be less given to reason and more easily swayed by passion. The impact of such views on Christianity gave rise to two perspectives on sexuality that have pervaded much of Christian tradition.

The first of these perspectives tends to view sexual activity as a concession to the frailty of human flesh, and therefore, if not strictly evil or sinful, at least not quite as good as *celibacy. It was in part as a result of such views—although also for social and economic considerations—that clerical celibacy became the norm, for it was inconceivable that a person "polluted" by sex could minister at the altar. (*See also* *Counsels of Perfection; *Asceticism; *Monasticism.)

The second such perspective sees the male as superior to the female, and therefore as solely capable of leadership in the life of the church. From this perspective, females, supposedly beings less given to reason and more to passion, are therefore less capable of guiding others in wisdom—the most notable exceptions being celibate women of great wisdom, who then are considered "almost as manly as men." By seeing women as temptresses, this second perspective in turn reinforces the first.

In more recent times, due in part to cultural changes and in part to new understandings of the reproductive process and of the psychology of sexuality, a number of issues connected with sexuality and its management have come to the foreground of Christian moral discourse—issues such as birth control, abortion, artificial insemination, in vitro fertilization, cloning, stem-cell research, and homosexuality.

Sheol In the Old Testament, the place where the spirits of the departed go after death. In most passages, it does not seem to be a place of reward or of punishment, but rather a place of shadowy existence. In some other passages, it is a place distant from God. With the advent of Christianity, Sheol was increasingly identified with *Hades or *hell. (*See also* *Soul; *Hell.)

Simony The medieval practice of buying and selling ecclesiastical positions. Named after Simon Magus, who according to Acts 8 sought to buy the power of the Spirit from Peter and John. Repeated reform movements sought to extirpate simony and to punish its practitioners, who were declared to be "simoniacs." During the sixteenth century, both Protestant and Catholic reformers declared it unlawful. By an extension of meaning, sometimes those who have received positions in the church in payment for services rendered or expected are also called "simoniacs."

Simul justus et peccator A phrase meaning "at the same time a sinner and justified," one of the trademarks of *Lutheranism. By this phrase, Luther meant that *justification is not an objective act that makes the sinner just, but rather God's acquittal of the sinner, who is declared to be just, not on the basis of the sinner's *merits or actions, but on the basis of the justice of Christ, which is imputed to the sinner. (*See* *Justice, Imputed.)

Sin A barrier that separates humans from God, standing between what we are and what we are intended to be.

Although in common language a "sin" is any action against the mores of society, most of Christian tradition has been aware that sin is both an action and a state. As an action, a sin is a willful violation of God's will, and therefore one may speak of "sins" in the plural and classify them according to various criteria. This is what is often meant by "actual sin"—an act or attitude that rebels against God's known will. However, in its deepest sense "sin" is not an action, nor even an attitude, but a state, a condition in which humans find themselves estranged from God and therefore also from each other and from the rest of creation. This is part of what is meant by *original sin—a condition into which we are all born and from which we cannot free ourselves. This vision of sin stands at the very root of the contrast between *Augustinianism and *Pelagianism. Pelagius tended to think of sins as actions or decisions against the will of God, and therefore insisted that it is possible for a person not to sin. For Augustine, in contrast, sin is a state, a condition in which sinners find themselves, and from which they cannot be freed by their own efforts. In such a state, humans have freedom to choose among a number of options; but all are sin—what Augustine would describe with the phrase *non posse non peccare*.

*Redemption is the action whereby God in Christ overcomes sin, and therefore each view of *atonement is paralleled by a distinct emphasis on a particular dimension of sin. If, for instance, sin is breaking the law of God, and therefore owing a debt to God, the work of Christ is in paying the debt owed for human sin. If sin consists in psychological or emotional alienation from God, then the work of Christ is essentially setting an example, showing a way, and providing inspiration and guidance. If, finally, sin consists of a form of slavery or subjection to death and to the power of sin itself, then Christ will be seen as the conqueror who overcomes the powers oppressing human-

kind. In similar fashion, many contemporary *liberation theologies see sin as inextricably related with various forms of oppression, and therefore see Christ as the liberator.

While generally agreeing that sin is a condition even before it is an act, theologians have not always agreed on the degree to which sin corrupts human nature. In this regard, the *Calvinistic doctrine of total *depravity insists that the effects of sin are such that not only are all human actions tainted by sin, but we cannot even discern within an action what is good and what is not. It is only through *grace—irresistible grace—that we are even made aware of the depth of our sinful condition.

In contrast, most medieval theologians—and with them *Tridentine Catholicism—while acknowledging that sin is a state, tend to focus on sin as an act—meaning by this both physical actions and inner attitudes—and therefore have paid more attention to the task of classifying sins according to their gravity. This has been particularly important given the pastoral needs connected with the administration of the *sacrament of *penance, where it is necessary to set an appropriate *satisfaction for each sin. Thus, sins may be either *mortal or *venial, according to the gravity of each. Another traditional listing, or classification, of sins, dating back at least as far as the seventh century, lists seven "deadly sins," in contrast to the seven *virtues. These seven deadly sins are pride, covetousness, lust, envy, gluttony, anger, and sloth.

It is significant that in much of this discussion sin is seen as essentially an individual's problem, and the social dimensions of sin, so prominent in Scripture, have long tended to be eclipsed by the more private dimensions—and particularly those having to do with *sexuality.

Socinianism An anti-Trinitarian form of *Anabaptism, receiving its name from the Italian Faustus Socinus (1539–1604), who took refuge in Poland and there gained many followers. Socinianism holds that the doctrine of the *Trinity, as well as the eternal generation of the Son, are not biblical, and should be rejected. It also rejects the theory that views the *atonement of Christ as *satisfaction for sins, declaring that it is not biblical and that in any case it contradicts the graciousness of God and the gratuity of forgiveness. During the seventeenth century a number of Socinian writings—among them the Racovian Catechism, written by Socinians in the Polish city of Raców (Kraków)—were introduced into England, and later into the United States. They contributed to the rise of *Unitarianism in the English-speaking world.

Sociology of Religion   The discipline of sociology, as first developed by Auguste Comte (1798–1857) and his contemporaries, was part of the general *positivistic trends of the time, and therefore sought to explain religion as a passing phase in the development of societies. This was the prevailing mood of sociological studies of religion until well into the twentieth century. For this reason, many theologians reacted with a general refusal to use methods of social analysis in their inquiries. A notable exception was Ernst Troeltsch (1865–1923), whose distinction between what he called "churches" and "sects," although much criticized and corrected, is still employed. In the early twentieth century, a student of Troeltsch, H. Richard Niebuhr (1894–1962), in studying *The Social Sources of Denominationalism*, showed how sociological factors affect theological and ecclesiastical stances. Thus, theologians were slowly moving toward the use of sociological analysis as providing material for their reflection. This was recommended by the Second Vatican Council (1962–65) in its document *Gaudium et spes*, and enthusiastically endorsed by the meeting of Latin American bishops in Medellín (1968). From that point on, the use of sociological analysis, not only for the understanding of religion as a phenomenon, but also for unmasking the hidden agendas (*Ideology) of religious stances and practices, has become quite common in *liberation and *contextual theologies. As a result of these developments, there is much debate on the traditional notion that philosophy is the best preparation for the study of theology, some suggesting that sociological and economic analysis are at least as important as is philosophy.

At the same time, partly as a result of the *postmodern critique of *modernity, sociologists were being called to recognize that they too are part of the phenomena they study, and that therefore an objective, positivistic sociology of religion such as Comte proposed is a false expectation.

Solipsism   The claim that all that exists—or all that can be proved to exist—is the self, and that the external world is, or may be, an illusion created by the self.

Soteriology   From the Greek *sōtēria*, salvation, and *logos*, treatise, reason. Thus, the study of the doctrine of *salvation. In the Old Testament, God's acts delivering the people from hunger, bondage, and other difficulties are usually called "saving" acts, and Yahweh is repeatedly praised as the Savior of Israel. In the New Testament, "salvation" may mean either healing or deliverance from sin—and sometimes both. Thus, salvation has to do, not only with one's eternal destiny, but with everything that stands in the way of God's purposes of communion with creation—and specifically with the human creature. Thus salvation includes both *justification and *sanctification.

In the Greco-Roman world in which Christianity was born, there were many religions offering "salvation." Most of these understood salvation mainly or exclusively as life after death, and often combined these notions of salvation with the ideal of escaping from the material world. Given that context, it is not surprising that quite often Christians lost the fuller notion of salvation that appeared in their Scriptures, and came to think of salvation merely as admission into *heaven—sometimes even seeing such admission as an escape from this physical world. Perhaps the most notable development in soteriology in recent decades has been the recovery of the wider notion of salvation as including, not only salvation from death and eternal damnation, but also freedom from all sorts of oppression and injustice (see *Liberation, Theologies of). Salvation, in its fuller sense, certainly includes *eternal life in the presence of God; but it also includes the process of sanctification, whereby we are brought greater communion with God; and it includes also the destruction of all the powers of evil that stand between God's purposes and the present order of creation (see *Fall).

Christians have always insisted that salvation is brought about by Jesus, whose very name means "Yahweh saves" and who is properly given the title of Savior. How Jesus achieves this has been explained by a series of metaphors, all helpful, but none sufficient by itself (see *Atonement). Thus, Jesus is Savior as the one who pays ransom for our sin, as the one who sets the example and shows the way to God, and as the conqueror over the powers of Satan and death.

One of the most debated points in soteriology has been the matter of human participation in our own salvation. Do we take the first step toward salvation, or is it God's *grace acting within us that brings about that initial step? (See *Initium fidei; *Pelagianism; *Augustinianism.) Are some *predestined to belief and salvation, and others not? Are we justified by *works, or by *faith? What is the relationship between justification and sanctification? (See *Simul justus et peccator.) How do we participate in the process? (See *Synergism.)

Soul While Christians have generally agreed that there is a soul, there has never been a clearly defined doctrine of the soul as such. In the Greek of the first few centuries of the Christian era, the "soul" was often understood to be the principle that gives life to a body, and therefore all living things—including animals and vegetables—are sometimes said to have a "soul." Paul and other early Christian writers sometimes refer to a full human being as "body, soul, and spirit," and sometimes as "body and soul," thus giving rise to a debate among some later theologians as to whether there are two or three components to the human creature—the *trichotomists* holding to "body, soul, and spirit," and the *dichotomists* insisting that the body and the soul are human, and that the "spirit" is God's presence in the soul. To complicate matters further, a similar ambiguity of language continues throughout the *patristic period, with a number of authors speaking of a "vegetative soul," that which gives life to all living beings—and a "rational soul," wherein reason and personality reside.

As to the origin of the soul, some early Christians, such as Origen late in the second century and early in the third, believed in the *preexistence of souls. Even Augustine (354–430) flirted with the idea for a time. In general, however, Christianity rejected such preexistence, thus leaving two options that different theologians have taken: *traducianism and *creationism. According to the first view, the soul is inherited from one's parents, just as the body is inherited. According to the second, each individual soul represents a new act of creation by God.

As to the final destiny of the soul (*Heaven; *Hell; *Resurrection), most Christian tradition has held that, although the soul can live without the body, a soul by itself is not a full human being, and that at the final consummation souls will be reunited with bodies— although now risen bodies, and therefore different from the present bodies.

Spiration   A traditional term employed to distinguish the manner in which the Holy *Spirit proceeds from the Father (and, according to Western theology, from the Son; see *Filioque), and the generation or *filiation of the Son. The Son is "begotten" from the Father, whereas the Spirit is "breathed" from the Father (and the Son).

Spirit, Holy   The Third Person of the *Trinity. In the Old Testament, the Spirit of God is present at the very act of creation, and is also credited with strengthening warriors, inspiring prophets, and guiding rulers. In the New Testament, the Spirit is active in the conception, *baptism, temptation, and *miracles of Jesus. The Fourth Gospel speaks of the Spirit as the "other Comforter" or "Paraclete"—from the Greek word employed there. Jesus promises the disciples that they will receive the Spirit after his departure, and this becomes true at Pentecost. There, the presence of the Spirit is manifested in tongues of fire over those present, and in communication across language barriers. In the case of Ananias and Sapphira, lying to the church is tantamount to lying to the Spirit. One of the criteria for the selection of the seven who are to administer the distribution of resources is that they be "full of the Spirit and of wisdom." In the early church, the gifts of the Spirit are manifested in many ways: speaking in tongues (see *Glossolalia), presiding, prophesying, teaching, healing, and others. Apparently this diversity of gifts was reason for jealousy and divisions, and it is to overcome such tensions that Paul insists that the greatest of all gifts is love (1 Cor. 13).

In spite of this long tradition, early Christian theologians did not attempt to say much more about the Spirit. It was in the second half of the fourth century, in the midst of the *Arian controversy, that the nature of the Spirit became a subject for discussion and definition. The *Macedonians, or Pneumatomachians, were willing to agree that the Father and the Son were of the same substance, but were not ready to say the same about the Holy Spirit. This prompted a number of writings on the Holy Spirit, of which the most influential were by Basil of Caesarea and Ambrose. In 381 the Council of Constantinople (Third Ecumenical), affirmed the full divinity of the Spirit, together with the Father and the Son.

After that, the next major controversy regarding the Holy Spirit, which eventually led to the final schism between the Latin-speaking West and the Greek-speaking East, had to do with the insertion of the *Filioque in the Nicene Creed. This addition, declaring that the Spirit proceeds from the Father *and the Son*, was rejected by the East, which held that the Spirit proceeds from the Father *through the Son*.

Augustine's doctrine of *grace, making it appear as a power infused into the believer by God, made it difficult to distinguish between such power and the Holy Spirit, with the result that one of the points debated during the Middle Ages was whether grace is created or uncreated. If the latter is the case, then grace is divine, and seems to be simply another name for the Holy Spirit.

At the time of the Reformation, some radical groups claimed that, because they had the Holy Spirit, they did not need to be subject to any authority. In most cases this meant civil or ecclesiastical authority, but in some cases it meant that the presence of the Spirit supersedes the authority of Scripture, which is no longer necessary.

John Wesley's (1703–91) insistence that the Holy Spirit was doing "a great work" through his movement led many of his contemporaries to accuse him of "*enthusiasm"—an accusation which he fervently denied, but was never completely able to leave behind. At any rate, it was early in the twentieth century, mostly out of *Wesleyan roots, that modern *Pentecostalism arose, first in the United States, and then throughout the world. The enormous growth of this movement has led to a new focus on the doctrine of the Spirit on the part of Pentecostals as well as others.

Spirit, Human   *See* *Soul.

State   In ancient times, it was inconceivable that a state not have a religious foundation. In some cases, conquered peoples were allowed to keep their gods, who were sometimes equated with the gods of the conquerors and sometimes simply added to the lists of gods. This was the case of the Roman Empire, which generally tolerated and absorbed the religions of most of the peoples it had conquered, and then sought to promote unity by equating some gods with others (*see* *Syncretism), and by the cult of the emperor and of Rome.

In the New Testament, there is ample cognizance of the government and its influence—the Roman government as well as its puppet government in Jerusalem. Sometimes it is implied that God uses governments for God's own ends—as in the case of Augustus's census, which takes the Holy Family to Bethlehem. Sometimes, obedience and subjection to the government are recommended —as by Paul in Romans 13. At other times, such as in the entire book of Revelation, resistance to government is encouraged and even expected of those truly faithful.

Such ambivalence is understandable, since the Roman Empire provided a measure of order and safety that was certainly a positive value, but at the same time made demands on Christians that were contrary to their faith. The ambivalence continued throughout the entire period of persecutions, for most Christians insisted on the need to resist the illicit demands of the state, and yet prayed for the emperors and other imperial authorities.

Once Constantine and most of his successors declared themselves Christian, and given the tradition of every state being religious, it was inevitable that Christianity would become the official religion of the Empire. While this took a few decades, by the end of the fourth century Christianity was the official religion, and others—particularly Judaism—were at best tolerated.

The rapid decline of imperial power in the West, connected with the Germanic invasions, led to a power vacuum that was progressively filled by the *hierarchy of the church, and particularly by the popes. By the time the Western Empire was restored, in the person of Charlemagne, it was restored by the church, and it was the pope who crowned the emperor (800). Thus, the Western church had an existence and a hierarchy quite independent of the secular government, and would often clash with that government. Powerful popes such as Gregory VII (ca.1020–85) clashed with emperors over the naming and investing of bishops; emperors tried to intervene in papal elections; popes declared kings and emperors deposed. Eventually the theory developed that there are "two swords"—the civil sword and the ecclesiastical—and that God has given one to the pope and the other to the emperor. At the high point of papal power, in the thirteenth century, it was claimed that God had provided the church and the state as two lights in the sky: the state to shine on bodies like the moon at night, and the church to shine on souls like the sun during the day. But just as the moon derives its light from the sun, so does the authority of the state finally derive from the church. Toward the end of the Middle Ages, as many attempted to reform the church and the papacy often resisted such reform, there were harsh criticisms of such views, to the point that a number of theologians claimed that the order should be reversed, with the "secular sword" holding sway over the religious.

Meanwhile, in the East, the Byzantine Empire continued for another thousand years, and therefore the ecclesiastical hierarchy was generally under the control of imperial authority.

The Reformation did not immediately put an end to the sort of relationship between church and state that had existed for over a thousand years. Some of the more radical Reformers did propose a separation of church and state; but even some of these, when given an opportunity, created their own, albeit ephemeral, theocracies. Among the major Reformers, Luther believed that God has established "two kingdoms," the civil and the ecclesiastical orders, and he related these two to *law and *gospel. Just as the law is valid for all, so are all to be subjected to the earthly kingdom. Believers, those who are justified, are subject to the spiritual kingdom. But, since they are still sinners (see *Simul justus et peccator), this does not exempt them from their civil obligations. Calvin, on his part, developed his views of the state in the context of his relationships with the City Council of Geneva. These relationships were not always cordial, and therefore it is wrong to say that Calvin established a theocracy. What Calvin did believe was that the state is necessary, not just to ward off evil or to limit the consequences of sin, but as an institution willed by God. In itself, the existence of a state and a government is good. Yet this also places the government under the obligation of complying with the law of God—and this was the reason for Calvin's conflicts with the City Council.

Guided by these principles, later Calvinists have often felt that they must demand justice and righteousness of their governments, and therefore it is not surprising that *Calvinism has resulted in a number of rebellions and revolutions—for instance, of the Dutch against the Spanish, of the *Presbyterians in Scotland and the *Puritans of England against the crown, and of the American colonies against England. (The influence of Calvinism may be seen in the American Constitution, whose system of checks and balances is based on the assumption that, people being corrupted by sin as they are [see *Depravity, Total], any branch of government given too much power will necessarily misuse it.)

Today's presence of large Christian minorities in traditionally non-Christian lands, as well as the growing secularism of traditionally Christian countries, is causing many theologians and ethicists to return to the question of the role of the state and the manner in which Christians are to relate to it.

Stoicism A philosophical school that was quite influential in the Greco-Roman world during the first centuries of the Christian era, and that therefore has also impacted Christianity itself. Stoics believed in the ultimate rationality of the universe. The reason underlying all things, they called the *logos, and therefore Stoic teachings regarding the logos impacted *Christology, as Christians sought to understand the person of their Savior in terms of the incarnation of the divine logos in Jesus.

Since this ultimate rationality pervades all of reality, the Stoics saw morality as adjusting to the natural, rational order of things. All of nature is ruled by this rationality, which the wise can also find within themselves. This "natural law" (see *Law, Natural), the basis for the wise life, was seen by many Christians as the foundation for a rational Christian ethics. Thus Thomas Aquinas (1225–74), for instance, argued for monogamous marriage on the basis of natural law.

Finally, the Stoics held that true wisdom is manifested in *apatheia*. Since all of reality is ruled by an orderly reason, wisdom consists in moderation and in accepting the order of reality, even though it may be painful. A spirit of rebelliousness or of grieving in the face of suffering is a sign of lack of wisdom. As a result of such views, much Christian *ascetic and *mystical literature promoted *apatheia*, and came to consider passion a shortcoming in the spiritual life. On the other hand, the Stoic emphasis on rational moderation served to counter the radical tendencies of some ascetic practices, giving *monasticism a more moderate tone.

Subordinationism Any doctrine that makes the Son (and/or the Holy Spirit) subordinate, or secondary, or less truly divine, than the Father. The best-known and most influential of the early forms of subordinationism was *Arianism.

Substance From the Latin *substantia*. A term derived from *Aristotelian *metaphysics, usually referring to the underlying reality of a thing, in contrast to its *accidents. The term has played an important role within theology, particularly in *Trinitarian and *Eucharistic theology.

In the formulation of Trinitarian doctrine, the term "substance" was used to refer to the divinity held in common by the three divine persons. This derived from the proposal by Tertullian (ca.155–ca.220) that in God there are three persons and a single substance. In the Greek-speaking East, however, *substantia* could be translated by either *hypostasis* or *ousia*. Etymologically, the first of these translations seemed closer, for both *substantia* and *hypostasis* refer to that which "stands under" a reality. But the Greeks spoke of "one *ousia* and three *hypostaseis*," thus employing *ousia* as the equivalent of the Latin *substantia*, and *hypostasis* as the equivalent of the Latin *persona*. These differences had to be clarified before East and West could finally agree on the formulation of Trinitarian doctrine.

In Eucharistic theology, the term "substance" has played an important role thanks to the explanation of the presence of Christ in the Eucharist, in traditional Roman Catholic theology, in terms of *transubstantiation.

Finally, from Descartes (1596–1650) on, there was much debate among philosophers and theologians regarding the "communication of the substances" —essentially, how the body communicates with the mind or the *soul. Kant (1724–1804) put a damper on such discussions by claiming that the very notion of substance has no empirical basis, but is rather a category in the mind.

Supererogation The earning of extra *merit by performing *works that are not simply "good," but "better." According to the *counsels of perfection, there are works, such as *celibacy and voluntary *poverty, that are not required, but which are better than what is actually required. Such "works of supererogation," not necessary for salvation, earn merits that then are added to the *treasury of merits of the church.

Supralapsarianism A view developed within orthodox *Calvinism during the period of Protestant *scholasticism, when theologians debated on the order of the eternal *decrees of God. According to the supralapsarians, the decree of election (see *Predestination) is prior to the decree concerning the *fall—*lapsus* meaning "fall," and hence the name for this tenet. Note that the issue debated is not whether predestination preceded or followed the fall. On this point all orthodox Calvinists were agreed: election and damnation are not God's response to the fall, but part of the eternal decrees of God. The debate had to do rather with the order of the decrees determining these events. (See also *Infralapsarianism.)

Sursum Corda Latin words usually translated into English as "Lift up your hearts," which the *eucharistic celebrant addresses to the congregation. They in turn respond, "We lift them up unto the Lord." The use of this formula is attested as early as the middle of the third century.

Symbol Something that stands for or represents something else, bringing it to mind. Strictly speaking, all words are symbols, for a sound or a set of characters bring the signified to mind. However, some prefer to limit the use of the term "symbol" for a sign that is so imbued with what it signifies that it actually makes the signified present. Such is the case of a national flag or, in the case of Christianity, the cross.

In traditional Christian theology, the term "symbol" appears most frequently in two different contexts. The first of these is *eucharistic theology, in which some declare that the presence of Christ in Communion is "symbolic" rather than corporeal or physical. The second context has to do with the *creeds, which in Greek were originally called "symbols." Thus, for instance, the Old Roman Symbol is the ancient creed from which the present Apostles' Creed evolved.

Syncretism The act of combining seemingly contradictory elements from religious or philosophical systems. Thus it is commonly said that the religious practices of the Roman Empire were syncretistic. Most often, the term is used pejoratively, implying that in accepting an alien influence one has denied a basic tenet of Christianity. Contemporary third-world theologians debate the very notion and accusation of syncretism as a way in which the old missionary centers sought to retain their control by raising the specter of syncretism whenever a younger church sought to inculturate the gospel (*see* *Inculturation) in ways that threatened the hegemony of the traditional centers.

The term was also applied in the seventeenth century to the proposal by Georg Calixtus (1586–1656), that all churches come together in what he called "the consensus of the first five centuries."

Synergism From Greek roots meaning "to work together," this term is applied in theology to any explanation of the participation of humans in their salvation that makes it appear that the *initium fidei* is not solely on the part of God. The term was first used by the stricter Lutherans

against Melanchthon (1497–1560), who sought to build bridges with the more moderate Roman Catholics by proposing a collaboration between the divine and the human in the act of conversion. Similar tendencies appeared within Roman Catholicism in the Council of Trent (1545–63), and were further strengthened with the ascendency of *Molinism and the rejection of *Jansenism. Among Calvinists, many accused *Arminianism of being synergistic.

Synoptics A term used to describe the first three Gospels, whose general outline and vision is common—hence the word "synoptic," having a common vision—and in some ways contrast with the Fourth Gospel. The "Synoptic problem" refers to the need to explain the commonalities as well as the differences among the three Synoptic Gospels. The most common view is that Mark is the earliest of the three, that both Matthew and Luke used Mark as their basic outline, but also had a common, now lost, source—which scholars call "Q"—as well as their own independent fragmentary sources. While there is a general consensus on these points, they are by no means uncontested.

Synteresis (also synderesis) A term in medieval moral psychology, usually referring to the knowledge the soul has of the principles of ethical action. According to some *mystics, it is the very heart of the soul, where the soul meets the divine.

Teleology The notion that things move toward a designed end. The notion appears in philosophy at least as early as Plato and Aristotle, and was incorporated into Christian theology, particularly by *scholasticism, which spoke of the "efficient cause" and the "final cause" of a thing or event. The "efficient cause" is what we commonly call the "cause": a billiard ball moves because another hits it. The "final cause" is the goal toward which a thing or an event is moving. Thus, as the efficient cause of all things, God made them all in the beginning; but as their final cause, God is also the purpose for which they were created, and they are all moving toward that purpose. The notion of teleology and of teleological or final causes fell into disuse during *modernity, mostly due to the practical success of the physical sciences, all of which study efficient, and not final, causes. There were in the twentieth century some theologians who stressed the movement of creation toward its intended end—most notably, Teilhard de Chardin (1881–1955). More recently, some of the *postmodern critique of modernity has led to a revival of teleological thought.

Theandric From two Greek words meaning "God" and "man." A term sometimes used to refer to the presence of both the divine and the human in Jesus. (*See also* *Christology.)

Theism A term coined in the seventeenth century as the opposite of atheism, and therefore originally meaning simply belief in God. With the passage of time, it has come to imply also the rejection of *deism and of *pantheism, and therefore it means belief in one *God, transcendent and personal, who created and preserves all things. As such, it is a view held in common by Judaism, Christianity, and Islam.

Theodicy A term first employed by Leibniz in 1710, as part of the title of an essay in which he sought to refute those who claimed that the existence of evil proves that a good and loving God does not exist. The word itself is derived from Greek words meaning God (*theos*) and justice (*dikē*).

The problem of evil, which is the main concern of theodicy, has long haunted philosophers and theologians of *theistic persuasion. Obviously, if there is no God, evil requires no explanation; and if there are several gods or eternal principles, evil can be explained

as the result of a conflict among them. Theism, however, must deal with the question, If God is good and omnipotent, how is it that evil exists? In the final analysis, most suggested solutions deny at least one of three points—divine goodness, divine omnipotence, or the reality of evil. Since Christians would never deny the goodness of God, most Christian theologians and philosophers have looked for answers in attempts to redefine either evil or divine omnipotence. Leibniz himself claimed that evil was the necessary background for good, for the only way we know good is by contrasting it with evil. This means that what appears as evil from our perspective is not really such from God's perspective—and thus this particular "solution" simply denies the reality of evil. Others—most notably some *process theologians—have argued that we misunderstand God's omnipotence, for God is in the process of becoming, and is therefore struggling with evil. In this "solution," God is good and evil is real, but God is not omnipotent.

Christian theology has consistently attributed *sin to the misuse of freedom, which is sometimes suggested as a solution to the problem of the existence of evil: evil originated in the free will of creatures—humans and angels—and not in God's will. This simply postpones the issue, however, for one must still ask the question, Why would an omnipotent and loving God make creatures and provide them the opportunity to sin?

Perhaps the best solution is no solution at all, for what makes evil such, what gives evil its enormous power, is the very mystery of its existence—the fact that it cannot be explained, and yet it is there.

Theologia crucis Literally, the "theology of the cross." While this phrase sometimes refers to the emphasis of late medieval devotion on the contemplation of the cross, it is most often used to refer to Luther's insistence that God is best known, not in glory or through metaphysical or philosophical speculation, but where God chooses to be revealed, namely, in the weakness and folly of the cross. Luther contrasts this true "theology of the cross" with a false "theology of glory," and on the basis of this contrast rejects all attempts on the part of theologians and philosophers to determine or describe the nature and activity of God on the basis of purely rational constructions. (*See also* *Reason and Faith.)

Theology The etymology of the word indicates that it refers to a discourse or a study of God (or of the gods). In classical Greece, the poets came to be called "theologians," because they spoke of the gods. In the early church, speech about God was sometimes called "theology." In many of the writings of the first five centuries of Christianity, "theology" is a discipline that leads the *soul to the contemplation of the divine. In this sense, a "theologian" is a *mystic. However, already by the time of Augustine (354–430) we find the use of the term as referring to the discipline that speaks about God. For Augustine, and for most writers in the next few centuries, "theology" did not deal with the entire corpus of Christian doctrine, but only with God. It was reflection and teaching about God, just as *ecclesiology is reflection and teaching about the church, and *Christology is reflection and teaching about Christ.

It was mostly *scholasticism that began using the term "theology" to refer to the entire corpus of Christian doctrine, and eventually to reflection about it. It is in this sense that it is most commonly employed in the latter part of the Middle Ages and until this day.

As to the purpose and method of theology, there has been much debate. For some, the purpose of theology is to discover truths about God and about life that one can attain by the sole use of reason (*see* *Reason and Faith)—and sometimes of experience. For others, theology has an apologetic purpose, trying to convince those who do not believe—or, in a variant of this position, at least trying to tear down the intellectual barriers to belief. Another position holds that theology is an intellectual exercise whereby the faithful come to understand better what they already believe, and that therefore theology, rather than seeking new truths, rejoices in discovering the depths of the truths already believed. For still others, theology is the systematization of Christian doctrine on the basis of Scripture—and, in a variant of this position, of Scripture and tradition. Many contemporary theologians argue that at least one of the functions of theology is to relate the Christian message to the historical situations in which people live—thus dealing, for instance, with sexist, racist, or class oppression. Finally, some hold that the task of theology is to critique the life and proclamation of the church in the light of the gospel.

Naturally, each of these views on the purpose of theology has important consequences for the method that theology is to follow. Thus, some would hold that the best preparation for the task of doing theology is the study of philosophy, while others argue that the social sciences are at least as important as philosophy as a background for theology. Likewise, some declare that theology is an intellectual discipline that may be carried on quite apart from the church, while others hold that theology is properly the task of the community of believers, and that theologians are truly such only inasmuch as they are immersed in and reflect the life of the church.

Theonomy Paul Tillich's (1886–1965) proposal for authentic existence. Such existence, in contrast with *heteronomy and with *autonomy, is built on the ground of all being, God. This, however, is not attainable during our historical existence, but serves as a hope questioning our tendencies toward heteronomy and autonomy.

Theopaschism A form of *Alexandrine *Christology that came to the foreground early in the sixth century, during the reign of Emperor Justinian. A group of monks, mostly from Scythia, proposed that the formula "one of the Trinity has suffered" be proclaimed as official doctrine of the church. Because of its origin, the theopaschite controversy is sometimes called the "controversy of the Scythian monks." At any rate, what the proposed formula sought was to reinstate the traditionally Alexandrine affirmation of a Christology in which the unity of the divine and the human is such that what is said of one must be said also of the other (what is known as the principle of the *communicatio idiomatum*). Justinian, who was eager to build bridges with the *monophysites of Syria and Egypt, gave his support to the Scythian proposal, and pressured Pope John II to declare it orthodox, even though it had earlier been rejected by Pope Hormisdas. Other controversies soon overshadowed the issue of theopaschism; and, when a century later most of the lands where monophysism was popular were conquered by Islam, Byzantium lost interest in a formula whose main asset was its overture to monophysism.

Theophany   A term derived from the Greek *theos*, God, and *phainō*, to appear or to show, and thus meaning a manifestation of God. It is used of any revelatory event in which God's presence is seen, such as Moses' burning bush, the dove in the baptism of Jesus, and Jesus himself—in Christian theology sometimes declared to be the supreme theophany.

Theopoiesis   The process of being made like God, also called *divinization. Most Western theologians have rejected it, or at least downplayed it, for fear that it may lead to notions of being absorbed into God, as has happened in some *mystical traditions. A fairly common notion in several early Christian writers, such as Irenaeus (died ca.202) and Athanasius (ca.293–373), it has remained

part of the spirituality of the Eastern churches, where it plays a role similar to the Western emphasis on *sanctification. Its goal is not the disappearance of all distance between God and the believer, but making the believer more capable of being in the presence of God.

Theosis   *See* *Theopoiesis.

Theotokos   A title often applied to Mary, meaning "mother [or, more exactly, "bearer"] of God." It was the focus of the debate around *Nestorianism, and was finally affirmed by the Council of Ephesus in 431 (Third Ecumenical Council) as an expression of the *communicatio idiomatum.* Although at the time of the original debate the issues were essentially of *Christology, many Protestants have rejected this title as an expression of what they felt was an excessive emphasis on *Mary and her role in salvation.

Thomism   The school of philosophy and theology emerging from Thomas Aquinas (1225–74). Thomas lived at a time when many of the writings of Aristotle were being reintroduced into Western Europe and leading a number of philosophers to claim that philosophical reason led to conclusions contrary to the established teachings of the church (*see* *Averroism). Most reacted by rejecting *Aristotelianism, or by accepting a few of its theses and incorporating them into the traditional *Augustinian framework of theology. A few, however, felt that the new philosophy provided a significant opportunity for recasting much of theology in a new framework without abandoning the old. Most notable among these were Thomas Aquinas and his teacher Albert the Great (ca.1200–1280).

One of the main points at which the new philosophy departed from the traditionally dominant *Platonism and Augustinianism was in its *epistemology. While traditional theologians believed that the best knowledge is that which is not dependent on experience,

Thomas followed Aristotle in affirming that all knowledge begins in experience, thus giving sense perception an important role in the process of knowing, and the body a significant role in the life of belief. As a result, Thomas's work may be said to open the way for modern experimental research and therefore for the technological developments of *modernity.

While adopting Aristotelian metaphysics, Thomas rejected some of the conclusions of the newly reintroduced philosophy, such as the eternity of *matter, the notion that all souls are ultimately one, and the claim that reason, properly used, can reach conclusions that are contrary to faith. He did believe that there are truths—such as the *Trinity and the *incarnation—that are beyond the reach of reason; but this means that they are *above* reason, not *contrary* to it. (*See* *Reason and Faith.)

On the basis of Aristotelian philosophy and received Christian doctrine, Thomas built an impressive system of theology whose greatest monument is his own *Summa theologiae*.

Thomism did not immediately gain wide recognition. In 1277 the Archbishop of Paris condemned 219 theses that he considered heretical, several of which had been held by Thomas. Similar action was then taken at Oxford. A number of distinguished theologians, many of them Franciscans, wrote against Thomism. The Dominicans came out in defense of their deceased teacher, forbidding members of the Order to attack his ideas, and in 1309 declaring that the teachings of Thomas were the official teachings of the Order. A few years later, in 1323, Pope John XXII *canonized Thomas. In the sixteenth century, the Jesuits also adopted his theology, although with some differences with the Dominicans as to how it was to be interpreted. Many of those present at the Council of Trent (1545–63) were Thomists, and therefore the Council adopted much of his teaching and even his phraseology.

In 1879 Leo XIII, in the bull *Aeterni Patris*, recommended the study of Thomas to all the church, and established a program for a critical edition of his works. By then, Thomism suffered from the general attitude of Roman Catholicism during the nineteenth century, of rejection of all things modern. Therefore, apart from ecclesiastical circles, Thomism was considered outmoded and irrelevant. However, partly as a result of Leo's bull, in the twentieth century there was a revival of Thomism, first led by French Neo-Thomists such as Jacques Maritain (1882–1973) and Étienne Gilson (1884–1978), and then by Jesuits Karl Rahner (1904–84) and Bernard Lonergan (1904–1984), who sought to respond to the Kantian critique of traditional epistemology by developing what he called a *transcendental method.

Tongues   *See* *Glossolalia.

Tradition   The original meaning of the term had little to do with repetitive action, as it is commonly used today. A "tradition"—*traditio*, or in Greek *paradosis*—was something given by one to another. Thus the term is employed by Paul when speaking of what he has received and passes on regarding Communion, and it is also employed to refer to Judas's betrayal—handing over—of Jesus. In this sense, all teaching is tradition, as is the communication of any item of news. And the passing of Scripture from one to another, or the copying and recopying of its text, is also *traditio*.

During the second century, some *gnostic teachers began claiming that they had received a secret tradition, supposedly passed from Jesus to a particular disciple, and by him to others, thus reaching the teacher who now claimed it. Against such notions, the church claimed the authority of the open tradition of all the apostles, as it was openly taught in all the churches that could claim apostolic origin (*see* *Apostolic Succession). Thus, if any proposed an interpretation of the gospel, or of a text in Scripture, in such a way as to deny some of the fundamentals of the faith —for instance, and most commonly, the *incarnation—the tradition of the church, that consensus expressed in Scripture as well as in the teaching of the apostolic churches, was used to refute them. Thus developed a theological approach in which Scripture and tradition worked together for the preservation of *orthodoxy.

As centuries went by, a number of practices, beliefs, and theological perspectives developed that were generally considered to be part of the tradition, and therefore fully consonant with Scripture. It was the Protestant Reformation that, in its effort to return to biblical doctrine and practice, pointed to many of these accretions as not part of the proper tradition of the church, thus beginning a bitter and prolonged debate as to the relative authority of Scripture and tradition. Even among Protestants, there was much disagreement as to exactly what the primacy of Scripture meant. Does it mean, as the *Anabaptists claimed, that all that is not found in Scripture must be rejected? Or does it mean, as *Lutherans and *Anglicans argued, that tradition is to be kept, except in those cases where it clearly contradicts Scripture? For its part, the Roman Catholic Church, at the Council of Trent (1545–63), took the extreme position of practically equating the authority of tradition with that of Scripture.

In the nineteenth century, this conflict between Protestants and Roman Catholics reached its high point. Many Protestant theologians (see *Liberalism) not only rejected the authority of tradition, but came to interpret Scripture itself in very untraditional fashion, questioning its authority, its truthfulness, and sometimes even its relevance. Roman Catholics, on the other hand, staunchly sided with tradition, no longer just against Scripture, but also and most particularly against the encroachments of *modernity.

In the second half of the twentieth century this debate subsided, as both sides acknowledged that Scripture and a proper sense of tradition are inextricably interwoven, and also that tradition by itself, without the correction of Scripture, has a tendency to wander away from its original meaning and content.

Traducianism   One of the ways in which ancient theologians spoke of the origin of individual *souls: just as the body and its characteristics are inherited from one's parents, so is the soul and its characteristics. Rejecting this theory, others insisted on "*creationism"—the notion that each new soul is an individual creation by God. Although eventually most theologians rejected traducianism as implying too materialistic an understanding of the soul, it played an important role in early discussions of *original sin. Indeed, it was a simple matter to claim that, just as one's facial features are inherited, so is sin.

Transcendence   A term derived from the Latin, and meaning to go over, or to climb beyond. It is used in theology to affirm that, while God is present in the world (*Immanence), God is not part of the world, nor is the world divine (*Pantheism). God exists apart from and beyond creation.

Transcendental Method   A method in theology developed by Jesuit Bernard Lonergan (1904–84). Originally a Neo-Thomist, Lonergan felt that the Kantian critique of knowledge, which some claimed rendered *Thomism obsolete, required a reshaping of traditional Thomism. Thus, Lonergan focused his work, as had Kant earlier, on the very process of knowing—or, to use his phrase, "an inquiry into inquiry." According to Lonergan, there are four operations in knowledge: experience, understanding, judgment, and decision. While the latter is not properly a step in the process of knowing, it is what brings knowledge to bear on life. On this basis,

Lonergan reconstructs Thomist *epistemology and *metaphysics, now in a post-Kantian mode.

As to theological knowledge itself, Lonergan moves once again from a more traditional understanding of knowledge to one that includes its functioning in contemporary life. Just as the fullness of knowledge involves decision, so does theological knowledge lead to contemporary interpretation and decision. Each of these two steps involves four "specialties": research, interpretation, history, and dialectics in the first step; and foundations, doctrines, systematics, and communications in the second. Thus, each "specialty" in the first step is paralleled by one in the second, as follows: research/ foundations, interpretation/ doctrines, history/systematics, and dialectics/communications. The passage from the last specialty of the first step, dialectics, to the next step is parallel to the passage from knowledge in the traditional sense to decision, and thus involves a sort of "intellectual conversion," which serves as a starting point for the rest of the theological task.

Transcendentalism A movement, generally associated with the name of Ralph Waldo Emerson (1803–82) as its principal founder, developing out of *Unitarianism, but moving beyond it in terms of its positive valuation of human potential. Philosophically, transcendentalism was a combination of *idealism with *pantheistic *mysticism, holding that the entire universe is the expression of the "Oversoul," or mind of God, and that what we view as evil, sin, pain, and all other negative realities are but passing moments in the thought of the Oversoul. Mary Baker Eddy (1821–1910), the founder of Christian Science, was influenced by transcendentalism.

Transignification A term suggested by some Roman Catholic theologians after the Second Vatican Council (1962–65), as a contemporary way to express the traditional doctrine of *transubstantiation. These theologians, notably Karl Rahner (1904–84) and Edward Schillebeeckx (1914–), suggested that, since *modernity no longer thinks in terms of *substance and *accident, it was best to speak of the *real presence of Christ in the *Eucharist in terms of a "transignification" (Rahner also suggested "transfinalization"), whereby the eucharistic elements no longer signify bread and wine, but the body and blood of Jesus. While these theologians did not deny the real presence of Christ in the Eucharist, and they offered these terms, not as substitutes, but rather as complements to transubstantiation, and as an attempt to show that at the Council of Trent (1545–63) the church had not canonized *Aristotelian metaphysics, many accused them of holding to a purely "symbolic" presence of Christ in the Eucharist. In 1965, in his encyclical *Mysterium Fidei*, Paul VI, while not quite declaring transignification a heresy, raised important caveats against it.

Transmigration of Souls *See* *Preexistence of Souls.

Transubstantiation The official doctrine of the Roman Catholic Church regarding the presence of Christ in the *Eucharist, where, according to this doctrine, the *substance of the bread and the wine is replaced by the substance of the body and blood of Christ, while the *accidents of the bread and wine remain. From a very early date, Christians have held that Christ is uniquely present in the Eucharist. At least by the fourth century, it is common to find claims that this presence is the physical body of Christ. In the ninth century, Paschasius Radbertus claimed that after the eucharistic consecration the bread and the wine are no longer such, but are transformed into the flesh and blood of Jesus Christ—the same flesh and blood that were born of the Virgin Mary and suffered under Pontius Pilate. This, however, was denied by Ratramnus of Corbie and others, thus showing that by that time the issue was still controverted. Yet, later in the same century Haymo of Halberstadt insisted that in the Eucharist, by a miraculous action of God, "this substance of bread and wine is substantially turned into another substance, that is, into flesh and blood." In the eleventh century, the controversy revived, now centering on Berengar of Tours, who defended the position of Ratramnus and was repeatedly forced to recant. This practically put an end to all discussion of the matter. In 1215, the Fourth Lateran Council proclaimed the doctrine of transubstantiation as the official teaching of the Roman Catholic Church. (Slightly later, the Eastern churches made a similar proclamation.) Later in the same century the reintroduction of *Aristotelianism into Western Europe made it possible for Thomas Aquinas (1225–74) to undergird this doctrine with more careful metaphysical considerations and clarifications. In the sixteenth century, the Council of Trent (1545–63) reaffirmed the doctrine of transubstantiation, which was under attack from Protestants.

Treasury of Merits   According to medieval penitential theory (*see* *Penance; *Satisfaction), the sum total of the *merits of Christ, and of the merits of the saints' works of *supererogation, which the church can now administer through its *sacramental system. This doctrine is in the background of the controversy over *indulgences and their sale.

Tridentine   Relating to the Council of Trent (1545–63)—in Latin, *Concilium Tridentinum*. This council, called in order to respond to the Protestant challenge and at the same time to reform the Catholic Church, both rejected practically all the claims of Protestantism and issued a series of decrees for the reform of the church. In this, it reflected the mood of the entire Catholic Reformation, which centered on the reform of mores, on the promotion of scholars capable of refuting Protestantism and other "heresies," and on reorganizing the church in

a more centralized fashion, under a series of popes committed to moral reform and to traditional theology.

Since this attitude prevailed in Roman Catholicism from the time of the Council of Trent until the Second Vatican Council (1962–65), it is common to refer to Catholicism during that period as "Tridentine," and thus to distinguish it both from earlier Catholicism and from "post-Conciliar" (or post-Vatican II) Catholicism.

Trinity   The doctrine that God, while being one, exists eternally in three "*persons," usually called Father, Son, and Holy Spirit. The word "Trinity" itself does not appear in Scripture. The Greek form, *trias*, seems to have been first used by Bishop Theophilus of Antioch in the second century. However, the basic ingredients of the doctrine are indeed found in Scripture, where Jesus is considered worthy of worship, and yet is clearly not the One to whom he refers as "Father," and where the *Spirit is promised by Jesus as "another Comforter." Thus, it may be argued that the development of the doctrine of the Trinity is simply the clarification and definition of what was already implicit in Scripture.

On the other hand, it is important to remember that usually doctrine is not the development of purely intellectual considerations, but is also an attempt to express the faith the church experiences in *worship. We know that from a very early date Christians gathered on the first day of the week—the day of the *resurrection of the Lord—"to sing hymns to Christ as to God." We also know that Christians were convinced that the Spirit that dwelt in them was God. Thus, it is not surprising that theological inquiry soon moved in the direction of clarifying the relationship among these three whom the church experienced in worship, and how such worship, and the faith behind it, remained *monotheistic.

Some of the earlier attempts to express the relationship among these three took the route of what later came to be known as modalism or *Sabellianism, which claimed that the Creator Father had become the Redeeming Son at the time of the incarnation, and had then become the Inspiring Spirit at Pentecost. Thus, these three were but three faces or three "modes" in which the One came to believers. This and similar doctrines were soon rejected, because in its worship and in its Scriptures the church knew of a Son of God who was distinct from the Father, and who also promised and sent the Spirit. When Jesus walked on earth, he did not exhaust the Godhead. Furthermore, Christians prayed to the Father in the name of the Son, and under the guidance of the Spirit.

A very influential treatise refuting modalism was Tertullian's (ca.155–ca.220) *Against Praxeas*, where he employed legal and metaphysical terminology to argue that God is "three persons in one substance." Although it took a long time for this to become the official doctrine of the church, Tertullian's formula was eventually adopted as the classical expression of Trinitarian doctrine.

What led to the most serious debates regarding the Trinity, and eventually to the formulation of the doctrine itself, was the rise of *Arianism, which held that, while the Son may be called divine, he is not God in the strict sense, for he is not eternal, but is in fact a creature. To this the Council of Nicaea (First Ecumenical Council, 325) responded with a *creed that stated in no uncertain terms that the Son is "very God of very God; begotten, not made, of one substance [*homoousios] with the Father." Although after this there were extensive debates seeking other formulas (*homoiousios) as well as regarding the divinity of the Spirit (see *Macedonians), by the time of the Council of Constantinople (Second Ecumenical, 381) the controversy had generally come to an end—although there would later be a revival of Arianism as the Goths and other Germanic tribes that had been converted to Christianity by Arian missionaries invaded Western Europe. The final formula

employed henceforth by the Latin-speaking church was "one substance, three persons," while the Greek church spoke of "one *ousia*, three *hypostases."

One important principle developed during the controversy is the *circumincession or *perichōrēsis*, which means that the three persons so interpenetrate each other that in each action of one the others are present. Thus, although through what later theologians called "*appropriations" it is correct to speak of the *incarnation of the Second Person of the Trinity, there is a sense in which the entire Trinity is present in Jesus; and, while it is the Spirit who descends at Pentecost, it is the Godhead, in the person of the Spirit, who dwells in believers.

In the ninth century, a controversy arose around the word *Filioque, meaning "and from the Son," which had been added in the West to the Nicene Creed, thus declaring that the Holy Spirit proceeds "from the Father *and from the Son*." The Greeks protested against this interpolation in the creed, which also reflected a different view of the place of the Spirit within the Trinity, and this eventually became one of the issues leading to a schism between East and West that still persists.

Beginning in the sixteenth century, and reaching its climax in the nineteenth, there was much criticism of the doctrine of the Trinity, which was seen as an irrational claim that three can also be one, and lacking in practical significance for the life of believers. In more recent times there has been a revival of interest in the Trinity, with a number of theologians seeing it as a paradigm for life in community, and as requiring a redefinition of the oneness of God in ways that are less conducive to authoritarianism than is a simple, non-Trinitarian monotheism.

Trisagion   Ancient hymn, dating at least from the fifth century, and sung both in the Eastern and in the Gallican liturgies: "Holy God, Holy and mighty, Holy and immortal, have mercy upon us." It became a subject of controversy late in the fifth century, when the *monophysite bishop of Antioch Peter the Fuller (d. 488) added into it the phrase "who was crucified for us," which some felt was an undue and extreme expression of *Alexandrine *Christology. Later, the Scythian monks saw in Peter's formula a forerunner to their own *theopaschism.

Typology A tradition of interpretation that sees past events as "types" or "figures" of succeeding ones, and particularly of the life and work of Christ. Thus, while *prophecy focuses on the words of a text and how they announce future events, and *allegory tries to see hidden meaning in those words, typology focuses on the events themselves as part of a pattern of God's action whose culmination is in Jesus Christ, but which continues in the life of the church. Thus, for instance, the passages on the Suffering Servant in Isaiah are seen as referring to events in the time of Isaiah, but also to the Suffering Servant par excellence, Jesus, and by extension to the life of the church and of Christians.

Ubiquity The ability to be present everywhere at the same time. It is usually included among the traditional *attributes of God, where it is similar to *omnipresence. In post-Reformation theological debates, it became a central piece of the *Lutheran understanding of the physical presence of Christ in the *Eucharist. Luther argued that, due to its union with the divine, the risen body of Christ has been endowed with the power to be in more than one place at the same time, and that this ubiquity makes it possible for Christ to be physically present at several eucharistic services at the same time.

Ultramontanism A term derived from the Latin for "beyond the mountains," and therefore employed, particularly in France but also in Germany and in various parts of northern Europe, for the movement in the Roman Catholic Church that sought to centralize authority in the city of Rome and the person of the pope. Its main opponent was *Gallicanism, whose defense of "the ancient liberties of the Gallican church" stood in the way of ultramontane claims. Although the conflict began as early as the seventeenth century, in the nineteenth the ultramontanes gained the upper hand, partly as a result of the French Revolution, in which Gallicanism had appeared to buckle under the pressure of the state, and partly as a reaction to the threats of *liberalism, the secular state, and other such modern ideas. The promulgation of papal *infallibility by the First Vatican Council (1870) marks the high point of ultramontanism. Although this was a triumph for the ultramontanes, it fell short of their goal of having the pope declared to be infallible, not only in matters of faith and morals, as the Council decreed, but also in matters of church administration.

Unitarianism A modern movement of *rationalistic tendencies, which gained great impetus in New England in the nineteenth century. It received the name of "Unitarianism" because it denied the doctrine of the *Trinity; but it also denied the divinity of Christ, and tended to consider *sin a passing imperfection in a human nature that is essentially good. Thus, in its most common usage, the term "Unitarianism" refers to much more than the denial of the Trinity.

On the other hand, in some contexts any who deny the Trinity may be called "unitarians." Thus, for instance, since there has been much discussion on the Trinity among some *Pentecostals, there is a "unitarian" form of Pentecostalism —even though this has little to do with the rationalistic unitarianism that originated in New England.

Unity of the Church One of the major *marks of the church, and a point of theological debate through the centuries. While practically all Christians are agreed that in some sense the church is one—if it is the body and the bride of Christ, Christ can have no more than one body or one bride—there is wide disagreement as to the precise nature of this unity. In patristic theology, the emphasis often lay in the *Eucharist, so that as long as various local churches accept each other at the Table they are one church. Thus, the union between churches in various cities was expressed in the list of names in the "diptychs"—folders of two leaves in which the names of others were listed for prayer. The exclusion of someone—usually a rival bishop or theologian—from the diptychs of a church was an act of *excommunication, declaring that the person whose name had been erased was no longer a part of the church.

During the Middle Ages, the acceptance of the authority of the pope in the West, or of a particular patriarch in the East, became the touchstone for unity. Still, the significance of eucharistic unity was such that, although there had been tensions between Rome and Constantinople for a long time, the division did not become official and final until 1054, when the legates of the pope broke communion with the Patriarchate of Constantinople.

At the time of the Reformation the emphasis shifted toward unity of doctrine. While Roman Catholicism continued existing as a transnational church, most Protestant bodies became national or even regional churches, now linked with each other through the common acceptance of certain doctrines or of a statement of faith—for the *Lutheran tradition, for instance, the Confession of Augsburg. While this meant that unity was no longer defined in organizational terms—as having a single leader or authority—it also meant that minor points of doctrine could easily lead to divisions. The result was the proliferation of Protestant denominations, several of them claiming that their particular points of doctrine were suffi-

ciently important to sever ties with others, and some even claiming that they, and only they, were the true church.

In the nineteenth and twentieth centuries, the issue of church unity was revived, primarily in what was then called the "mission field," but also among biblical and other scholars. The result was the modern *ecumenical movement. Even then, however, while all participants in the movement agreed that the church is one, and that its life must manifest this oneness, there remains a wide variety of opinions as to what constitutes the outward unity that Christians must seek.

Universalism   The expectation that all will eventually be saved, that there is no final damnation, and that *hell is a temporary place whose function is to purify the souls before they can be in the presence of God. Its description of the final consummation often takes the form of an *apocatastasis—although a universalist position does not necessarily imply a return to the original state of all things, as in a true apocatastasis. In the United States, universalism has historic connections with the more rationalistic forms of *unitarianism.

Universals   In medieval philosophy, the ideas that hold genera and species together—as, for instance, all horses share in a common "horseness," which makes them be members of that species. The question that was then debated was whether these universals are real, or exist only in the mind. At one extreme of the debate, *nominalism held that universals are mere names, matters of convenience—as some would say, "the wind of the voice." At the other extreme, *realism held, not only that universals are real, but that they are more real than their particular instances, which derive their existence and their nature from them.

Each of these two extremes posed significant difficulties both for theology and for philosophy. If universals are mere names, capricious ways in which the mind puts things together, what is there to prevent us from linking things erratically? How can one claim to know anything if all one knows are particular instances, and the links that we use to generalize about them have no reality?

In the field of theology, extreme nominalism also created problems. If there is no such thing as humanity, but only humans, how is one to understand *original sin? How can the suffering of one man, Jesus, atone for others? What is it that holds the church together?

On the other hand, extreme realism leads to *monism. If the ultimate reality of individuals is to be found in the universal that holds them together, the reality of universals is to be found in higher universals—thus, the reality of a horse is in its "horseness," but the reality of "horseness" is in "animalness," and so on. Ultimately, the reality of all things is to be found in the one supreme universal, "being."

In theology, this would lead to *pantheism, and some have used an extreme realism regarding the universals to claim that ultimately all souls are one.

There were many intermediate positions, such as the "conceptualism" of Peter Abelard (1079–ca.1144), and the so-called nominalism of Ockham (ca.1285–ca.1349) and other late medieval theologians, who in truth were closer to conceptualism than to nominalism. But in general throughout the Middle Ages the problem of universals appeared an unsolvable enigma in which philosophers as well as theologians were repeatedly trapped.

Utraquists Those among the Hussites who held that the *Eucharist should be offered to all—including the laity—in both the bread and the wine [sub utraque specie]. Although their position was condemned by the Council of Constance in 1415, eventually the Roman Catholics had to concede the point, and allow those Hussites who were reconciled with Rome to receive Communion in both species—a concession that was later repeatedly withdrawn and reaffirmed, and that eventually, in the twentieth century, became common practice for all Catholics.

Venial Sin *See* *Mortal Sin.

Vestigia Trinitatis A principle developed by Augustine (354–430), who held that there are vestiges or signs of the *Trinity in all its creatures. It is not merely that things may be used as illustrations for the Trinity, but rather that, precisely because they have been made by the Trinity, all creatures bear the triune imprint. Augustine's favorite example of this is the mind, which shows the imprint of the Trinity in being memory, understanding, and will. Medieval theologians developed this principle further. Bonaventure (ca.1217–74), for instance, distinguishes the vestiges from the image and the likeness of the Trinity. All things bear vestiges of the Trinity, for they all bear being, truth, and goodness. All rational beings bear the image in their memory, intellect, and will. The likeness of the Trinity is found in those rational beings that have faith, hope, and love.

Victorines A theological school connected with the monastery of St. Victor, in the outskirts of Paris. Its founder was William of Champeaux (ca.1070–1121), but its most famous teachers were Hugh (1096–1141) and Richard (d. 1173) of St. Victor. They were characterized by their combination of mystical piety with rational inquiry, and for that reason are considered among the most important forerunners of *scholasticism.

Virgin Birth The virginal condition of Mary at the time of conceiving Jesus is attested in the Gospels of Matthew and Luke, but not in Mark or John. In the second century, some anti-Christian polemics claimed that Jesus was not conceived of a virgin—*parthenos*—but of a

Roman soldier whose name was Pantheros. Most scholars—including those who deny the virgin birth—consider this simply a bit of gossip invented by the enemies of Christianity, for there are no grounds for believing it to be true. At any rate, there is no doubt that by the second century—and in at least some cases in the first century, as Matthew and Luke indicate—Christians generally believed that Jesus was born of a virgin. The significance of the virgin birth was often understood *typologically, as the fulfillment of the theme of the barren woman giving birth to God's chosen instruments.

Significantly, most of the opposition in the second century to the virgin birth was not objecting to the idea that Jesus was born of a virgin, but rather to the notion that Jesus was born at all! What such people found scandalous and difficult to believe was not that a virgin would have conceived Jesus, but that God would have deigned to enter into the womb of a woman and be born as a babe. Thus, the reference to the virgin birth in the Old Roman Symbol—the forerunner of the present Apostles' Creed—is not directed against those who claimed that Jesus had an earthly father, but rather against those who claimed that he was not born.

By the late second century, and increasingly over the centuries, the virgin birth of Jesus tended to focus attention on *Mary, rather than on Jesus. As notions filtered into the church according to which sexual intercourse defiled a woman, it became increasingly common to claim that Mary had been a virgin, not only at the time of conceiving Jesus, but throughout her entire life. The "perpetual virginity of Mary" was defended by Ambrose and Hilary of Poitiers as early as the fourth century. By the ninth it was generally assumed, not only that Mary had never had intercourse and that therefore Jesus had no brothers, but even that in his birth Jesus did not destroy the physical virginity of his mother. Eventually, this led to other teachings regarding Mary, such as her *immaculate conception and her *assumption, as well as to the practice of praying for her intercession and even calling her "Co-Redemptrix."

Virgin Mary   See *Mary.

Virtualism   A term often employed to refer to Calvin's understanding of the presence of Christ in the *Eucharist, which takes place by the power—that is, the "virtue"—of the Holy Spirit. While the risen body of Christ is in heaven, and only there, in Communion he feeds believers "by the power [virtue] of the Spirit." This power is such that, rather than speaking of Christ's coming down from heaven to the Table, one may speak of the Spirit's raising the worshiping community to the presence of Christ, as a foretaste of the final heavenly banquet.

Virtues   *Aristotle defines virtue as "a disposition that makes one good." In classical Greek ethics, there were four main virtues, often called the "cardinal" virtues: these are prudence, justice, temperance, and fortitude. Prudence is the disposition that allows one to make correct judgments as to values and courses of action. Justice is the practice of rendering to all what is their due. Temperance is one's power over one's desires, particularly the desire to abuse that which is in itself good. Finally, fortitude allows one to stand for what is good in spite of difficulties, opposition, and consequences. To these four "cardinal virtues," Christian tradition has added three "theological virtues," which are infused into the believer by *grace. These are faith, hope, and love. Together, these seven virtues are the counterpart of the seven "deadly" or "capital" sins—in the sense that they are the root of all sin—which are pride, covetousness, lust, envy, gluttony, anger, and sloth.

Voluntarism   A term with two very distinct meanings. In much contemporary discussion on the nature of the church, particularly in the United States, voluntarism is the notion that the church is a voluntary association, formed by those who out of their own free will choose to join it, and supported by their freely given offerings and other resources. Quite often it is joined with a "low" *ecclesiology, which views the church, not as part and parcel of the gospel, but simply as an association of Christians who seek to support each other in their faith. (In this sense, the term is sometimes "voluntaryism.")

In more traditional theology, voluntarism is the notion that will is above reason. This position has been held by many in the *Augustinian tradition, thus reflecting Augustine's own experience of knowing what was true and good before being ready to believe or to do it. It received its classical expression in the theology of John Duns Scotus (ca.1266–1308), who agreed that in God there is no difference between will and reason, but also argued that from our point of view it is best to see God primarily as will, rather than as reason—and who also argued that this is certainly true of us, for reason does not usually govern the will. These notions were carried to an extreme by some late medieval theologians who argued that, given the primacy and freedom of God's will, it is more correct to say that whatever God does is good than to say that God always does what is good—in other words, that God's free will is such that it is not confined even by the idea of the good. (See *Potentia Dei absoluta.*)

Waldensians Also "Waldenses," and originally known as "the Poor of Lyons." The followers of Peter Waldo (d. before 1218), who devoted himself to a life of poverty, but was denied the right to preach by authorities in Rome. As a result, the group broke away from the church. Persecuted, its members hid in the valleys of Switzerland and northern Italy, where they were able to survive. At the time of the Reformation, they adopted *Reformed theology, thus be-

coming the oldest of all Reformed churches—the *Chiesa Evangelica Valdese.*

War While in the Old Testament there are many accounts of wars ordered by God, the preaching of Jesus regarding forgiveness and love for one's enemies, and rejecting violence as a response to violence, meant that early Christians refrained from participating in wars. This was a tenable position in a situation in which Christians were a small minority of the population, and in any case the state did not trust them and often even persecuted them. In the second century, the pagan Celsus charged that if all were to follow Christian principles the Empire would soon be overrun by barbarians—to which Origen replied simply that in that case the barbarians also would be Christians, and there would be no need to fight them. But later that century, to the great dismay of church leaders, there were already Christians in the army—probably at first soldiers who were converted while in the army, and who had to fulfill their commitment to the military.

After Constantine, as the population of the Empire became increasingly Christian, the earlier *pacifist attitude was greatly modified. Some joined the army but postponed *baptism until after their military service, so that if they had to kill someone they would be forgiven at baptism. Eventually, the original pacifist stance was abandoned, although reluctantly. In this process, Augustine (354–430) developed what has come to be known as the "just war theory." Preferring nonviolence, and deploring the need to resort to war, Augustine offered a number of criteria that a war has to meet in order to be justified. As to its goal, it must be intended to promote justice and to restore peace. As to its leadership, it must be waged only by proper authority—a principle that later would be used against various revolutionary groups. As to its conduct, it must be waged without cruelty or hatred toward the other, with no violence done to noncombatants, and with no looting or mass destruction.

Although Augustine himself did not intend his principles to be employed for the wholesale justification of war and violence, this is what in fact happened. Augustine died precisely at the time when the Germanic peoples were invading the ancient Roman Empire. These were bellicose societies, with a longstanding tradition of violence and wars of vengeance. The result was that Augustine's principles, intended to make war an exceptional option of last resort, became the justification for constant wars.

By the late eleventh century this process led to the Crusades. At that point Augustine's principles of seeking to establish peace, and his limitations on the actions that soldiers could take, were generally ignored. The enemy was demonized, and cruelty and mass murder were often seen as acts of valor and even of virtue. While originally intended against the Muslims who held the Holy Land, eventually the principles of the Crusade were extended to wars against the *Albigensians in southern France, and later against the natives of the Western Hemisphere as it was conquered by European powers. Similar attitudes of cruelty and demonization of the enemy prevailed in Europe during the wars of religion of the seventeenth century.

In response to all of this, a number of groups have reverted to pacifism as the only Christian alternative to war—such are, for instance, the *Mennonites and the *Quakers. After enduring persecution at the hands of states that feared that such teachings would weaken their defensive capabilities, such Christian pacifists have gained general recognition in a number of countries. Still, however, most Christians—particularly in traditionally Christian nations—follow some form of the just-war theory, or are simply so committed to nationalism that they do not even ask questions about the rightness of war. One factor that compli-

cates the application of the "just war" principles is that modern weapons make it very difficult to spare noncombatants.

Wesleyans   The heirs of the revival in eighteenth-century England led by John Wesley (1703–91) and his brother Charles (1707–88). This includes the various *Methodist churches as well as much of the *Holiness and *Pentecostal movements. Thus, there is great variety among Wesleyans, although they are generally *Arminians and stress personal experience and holiness of life (see *Sanctification; *Perfection).

Wisdom   In the latter books of the Old Testament, as well as in the intertestamental period, much was written about the Wisdom of God, both equating wisdom with God and making wisdom a being next to God. (See, for instance, Prov. 8, from which much later literature on the subject is inspired.) In the New Testament, the prologue to the Fourth Gospel speaks of the Word or *Logos who was *incarnate in Jesus, and most of what is said there about the Word had been said earlier about the Wisdom of God—except for the line "and the Word was made flesh." Thus, in much early Christian literature Jesus is said to be the incarnate Wisdom of God. This may be seen in the very name of the cathedral of Constantinople, which was dedicated to "Holy Sophia," or Holy Wisdom—not a saint by the name of Sophia, but Jesus himself.

In the late twentieth century much was made of "Sophia" as the feminine name of God, and of the revival of the worship of Sophia as a return to the femininity of God, or to "the Goddess." While it is true that the word *sophia* is feminine, the same is true of most abstract names in Greek, and therefore not only wisdom, but also truth, folly, power, weakness, Trinity, and many others are grammatically feminine nouns.

Within entirely different contexts, traditional theology has also distinguished between wisdom—*sapientia*—

and knowledge—*scientia*. Toward the end of the twentieth century, there was a repeated call to recover those aspects of the theological enterprise that are best described as wisdom, and which have often been eclipsed by intellectual knowledge.

Womanist Theology That form of *contextual *liberation theology done from the perspective of African American women. Such theology is deeply aware of the manner in which theology and Christianity have been used to justify the oppression of both African Americans in general and African American women in particular. Thus, while sharing in the black struggle (*see* *Black Theology), womanist theologians insist on the significance of a feminine perspective; and, while sharing in much of the feminist struggle (*see* *Feminist Theology), they insist on keeping the issue of race and the consequences of slavery in the foreground. Thus, womanist theology includes analysis of gender, race, and class. From this perspective, it then seeks to reinterpret the Christian faith, and to read Scripture anew, in such a way that they reflect the experiences of and are liberating for African American women. Among the leaders of this movement are Jacquelyn Grant (1948–) and Delores Williams (1929–).

Word of God Although in most common contemporary usage the phrase "Word of God" is practically synonymous with *Scripture, the meaning of the phrase is much wider. In the Bible itself, both in the first verses of the Fourth Gospel and in the book of Revelation (Rev. 19:13), the Word, or *Logos, of God is none other than the Second Person of the *Trinity, who has become *incarnate in Jesus Christ. Significantly, the Bible never refers to itself as "the Word of God"—although some of the prophets declare that what they have spoken is "the Word of the Lord"—but it does say that the Word is the one who was in the beginning with God. For this

and other reasons, in much of the early Trinitarian debate there were those who preferred to speak of the Second Person as the Word, or Logos, rather than as Son.

In the Fourth Gospel, and in most Christian theology, the Word, or Logos, of God is eternally present with God, and takes part in the *creation of all things. Indeed, we are told that "all things came into being through him, and without him not one thing came into being." This corresponds to the story of creation in Genesis, where God creates by speaking: "Let there be . . . and there was."

Thus, the function of the Word of God is not limited to communicating ideas, principles, or commandments; the Word of God is God's very action, creating and effecting what God speaks.

This means that, although strictly speaking the Word of God is none other than God, there is a sense in which the phrase can be applied to instruments or means that God employs to speak and to effect what God pronounces. The first of these is Scripture itself, and it is for this reason that it has become common to equate it with the Word of God. In Scripture the Word of God—the Word through whom all things were made, and through whom all things are still made—comes to us. Obviously, at this point there is some disagreement among Christians, for some see Scripture as witnessing to the Word, to Jesus Christ, while others see it as an *inerrant collection of propositions or statements, not only about Jesus, but also about the world, its origin and functioning, and so on (*see* *Fundamentalism).

Finally, it must be added that for many early Christian writers, as well as for Luther and most of the Reformers, and for many theologians, the Word of God acts also in the *sacraments and even in the act of preaching—which does not make the preacher infallible, but merely an instrument through which the Word of God accomplishes that for which it was sent.

Work of Christ   *See* *Atonement.

Works   All Christians are agreed that God calls them to do good works—by which are meant works of mercy as well as works of devotion. Since the controversy of *Augustine with *Pelagianism, most Christian theologians have also agreed that in a state of sin it is impossible to do works that are not sinful (as Augustine would say, a sinner is in a state of *non posse non peccare*). The question then that has been debated among Christians, particularly between Catholics and Protestants since the time of the Reformation, is what is the role of good works in the process of salvation. In the medieval Catholic tradition, and in its continuation in *Tridentine Catholicism, it is held that *salvation is attained by the *merits of good works, as well as by the merits of Christ (*see* *Atonement). Following Augustine on this point, it is held that the *grace of God, after initiating faith, collaborates with the believer in performing good works worthy of salvation.

Luther held that salvation is an act of God's grace, quite apart from our merits. In his view, even after being justified a sinner remains a sinner (*Simul justus et peccator*), and therefore all the works of such a person remain sinful and merit nothing. Good works are to be commended. However, they are not a means to salvation, but rather a result and a sign of it. Nothing that we do—neither works of mercy, nor works of devotion, nor the "work" of believing—earns our salvation, which is entirely in the hands of God.

Worship   An English word derived from "worthship," commonly used to translate the Greek *latreia* and *leitourgia*, or the Latin *adoratio*. To worship means essentially to recognize, celebrate, and praise God's majesty; and, as a result, it also means to acknowledge our own sin and unworthiness before God. Thus, worship is above all a recognition of God's majesty and *grace.

From a very early date, the worship of the Christian church centered on the *Eucharist, which was normally celebrated on the first day of the week, because this was the day of the *resurrection of Jesus. The Eucharist, rather than a funereal service centering on the cross, was a celebration of the victory of Jesus through the cross, and an announcement of his coming again in glory in the final day. In this sense also, the first day of the week was significant, for the first day is also the eighth, and there was a tradition that the day would come when the weekly cycle would cease—the day of the final consummation that the Eucharist also celebrated. While in the very early church the Eucharist involved a complete meal, by the second century the meal had been separated from the Eucharist itself, and two hundred years later the meal had practically disappeared—apparently because, now that church attendance had soared, such a meal was easily susceptible to abuse and disorders.

The Eucharist or "service of the Table" was preceded by the "service of the Word," in which Scripture was read, explained, and applied to the lives of believers. While this earlier part of the service was open to all, before the beginning of the service of the Table all those who were not yet baptized (*see* *Baptism for the early baptismal practices), and those who for other reasons were excluded from Communion (*see* *Excommunication), were dismissed.

These early services seem to have been quite simple, and rather spontaneous, even though a certain order was normally followed. However, after the time of Constantine there was an increasing tendency to bring into Christian worship the protocols and the pomp of the imperial court and of imperial celebrations, and thus worship became more elaborate. Also, partly in order to avoid disorders now that there were masses attending worship services, the order of worship was much more structured, eventually resulting in a series of liturgical traditions that were typical of particular geographic areas—even though these various traditions had much in common. All of this also tended to limit the active participation in worship of many in the laity, whose function was to attend worship while others spoke, sang, and performed other ritual acts.

The dark periods of the early Middle Ages in the West brought about a preoccupation with death and with the possibility of damnation, thus leading worship, and particularly the Eucharist, to take on increasingly penitential tones. This was not changed by the Reformation, which basically inherited the traditions of the Latin Mass, and was often satisfied with eliminating from it those elements that were clearly contrary to biblical teaching as the Reformers understood it—the Eucharist as a sacrifice, the practice of celebrating private masses, worship only in Latin, and the like. Thus, in spite of the changes introduced by the Reformation, the Eucharist —which still was the center of the worship life of the church—remained a funereal rite more appropriate to Good Friday than to Easter. One element that the Reformation did reintroduce was the importance of preaching, which became the modern equivalent of the ancient "service of the Word."

At any rate, before, during, and immediately after the Reformation, most churches continued centering their worship on the Eucharist, which was normally celebrated at least once a week, on Sundays. Although some Protestant groups led the way in the process, it was during the eighteenth and nineteenth centuries, and particularly in new territories like the Americas, where ordained ministers were scarce, that the practice of frequent Communion began receding. Among Protestants, this was partly the result of the great revivals of the time, which centered on preaching and awakened the faith of many people but did not always provide for them the opportunity or the stimulus to partake of Communion. Soon it became customary among Protestants in areas such as the

United States to regard the sermon as the focus of worship, and to limit Communion to an occasional service, sometimes celebrated once a month, sometimes quarterly, and sometimes even less frequently. Among Roman Catholics, particularly in the Spanish and Portuguese colonies, the scarcity of ordained priests led to greater emphasis on lay-led services, such as the rosary, while the use of Latin in the Mass continued making believers passive spectators of the holy mysteries.

During the twentieth century there was a movement of "liturgical renewal" that spread through many denominations. This was fostered in part by the rediscovery of ancient documents describing worship in the early church, in part by the need to make worship more relevant to the lives of believers, and in part by the necessity to use worship as a means to strengthen and guide believers in an increasingly secularized society. The Second Vatican Council (1962–65) proposed and initiated a far-reaching series of changes in the Roman Catholic liturgy, including the renewal of the practice of celebrating the Mass in the language of the people. The survival of Russian Orthodoxy even after more than eight decades of governmental hostility and even persecution, and the fact that one of the elements making such survival possible was the worship life of that church—centering on a very structured and fixed liturgy—convinced many Protestants that there is in worship a power that goes far beyond the power of persuasive words or eloquent sermons. Among Protestants, and particularly *Pentecostal Protestants, there was a sense that the worship of the church needed to be renewed so as to allow greater freedom for the *Spirit. Although this led in very different directions from the rest of the movement of liturgical renewal, there is a sense in which this too is part of the same movement, seeking to make worship more meaningful and powerful. Thus, although early in the twenty-first century several of these tendencies seem to be opposed to each other and vying for the support of the faithful, it is to be expected that, as time passes and the more valuable elements of each prove their worth, the net result will be a renewal of the worship life of the entire church, both reaffirming some of the more traditional elements that some now declare to be meaningless and incorporating some of the innovations introduced more recently.

Year, Liturgical   The annual cycle in which the church celebrates and focuses on specific events of *redemption. Before there was a liturgical year, there was a weekly cycle of celebration and remembrance. This centered on the first day of the week, the day of the *resurrection of Jesus, and therefore often called the "day of the Lord"—hence the Latin *dominica*, from which many Romance languages derive their name for this day: *domingo*, *dimanche*, and the like. Sunday was a day of celebration focusing on the resurrection of Jesus and on his *Parousia and coming *kingdom. The Sunday service, usually very early in the morning, culminated in the *eucharistic celebration. Friday was then a day of remembrance of the cost of redemption, the crucifixion, and was therefore a day of *penance and fasting. At least in some churches, Saturday was also a day of fasting and meditation—and of rest, in the rare cases where the authorities and the social order allowed it.

Out of this liturgical week developed the liturgical year. Although every Sunday was a celebration of resurrection, from a very early date—at least as early as the second century—there was a special Sunday every year, a sort of "Great Easter," which eventually became one of the two foci around which the liturgical year developed.

Already in the second century, however, there was disagreement between churches in Asia and in the West as to how the date of this great Easter Sunday was to be determined. While both sides

agreed that there was an original connection between this date and the Jewish Passover, they disagreed as to how the date of Easter was to be determined in an increasingly Gentile church—a disagreement that continues to this day, with the result that the celebration of Easter in the Eastern churches seldom coincides with the celebration in the churches of Western origin—Roman Catholics and Protestants.

The Eve of Easter Sunday was also the day in which neophytes were normally baptized (*see* *Baptism). In connection with that baptism, the rest of the church renewed its baptismal vows. In preparation for that great event a time of several weeks was set aside for the final instruction of the catechumens, and for the rest of the church to prepare to renew its vows. This is the origin of Lent, which eventually was fixed at forty days—not counting the Sundays, which even in the midst of Lent are supposed to celebrate the resurrection of Jesus.

Completing the cycle centering on Easter, the celebrations of Pentecost and, later, of the ascension of Jesus were placed at appropriate times after Easter.

The other main focus around which the liturgical year developed is the Nativity of Jesus. Long before December 25 became the feast of the Nativity of Jesus, January 6 was celebrated in the Eastern churches as the "Epiphany" or manifestation of Jesus and his mission, and therefore as the day of the baptism of Jesus. While many different dates were suggested as the day of the birth of Jesus, in the fourth century the Western church began celebrating this event on the twenty-fifth day of December, apparently in an attempt to counteract the pagan rites around the winter solstice and the birth of Mithras. Eventually, the Eastern observance of Epiphany passed to the West, and the Western day of Christmas gained acceptance in the East—except in the Armenian Church, which still celebrates the birthday on January 6. Thus the two central dates around the Nativity were set: December

25 as the date of the birth, and January 6 as the day of the Epiphany or the manifestation of Jesus in his baptism—to which were then added the coming of the magi and Jesus' first miracle, in the wedding at Cana.

Advent, the period immediately preceding Christmas, seems to have been originally a period of preparation, not for the birth of Jesus, but for his Second Coming or Parousia. For this reason it was placed at the end of the year, just before the coming of the new year, as a reminder of the coming new age. However, with the placing of the Nativity of Jesus on December 25, Advent became a period of preparation for the coming of Jesus, not only at the end of the age, but also on Christmas day. Later, in imitation of Lent, Advent became a penitential period.

Since Christmas is on a fixed date, and Easter is movable, the length of the periods between the Christmas and Easter cycles varies, and this is what has come to be known as "ordinary time."

In order to help the church focus on the themes of the various seasons and dates of the liturgical year, *lectionaries were developed, so that the texts assigned for a particular day illumine the theme or themes of that day.

Besides the Christmas and Easter cycles, various churches celebrate a number of special dates that sometimes obscure the liturgical year itself. Thus, from a very early date it became customary to commemorate the martyrdom of Stephen on December 27, and the slaughter of the innocents on December 28—with the strange result that the slaughter of the innocents takes place before the magi arrive! Besides the martyrdom of Stephen, celebrations soon arose in memory of other martyrs, apostles, and saints—to the point that in some traditions every day of the year is the day of at least one saint, and usually more than one. Protestant churches usually have fewer such celebrations, but it must be noted that many celebrate November 1 as "All Saints' Day," together with the Roman Catholic Church, and October 31 as "Reformation Day," and that *Methodists and others in the *Wesleyan tradition observe "Aldersgate" as the day of John Wesley's experience of personal salvation.

CPSIA information can be obtained
at www.ICGtesting.com
Printed in the USA
LVHW022051300321
682991LV00001B/1